The Decline (and Fall?)
of the Income Tax

Also by Michael Graetz

FEDERAL INCOME TAXATION: PRINCIPLES AND POLICIES
(with Deborah H. Schenk)

The Decline (and Fall?) of the Income Tax

MICHAEL J. GRAETZ

W · W · NORTON & COMPANY

New York   London

For information about permission to reproduce selections from this book, write to
Permissions, W. W. Norton & Company, Inc., 500 Fifth Avenue, New York, NY 10110.

The text of this book is composed in ITC New Baskerville
with the display set in ITC New Baskerville
Composition and manufacturing by
the Haddon Craftsmen, Inc.
Book design by Jacques Chazaud

Library of Congress Cataloging-in-Publication Data

Graetz, Michael J.
The decline (and fall?) of the income tax / by Michael J. Graetz.
p.   cm.
Includes bibliographical references and index.
ISBN 0-393-04061-5
1. Income tax—United States. 2. United States—Politics and
government. I. Title.
HJ4652.G697   1997
336.24´0973—dc20   96-36159
                                                    CIP

W. W. Norton & Company, Inc., 500 Fifth Avenue, New York, N.Y. 10110
http://www.wwnorton.com

W. W. Norton & Company Ltd., 10 Coptic Street, London WC1A 1PU

1 2 3 4 5 6 7 8 9 0

To Brett

Acknowledgments

The tax professionals who have made it possible for me to write this book are too numerous to name; I have been rich in mentors and friends. My students deserve special thanks. They make sure that I keep learning as I am teaching. In particular, Tom Thurston and Neera Tanden provided essential research for this book, and David Kennedy commented on the entire manuscript. My good friends and colleagues Jerry Mashaw and Alvin Warren provided crucial support and wise counsel throughout this endeavor. Anne Alstott offered important comments as I neared completion. Gene Coakley of the Yale Law Library answered endless requests for materials in an ongoing demonstration that he cannot conceal a kind heart by a gruff affect. Laura Orr, also of the Law Library staff, provided lessons in the quality of research that can be mustered when good training is combined with determination. Marcia Mayfield typed, retyped, and retyped again and again with consummate skill and unfailing good humor; it is simply not possible to thank her enough. Boris Bittker read and commented on the entire manuscript, demonstrating for the umpteenth time why he has been the clearest and most insightful tax scholar in a generation, and by far the best writer. Each time I rejected a change he proposed—which wasn't often—I felt certain I was making a needless mistake.

In writing a book intended for people whose main contact with tax law and tax policy is only an annual unpleasant experience, I wanted to limit the amount of distracting superscript so I have kept footnotes to a bare minimum. I fear that my footnoting decisions have been quite arbitrary. I hope that in my effort to avoid scholarly excesses, I have not slighted anyone or any publication.

I am extremely grateful to the people at W. W. Norton who encouraged and advanced this project. Special thanks are due my editor, Hilary Hinzmann, for his unwavering faith in this book and his insightful suggestions throughout its development. I also want to thank my deans at the Yale Law School, Tony Kronman and Guido Calabresi, for both financial and moral support.

Last, but certainly not least, I thank my family. My children, Luke, Dylan, Jake, Sydney, and Casey, made sure that no day was devoted solely to work on this or any other project. For that constant injection of wise perspective and their exceptional companionship always, there are no adequate words. Finally, to Brett, who makes everything possible.

Michael J. Graetz
October 1996

Contents

---

1. Introduction   *3*

PART I. THE DECLINE

2. It's a Sin to Get a Mexican Divorce   *29*
3. Chasing Chinchilla Coats
     and Other Tax Shelter Aerobics   *41*
4. Disappearing Dollars   *52*
5. Dad Is Not at the Dining Room Table Anymore   *68*
6. Have We Become a Nation of Tax Cheaters?   *89*

PART II: THE SAUSAGE FACTORY

7. A Visit to the Sausage Factory   *111*
8. Rosie Scenario Becomes the Belle of the Ball   *123*
9. The Madness of Two Georges   *140*
10. Sin Looks Pretty Good When the Alternative Is Taxes   *149*
11. Read My Hips   *160*
12. Just the Facts, Ma'am   *177*

PART III: THE FALL?

13. Taxing What You Spend Instead of What You Make   *195*
14. The Flat Tax, the "USA" Tax,
      and Other Uncommon Consumption Taxes   *212*
15. Back to the Future   *244*
16. Seeking Protection from the Politicians   *277*

NOTES   *293*
INDEX   *311*

The Decline (and Fall?)
of the Income Tax

I've often thought that only Proust and our tax structure stand up to a good Persian carpet. . . . [I]n one sense the tax structure is art—a subsuming of the infinite muddle of human activity under a single rubric, as though it had a single purpose and could be ordered by a mind heaving the line of a single vision. Everything that everyone is doing this very instant in this part of town has tax consequences.

—JOHN CASEY
Testimony and Demeanor

1

Introduction

In 1913 the Sixteenth Amendment empowered Congress to impose an income tax and it quickly did so. For the rest of the twentieth century, the income tax has played a central role in America's financial and political life. The income tax has been the nation's principal source of revenue since World War II, and—despite its shortcomings, which are serious indeed—it has long been the fairest tax in our fiscal system. The income tax has served the nation well during this century. Now, for the first time, its survival is being threatened.

The Threat to the Income Tax

In 1972, a plurality of Americans considered the federal income tax the fairest of all the taxes used by the various levels of government.

But beginning in the middle of the 1970s, people widely came to regard the income tax as badly broken. Although he proved incapable of turning the thought into action, Jimmy Carter captured a widespread sentiment in his 1976 presidential campaign when he described the income tax as a "disgrace to the human race." By 1979, a seismic shift had occurred; most people rated the income tax as the least fair.[1] Increasingly through the 1980s and 1990s people criticized the federal income tax as inequitable, economically inefficient, and unnecessarily complex.

Now politicians have discovered a guaranteed applause line: just promise to cast out the income tax, root and branch. Washington pundits have come to regard replacement of the income tax as virtually inevitable; the McLaughlin Group predicted its demise as approaching "metaphysical certainty." *BusinessWeek* and *Fortune* magazines joined in, assuring us that a "massive restructuring" or "radical" tax reform is coming.

The field for the presidential election of 1996 was crowded with candidates determined to eliminate the income tax. Steve Forbes, the dynastic heir to a fortune and a magazine bearing his name, entered the race to promote replacing the income tax with the "flat tax," which he claims would reduce taxes for all and also get the country moving in the right direction. He insisted it would not save him enough money to pay his campaign costs. A flat tax proposal also was embraced by the presidential candidate Senator Arlen Specter of Pennsylvania and by House Majority Leader Dick Armey of Texas. Richard Lugar, Indiana's senior senator and another Republican presidential candidate, wants to replace the income tax with a national sales tax collected by the states, which he says will get rid of the IRS. Ways and Means Committee chairman Bill Archer of Texas also wants to replace the income tax with a consumption tax, and apparently so does a tax reform commission appointed by Robert Dole and Newt Gingrich and headed by Jack Kemp, former professional quarterback, congressman, secretary of Housing and Urban Development, and Bob Dole's choice for vice-president. Rather than calling directly for replacing the income tax with a consumption tax, the Kemp Commission instead described principles for tax reform that can be met only by a flat-rate consumption tax. The refusal of both the Kemp Commission and many flat-tax proponents to admit that they are proposing substitution of a tax on consumption for the income tax suggests, however, that there may be important residual public support for a tax on income, even if not for the income tax in its current form.

The Republican presidential nominee Bob Dole may have been trying to capture the votes of people clamoring for fundamental change, while retaining the support of people reluctant to abandon income taxation altogether, when he decided to campaign on a promise of large specific income tax cuts, coupled with a vague suggestion that he would "repeal the entire tax code and replace it with a simpler, fairer, flatter system that will allow Americans to file their tax returns without the help of a lawyer, or an accountant, or both." Dole also tried to tap into widespread anti-IRS sentiment, promising to "free the American public from tax tyranny" by proposing to privatize certain IRS functions, halt what he described as "KGB-like tax audits," and "eliminate the IRS as we know it."[2] Steve Forbes had gotten his greatest applause when he told audiences that his tax plan would turn the IRS into R.I.P.

Never before has such a prominent cast of politicians promoted replacement of the income tax. This remarkable effort to tap into an obviously widespread public attitude is a major event regardless of the personal political fortunes of these people. Even those who defend the income tax now call for radical surgery. Richard Gephardt of Missouri, the Democratic leader in the House of Representatives, advanced a proposal to eliminate many of the current income tax deductions and exclusions and reduce the tax rates to two: 10 percent and 25 percent. The conservative *New York Times* columnist William Safire called for something similar. A majority of both Republicans and Democrats apparently favor a "complete overhaul" of our nation's tax system.

How did the income tax come to its current state of disrepute and disfavor in such a relatively brief time? There are two common explanations why anti–income tax sentiment runs so deep in today's public life. The first, which led the journalist Robert Kuttner to label Proposition 13, California's property-tax-limiting constitutional amendment, the "Revolt of the Haves," has more recently been expressed with simple elegance by Paul Thrasher, a retired foreman from Springfield, Illinois: "Everybody wants everything and nobody wants to pay for it."[3] This is, of course, exactly what Russell Long, the Democrat from Louisiana, had in mind when, as chairman of the Senate Finance Committee, he coined this ditty as the first principle of tax reform: "Don't tax you. Don't tax me. Tax the fellow behind the tree." In 1992, bowing to the force of the new world economy, Dan Rostenkowski, then chairman of the House Ways and Means Committee, added a second stanza: "Don't tax you. Don't tax me. Tax the companies across the sea."

The second explanation for the precarious state of the income tax views the anti-tax movement simply as an integral part—perhaps the most visible symbol—of the general anti-government attitude so prevalent in America today. A surprising number of Americans insist that all levels of their government—local, state, and federal—are rife with mismanagement, fraud, waste, and abuse. Recently retired congressman Berle Anthony of Arkansas clearly linked anti-government sentiment and tax resistance: "The voters believe government is not giving anywhere close to a dollar's worth of value for a dollar's worth of taxes." The singer and songwriter Richie Havens captured this sentiment more graphically when he said, "We should pay for what we get, not for what we don't get. What we don't get is just about everything."[4]

Long ago and far away, Supreme Court Justice Oliver Wendell Holmes dissented from the common sentiment in an oft-quoted phrase, claiming "I like to pay taxes. They are the price we pay for civilized society." Department store mogul Edward A. Filene also refused to join the anti-tax brigade, asking, "Why shouldn't the American people take half my money from me? I took it all from them."[5] But this high-minded attitude has always been a minority position, and no one likes to pay taxes for an uncivil society. Unfortunately, that is what we now seem to have: fragmented and dysfunctional families; metal detectors, not only at our airports but also in our public schools; fear and distrust all around.

It is not only our society that has lost its civility. The way we are governed—our political process—has also turned uncivil. Public hearings before the Congress are no longer places for learning, dialogue, and analysis. Television coverage has made them occasions for political posturing, just another opportunity to get today's screaming on the evening news. The thirty-second commercial is now the nation's highest political art form, seen by far more people than candidates' debates. Bipartisanship in domestic policy should be added to the endangered species list.

Don't forget the money. The days when a PAC was six beers (or a West Coast athletic conference) are long gone. It is common for fundraisers like Nancy Maxwell, who raises money for Republican candidates, to brag openly about their direct access to members of Congress. She says she has eighteen she can see at any time, and she boasts that this makes it easy for her clients to "get to the member."[6] The exchange of fundraising cash for legislative favors has become so commonplace that we no longer even notice the stench.

At an October 22, 1995, meeting on Medicare proposals that the Congress then was considering, John Hill, of Fort Pierce, Florida, a seventy-two-year-old retired manager of a manufacturing company, told his congressman, Mark Foley, a freshman Republican: "I just have trouble believing anything that comes out of Washington these days."[7] Don't we all.

It's more than enough to make anyone hate paying taxes. But neither the selfishness of the haves nor the widespread indifference toward the have-nots nor the intrusiveness and wastefulness of government programs—not even the weakening of civil society—explain the public's current distaste for the income tax. I do not deny that all these are important, but to understand fully the public's antipathy for the income tax you have to look into the belly of the beast itself. The answers are found both in the substance of the Internal Revenue Code itself and in the political process that has created and feeds this monstrous statute.

First, the income tax has strayed too far from the values of the people it represents. When two-thirds of married couples are required to pay higher income taxes solely because they have married, the American public rightly loses respect for the law. Second, the average American family regards the income tax as unfair. Aware of the lobbyists' power over the government, people believe the income tax permits high-income individuals and large corporations routinely to avoid paying their appropriate share of taxes. Third, inflation during the 1970s and 1980s pushed more and more people into higher tax brackets, even though they had no more real spendable income. In the process, they became convinced that their own income tax burdens were excessive and unfair. Fourth, foolish and unnecessary complexities in the income tax law have driven a massive wedge between the people and their government. Preparing the most routine income tax forms is infuriating. Over time, the American people have had to waste more and more of their hard-earned money on tax advisers, tax-preparation manuals, computer tax programs, and tax-return preparers. This has diminished respect for and public approval of the income tax. These forces have combined to stimulate a serious decline in tax compliance. Instead of disdain for tax protesters, law-abiding citizens are increasingly tempted to shout "right on."

Today's proposals for radical change in the income tax—such as those for the flat tax, which, as I shall subsequently demonstrate, have serious problems of their own—are in large part a response to the public's well-founded dissatisfaction with the current income tax.

The tax law did not become the way it is by accident. Congress made it what it is today. Here lies the other shoe of the anti-tax movement: people's determination to constrain politicians' endless tinkering, to rein in the raw power of the political process. This is why the tax limitation measures in most states and the tax reform measures proposed in the Congress not only would radically restructure the substance of the tax law but also would adopt new procedural or constitutional constraints on the political process. For example, many proposals would require a two-thirds majority vote to increase tax rates; others would require public initiatives to raise taxes. Dissatisfaction with politics as usual accounts for the popularity of proposals for new constitutional restrictions on Congress, including the balanced budget amendment, term limits, and the line item veto.

It has been more than two decades since late 1974, when Wilbur Mills, the powerful chairman of the House Ways and Means

Committee, lost his sway, and the congressional budget process was drastically altered. During that time, the power of special interests expanded greatly, the number of congressional staff has exploded, and Congress has become much more partisan in tax matters. Political leadership during that period has been diffuse, often absent altogether. Congress has far too frequently relied solely on predictions about the revenue consequences of change to guide their policies and, in so doing, has avoided making difficult substantive judgments about how to improve the equity, economic efficiency, and simplicity of the tax law.[8]

Only Four Things to Tax; Infinite Ways to Tax Them

Two fundamentally conflicting facts about taxation combine to confuse, confound, and undermine people's understanding of taxation. First, most people properly feel that everything but the air they breathe (and sometimes even that) is taxed by some level of government. As we have all come to know through experience, virtually any product or transaction can be taxed, and politicians enjoy limitless potential to do mischief in deciding whom and what to tax. Second, within any tax there are virtually unlimited potential variations on the amount of tax that can be imposed as specific circumstances change.

Over time, the federal government has imposed more than fifty kinds of taxes. These include, for example, taxes on incomes, estates, gifts, capital stock, excess profits, admissions, club dues, documents, playing cards, safe deposit boxes, circulation of bank notes, cotton futures, tobacco, snuff and cigarettes, oleomargarine, filled cheese, firearms, and liquor, as well as taxes on the manufacture of many articles, including tires, tubes, toilet preparations, automobiles, radios, refrigerators, matches, electrical energy, gasoline, and lubricating oil, on the transportation of oil by pipeline, and on telegraph, telephone, radio, and cable messages. Many of these taxes no longer exist.

In sharp contrast, however, to the freedom politicians enjoy in determining how, when, and where to impose taxes, financial reality severely limits the kinds of taxes that can serve effectively to finance government expenditures. All the governments of the world—including the United States—are generally financed by only four kinds of taxes: taxes on income, wages, consumption, or wealth. In the United States today the individual and corporate income taxes and the payroll tax are the major sources of federal revenues and, along with the estate and gift taxes, also account for virtually all federal tax controversies between the public and the Internal Revenue Service. In addition to income, payroll, and inheritance taxes, state and local governments rely on sales and property taxes for their revenues.

This is not mere coincidence. Income, wages, consumption, and wealth are the four general tax bases sufficiently robust to produce the revenues required that also can generally be said to satisfy the dominant criterion of a good tax, namely that it be fair—that the tax be connected in some way to a person's ability to pay. Modern governments' appetites for revenues have been so voracious that they routinely use all four of these tax bases rather than choosing among them. The key question usually is the mix of these four taxes, not whether any of them will be avoided entirely. It is the complete replacement of the income tax with some form of consumption tax that makes today's tax reform proposals radical.

The Principles of Taxation

How do we decide whether a particular tax or a nation's tax system is good or bad? Most everyone agrees that we should ask the following five questions:

1. Is the tax fair?
2. Is the tax easy to comply with and administer?
3. Does the tax interfere as little as practical with private economic decisions?
4. Is the tax conducive to economic growth?
5. Does the tax produce adequate revenues?

Of course, the relative priority to be given to each of these questions is controversial and the actual effects of taxes are uncertain. Conflicts among the criteria are commonplace; compromise is inevitable.

There is also debate about what the criteria mean. Fairness, for example, suggests that people who are in similar circumstances pay similar taxes, but this principle often just starts an argument about who is in similar or different circumstances. Even so, it is not—as some have suggested—utterly hopeless to strive for an income tax which collects the same tax from people who have identical incomes, regardless of the sources or uses of their incomes.

Likewise, to insist that a tax or mix of taxes be imposed in accordance with people's ability to pay does not tell you what the tax rate or rates ought to be. But *New York Times* columnist William Safire is right when he says: "Most of us accept as 'fair' this principle: the poor should pay nothing, the middlers something, the rich the highest percentage."[9] If a tax system is not perceived as fair by the people, its political support will evaporate and widespread noncompliance may result.

Economic efficiency demands that a tax interfere as little as possible with people's economic behavior. The economists' benchmark typically is the allocation of goods and services that would occur in a market economy in the absence of taxes. In some fundamental sense, however, describing economic efficiency this way is nonsensical. A market economy simply cannot function in the absence of government institutions, such as courts to enforce private contracts, and these institutions, along with spending on such things as police and national defense, must be financed through taxation. Nevertheless, people are rightly concerned with the potential reductions in the economy's ability to satisfy people's desires that might occur because taxes will change people's incentives to engage in important economic activities, such as work, savings, risk taking, or consumption.

Taxes are not neutral because they change people's incentives to engage in various activities and thereby will affect the allocation of resources. Congress sometimes consciously uses a tax provision to affect behavior or to reallocate resources. That is why, for example, the income tax allows deductions for gifts to charity. But often tax distortions are undesirable. Generally, a "good" tax is one that has as few efficiency costs as practical, given the need to satisfy other values.

Taxes also are often said to be efficient when they promote economic growth and inefficient when they inhibit such growth. Economic growth obviously is a key factor in determining people's well-being; greater output is how a nation raises its standard of living.

On some important issues of tax policy, equity and economic efficiency are in harmony. For example, both economic efficiency and equity generally support uniform income tax treatment of all sources and uses of income. In other circumstances, however, equity and efficiency conflict. For example, tax fairness might support taxing all sources of income when economic efficiency argues for taxing consumption or wages. Likewise, the disincentives for earning income may be greater under a progressive rate structure that applies higher rates to greater amounts of income, but a society's sense of tax justice may demand such progressivity.

Typically, the choice of a nation's mix of taxes or of the structure and details of a particular tax requires political compromise among conflicting norms based upon judgments of the likely economic and social consequences of the various choices presented. Occasionally, however, someone denies that a particular criterion is at all relevant. A *Wall Street Journal* editorial, for example, described the "fairness issue" as a "cynical exercise" which Democratic leaders in Congress "George Mitchell and Danny Rostenkowski concocted" in the 1980s.[10] In addition to ignoring Adam Smith's eighteenth-century call for distributing taxes in accordance with people's ability to pay, this extreme view also denies the fundamental motivation of the American people in choosing to tax income.

In deciding whom to tax, what to tax, and when, Congress routinely makes social as well as economic judgments. Tax policy decisions affect the general condition of the economy, its direction and growth. In addition to their effect on the overall functioning of the nation's economy, the tax provisions that emerge from the political process have a major impact on the nation's use of specific resources: who works and who doesn't, how much the people save and in what form, how much people spend on this or that.

The most fundamental issues of public policy are at stake when Congress enacts tax laws, and the Internal Revenue Code is laden with legislative judgments about social policy. Alexander Hamilton, the nation's first secretary of the Treasury, regarded taxation as a "means for shaping the national economy, bringing foreign nations to fair commercial terms, regulating morals, and realizing . . . social reforms"—thereby reflecting a thoroughly modern view of taxation.[11] Issues of equity in taxation raise issues of justice generally. Asking how much revenue to coerce from various classes of individuals in our society is often a way of asking how much economic inequality society will tolerate. Acceptance or rejection of any tax increase or, indeed, of any specific kind of taxation depends not only on the economic conditions of the moment and the government's current need for finance, but also on public values and opinions. The current status of the income tax as the major source of federal revenues reflects a long-standing American commitment to a particular vision of fairness in taxation. However, as the following brief look back at our nation's tax history shows, this vision did not flower until the twentieth century.

A Bird's-Eye History of Taxation in the United States

In 1791, the first secretary of the Treasury, Alexander Hamilton, convinced Congress to impose taxes on distilled spirits and carriages "more as a measure of social discipline than as a source of revenue."[12] Politicians have been tinkering with the tax system ever since. The first year's receipts from internal taxes netted the federal government a grand total of $208,942.81. The first "commissioner of the revenue" was appointed on May 8, 1792.

In 1798 a tax was enacted on real property—houses and land—as well as a tax of 50 cents on all slaves between the ages of twelve and fifty. These two taxes, like the taxes on distilled spirits,

proved both unpopular and difficult to collect and, along with opposition to the Alien and Sedition Acts, contributed to Thomas Jefferson's presidential victory over John Adams in 1800.

In 1802, at the initiative of President Jefferson, all internal
taxes (except a tax on salt) were repealed, reflecting Jefferson's determination to reduce federal taxes, expenditures, and the national debt. The connection between death and taxes—made
famous in an oft-quoted remark, describing them as the only two
certain events, first attributed to Benjamin Franklin in 1789—became all too real shortly thereafter, as the nation's major changes
in tax policies began their long pattern of accompanying wars.

The War of 1812 demonstrated the risks of Jefferson's policy
of relying entirely on tariffs as the sole source of federal government finance and also offered the nation's first proof that higher
rates need not necessarily produce higher revenues. Tariff rates
were doubled in 1812 and in 1814 produced just half of the revenues collected prior to the increase due to the wartime decline in
imports. A peacetime deluge of imports the following year, however, led domestic manufacturers to embrace additional protec-
tionism, and the Tariff Act of 1816 raised duties on imports to a
new high. Trade tariffs remained the most significant single source
of federal revenues until 1894. Thus, although Congress had raised
some revenues from taxes on internal sources since the first days
of the Union, tariffs produced the bulk of the money required to
finance federal expenditures for most of this nation's first century.

The federal government's reliance on tariffs as its principal
funding source initially suited both the young nation's manufacturers and farmers. High duties on imports served to protect the
country's manufacturers from foreign competition and imposed little or no burden on the farmers, who were largely self-sufficient
from items they produced themselves. Do not think, however, that
tariffs avoid imposing burdens similar to those which accompany
other forms of consumption taxation. Tariffs produce higher prices
for both imported goods that are subject to these duties and domestically produced substitutes and therefore impose significant
burdens on consumers, similar to those associated with sales or excise taxes, but varying greatly depending on the linkage between

the tariff schedule and each family's mix of purchases of goods and services.

The income tax made its debut to finance the Civil War. On July 1, 1862, President Lincoln signed an income tax, which taxed amounts between $600 and $10,000 at a 3 percent rate, with income exceeding $10,000 taxed at 5 percent. The Supreme Court upheld the constitutionality of this income tax.[13]

The income tax was increased in 1864—with the top rate doubled to 10 percent—was reduced in 1867 and again in 1870, when the inheritance tax was repealed, and was repealed in 1872 during the Grant administration when the federal government was enjoying large budget surpluses. During this time, James A. Garfield proved himself a thoroughly modern politician by railing in 1867 against the income tax he had avidly supported in 1865 and subsequently riding a conservative tide to become president in 1880.

Tariff issues dominated the presidential campaigns of both 1888 and 1892. Tariffs were increased to an average rate of nearly 50 percent in the McKinley Tariff Act of 1890, but by 1892 it had become apparent that further tariff increases would be counterproductive and that only a decrease in tariff rates would increase revenues.

The income tax was reinstated at the insistence of the Democrats in 1894 after intense controversy to compensate for the reduction in tariffs anticipated to result from the 1894 Tariff Act. The tax was modeled after the Civil War income tax and imposed a rate of 2 percent on all income over $4,000. In an interesting innovation that since has been lost, gifts and inheritances were taxed as income to the recipient.

Contrary to its prior determination that the Civil War income tax was constitutionally permissible, in 1895 the Supreme Court struck down the entire income tax as a direct tax not apportioned among the states as the Constitution requires.[14] That decision was highly controversial, with the Court's majority suffering accusations that they had forgotten they were a court and not a legislature—something courts often are accused of forgetting. The case ultimately led to the dramatic step of amending the Constitution, and, with the widespread support of the public and their state and national legislators, the Sixteenth Amendment was adopted in 1913, permitting Congress to tax income "from whatever source derived." The Sixteenth Amendment took effect on February 25, 1913, and it took Congress only until October 3 of that year to enact a tax on the net income of individuals and corporations that was to commence in 1916. In 1916, the Supreme Court sustained the income tax enacted in 1913 under the explicit power the Sixteenth Amendment granted to Congress.[15]

During the period 1925–1932, Secretary of the Treasury Andrew Mellon became a role model for Ronald Reagan by lowering the top rate from its previous high of 73 percent when he took office in 1921 to 25 percent in 1925. (President Reagan started three points lower, at 70 percent in 1981, and ended three points higher, at 28 percent in 1986.) The period of a 25 percent top rate, which lasted from 1925 to 1932, was something of a mixed economic bag: times were very good for a while; then times became very bad. By 1932, the depression had depleted federal revenues and was producing large and growing deficits. Economic science was so bad in those days that agreement was universal that taxes had to be raised. As a result, the Revenue Act of 1932 enacted a major tax increase that could have served only to prolong the depression. During the subsequent five decades from 1932 to 1982—also a period of some good and some bad years—the top rate never dropped below 63 percent. President Kennedy is now often cited by tax cutters, along with Andrew Mellon, as a godfather of supply-side economics because in the 1960s he cut the top income tax rate from 91 percent to 70 percent.

From his first days as president, Franklin Delano Roosevelt preached from a populist's hymnbook, railing against the rich and big business, but in tax legislation, at least, his bark was generally far worse than his bite. The most significant tax legislation of the years between the First and Second World Wars clearly was the Social Security Act of 1935 and its amendments in 1939. This legislation created the federal retirement, disability, and unemployment insurance system, financed through a regressive flat-rate payroll tax on a specified amount of wages. The benefits paid for by this tax, however, are sharply progressive.

Originally, the Social Security tax rate was set at 1 percent of wages to grow to 5 percent, split evenly between employees and their employers. Today the combined tax rate on employers and employees exceeds 15 percent and an additional tax of nearly 3 percent of wages is imposed to pay for hospital insurance under Medicare. The share of federal revenues supplied by these payroll taxes has grown substantially over time, and they now account for nearly 40 percent of federal revenues.

The First World War had served to secure for the income tax an important place in this nation's fiscal system, and the Second World War converted this limited tax into a tax on the masses. The income tax originally was imposed at low rates and applied to fewer than 400,000 individuals. It was not until the World War II era that the income tax came to be paid by middle-income Americans. Income tax rates reached their peak of 94 percent during that period. Following the Second World War, taxes—as usual following a war— began to decline, but that trend came to an end with legislation in 1950 and 1951 to finance the Korean War.

Beginning with the election of President Kennedy in 1960, the use of tax cuts as a short-term economic stimulus became commonplace, and since the early 1960s the government frequently has used tax reductions to stimulate economic growth. Income taxes were reduced to stimulate a lagging economy in 1964, 1971, 1975, and 1981. The 1981 act provided the largest tax reductions in the nation's history in an attempt to stimulate investment by business and savings by individuals. Ironically, this legislation was followed one year later in 1982 by what was the largest peacetime tax increase in the nation's history until 1993. Tax increases were again enacted in 1984, 1990, and 1993 in an effort to combat large federal deficits.

With considerable hyperbole, the Tax Reform Act of 1986 was heralded as the most significant tax change since the income tax was extended to the masses during the Second World War. This legislation, however, ultimately must be judged only a slight improvement of tax policy. Nevertheless, the rate-reducing and base-expanding contours of the 1986 act were copied throughout the industrialized world.

As its coverage broadened and its missions became more numerous, the income tax has grown more cumbersome. Extraordinary complexity is an income tax hallmark. In no small measure this is due to policymakers' tendencies to compromise among competing purposes, although the taxation of businesses and of some investment income is inherently complicated. More than 100 different federal tax forms are used each year by individuals. The 1986 legislation did achieve some simplification for low-income and some moderate-income taxpayers, but even these gains soon were eroded by subsequent expansions and changes in a refundable earned-income tax credit available to low-income families.

In 1990, after months of tortuous negotiations, Congress passed a budget act, which, through a combination of tax increases, provisions to slow the growth of federal expenditures, and new budget-enforcement procedures, was supposed to reduce deficits by about $500 billion in the subsequent five-year period. The 1990 act, with tax increases that no doubt contributed to President Bush's failure to win reelection, served as the blueprint for President Clinton's 1993 tax and spending proposals.

In early 1993 President Clinton tried to enact a short-term fiscal-stimulus package but this effort was thwarted by a Republican filibuster in the Senate. The 1993 budget legislation, which ultimately passed by only one vote and with no Republican support, strengthened and extended the budget process adopted in 1990 and lowered projected deficits through tax increases and reduced expected growth in federal spending, especially for defense.

Notwithstanding more than a decade of legislation between 1982 and 1993 aimed at curbing deficits and promises in 1996 by Republicans and Democrats alike for a balanced budget by the year 2002, deficit policy and tax policy remain inextricably intertwined. The cumulative federal debt held by the public, including foreigners, in 1995 totaled more than $3 trillion and may rise to more than $6 trillion shortly after the turn of the century.[16] Interest on the federal debt paid to the public in 1994 was more than $200 billion—about 14 percent of total federal outlays and 3 percent of gross domestic product (GDP). The share of federal spending to pay interest on the federal debt is historically extremely high, either as a percentage of federal outlays or of GDP.

Although the total national debt quadrupled during the 1980s, federal deficits are not a recent phenomenon; 1969—nearly three decades ago—was the last year of a balanced federal budget. Contrary to popular notions, tax reductions in the 1980s do not explain the nation's recent deficit condition. Taxes in fiscal year 1995 were $1.35 trillion, 18.9 percent of GDP. Outlays were $1.52 trillion, about 21.2 percent of GDP. Despite thousands of pages of tax law changes, federal taxes have been a relatively constant share of GDP over a long period of time: around 18 percent from 1950 through 1975 and usually about 19 percent since then. Current and projected deficits exist principally because, while the level of taxes has remained constant, federal spending has increased as a share of GDP over time—beginning in the late 1970s from about 20 percent to as much as 23 percent, remaining about 23 percent of GDP today. Major increases in spending during that interval have included defense, income security, health care, and interest on the federal debt.

Because of economic growth and the decline in the value of the dollar, total receipts have grown dramatically, even though they have remained relatively constant as a percentage of GDP. In 1969, for example, total federal receipts were just under $187 billion; in 1996, they exceeded $1.4 trillion. Total federal revenues have increased consistently over time in both real and nominal terms because national output—GDP—has grown consistently over a long period of time. The important point here is that economic growth has long been the engine of federal revenues, not changes in the kinds or rates of tax or a dramatically more burdensome federal tax structure.

In thinking about the future, we should all be aware that estimates of both federal spending and federal deficits have long been unduly optimistic. One careful study of forecasts of future deficits made by the Congressional Budget Office (CBO) during the years 1983–1993 demonstrates that had the forecasts been correct, the U.S. budget would have enjoyed surpluses in the early 1990s instead of our actual budget deficits of $200 billion to $300 billion annually.[17] While there are no simple explanations for recurring overly optimistic deficit forecasts, we should not surgarcoat our expectations about the large long-term deficit problem we now face. Deficits are not going to behave like Alice's Cheshire cat and simply disappear with a smile. Our national debt is now equal to about one-half of GDP and, as a result, we face substantial future expenditures to pay interest on the federal debt.

Obviously, to reduce or eliminate the deficit, either federal spending will have to be reduced significantly, taxes increased, or both. Contrary to conservative dogma of the 1980s, tax reductions did not produce federal spending reductions or a shrinking of government's size. Nevertheless, the American people became very good at resisting additional taxes. It was no accident that Bob Dole chose a tax cut proposal as the policy vehicle to ignite his lagging presidential campaign. Despite the public's desire for deficit reduction and the general popularity of "soaking the rich," an overall increase in tax burdens can still be very costly to politicians. Together with the difficulty of enacting major spending cuts, these two facts make deficit reduction an extremely difficult task. We seem to be facing a public policy conflict between an irresistible force and an immovable object—not exactly what Cole Porter had in mind when he coined that phrase.

Although the public often complains about high taxes, the United States currently has the lowest top tax rate among our major trading partners and the U.S. average tax rate is also generally lower than abroad. Taxes in the United States are also lower as a percentage of GDP than in many other countries. When one adds state and local taxes to the federal take, total U.S. taxes are about 30 percent of GDP, a low level by international standards. The average of the more than twenty industrialized countries that are members of the Organization for Economic Cooperation and Development (OECD) is about 40 percent. Currently, only Japan, Australia, and Turkey enjoy total taxes lower as a percentage of GDP than the United States.[18]

The individual income tax has, for a long time, supplied a relatively steady source of federal revenues. It produced about 43 percent of total revenues in 1953, about 43.5 percent today. Despite the constancy over a long period of time of both the overall federal tax level relative to national output and the percentage contributed by the individual income tax to total revenues, the mix of federal revenues has changed dramatically. The most important development in the federal tax structure in the past forty years has been the growth of the payroll tax to finance social welfare programs, particularly Social Security and Medicare. These taxes on wages have risen from 10 percent of total budget receipts in 1953 to about 36 percent today. This increase in payroll taxes has had a major effect on the take-home pay of low- and middle-income workers. The promise of future benefits upon retirement does not serve to offset the perception of both the public and politicians that the wages of the middle class are being overtaxed. There is also considerable evidence that the Social Security and Medicare systems have had a substantial adverse impact on the nation's level of savings.

In contrast to the enormous growth in taxes on wages, the percentage of total revenues generated by the corporate income tax has declined sharply in the past forty years. The corporate income tax produced more than 30 percent of federal revenues in 1953, but now produces only about 12.5 percent.

The federal government's only tax on wealth, the estate and gift tax, which applies only to the richest 1 percent of Americans, has accounted for a very small portion of federal revenues for a very long time. Today these taxes produce about $15 billion annually, about 1 percent of total revenues. Federal estate taxes once were a significant revenue source, producing nearly 11 percent of federal revenues in 1936, but have not produced more than 2.5 percent of total revenues since the end of World War II. These taxes are far more important for their contribution to the progressivity of the tax system than as a revenue source.

Nor do federal excise taxes, such as those on gasoline, tobacco, and liquor, produce a substantial portion of total federal revenues today. Excise taxes yield less than $60 billion a year, less than 5 percent of total federal revenues. In the 1930s, before the income tax was extended to the masses, excise taxes produced nearly half of all federal receipts, and as recently as 1965 they contributed about 12 percent of the total. Many federal excise taxes were repealed or reduced in 1965 and it was not until the 1990s that they experienced something of a revival as a potential source of revenue to narrow the federal deficit.

Since the federal government does not employ a general tax on consumption, such as the retail sales tax imposed by the states or the value-added taxes of other nations, excise taxes are the only federal taxes on consumption. A comparison of this nation's tax system to those of our trading partners reveals that the greatest disparity is their greater reliance on consumption taxes. The OECD countries, on average, collect about 30 percent of their tax revenues from such taxes, and only Japan relies less than the United States on revenues from such taxes. In the United States, consumption taxes raise less than 20 percent of total federal, state, and local revenues, and the federal government's share of that is quite small.

The Central Role of Tax Politics

The political role of taxes is every bit as important as their economic and social roles. In the seventeenth century, Charles I attempted to make residents of England's coastal cities pay "ship money" to the Crown without any approval by Parliament. John Hampden, a prominent parliamentarian who had specialized in tax issues, refused to pay. Despite narrowly losing his challenge in the courts, Hampden sparked a taxpayer revolt and raised a fundamental question of the proper balance of power between the monarch and Parliament. Parliament's ultimate victory profoundly affected the structure of English government.

Likewise, American resistance to the power of Parliament to impose taxes on the American colonies raised a fundamental question about Parliament's constitutional authority and sparked passions that led to the Revolutionary War. Years later, when Alexander Hamilton imposed federal taxes on distilled spirits in 1791, he had the financial purpose of raising money to pay the small national debt, but, more important, he wanted the tax imposed to advance and secure the power of the new federal government.

This distilled-spirits tax produced the 'Whiskey Rebellion' of

1794, a tax resistance movement led by farmers of western Pennsylvania, Maryland, Virginia, and North Carolina, who—being consumers as well as producers of substantial quantities of whiskey—regarded themselves as the targets of the tax. In July 1794, about 500 tax protesters burned a tax collector's home and soon thereafter, with the approval of Congress, George Washington sent 13,000 troops into the troubled area. This ended the rebellion. Suppressing these tax protesters demonstrated the ability of the recently formed federal government to enforce its revenue laws within the states. In so doing, it served to secure the power of the national government and to fulfill, at least temporarily, Hamilton's policies.

In recent years Proposition 13 and its progeny have had profound effects on the relationship between state and local governments in the United States. The tax limitation provisions of Proposition 13, for example, shifted great power from local governments to the state of California.

Taxation has long been the primary link between the people and their government. The gesture chosen by Henry David Thoreau, later by Vietnam War protesters, and more recently by a wide variety of anti-government groups to question the validity of government action was a refusal to pay taxes. In the United States today, far more people file tax returns than vote in presidential elections, and the politics of taxation currently dominates electoral debate at every level of office seeking, including the presidency.

For both the long and short term, the goals of the nation's tax and fiscal policies will be what they always have been: to facilitate growth of the nation's economy and to do justice in the distribution of the burdens and benefits of government. But tax policy inevitably is constrained by the difficulties of achieving political majorities.

Tax policymaking always has been marked by conflict. In 1928, when the income tax was just a teenager, a Treasury tax official characterized tax lawmaking as a "group contest in which powerful interests vigorously endeavor to rid themselves of present or proposed tax burdens."[19] In the nation's infancy when adequate revenues could be produced by tariffs, geographical regions competed in an effort both to shift tax burdens to others and to protect local industries from competition. These kinds of battles still ring familiar two centuries later. In 1993, for example, northeastern legislators fought to avoid energy taxes on home heating oil, while western senators struggled against large increases in gas taxes, and West Virginians sought preferential treatment for coal. Today, regions battle, industries battle, young workers and the retired elderly battle, labor and business interests battle. Conflicts to shift tax burdens to others abound.

Conclusion

At a minimum, the anti-tax attitude of the public that has dominated federal tax policy since the late 1970s—coupled with the willingness of key politicians to camouflage ideology as fact and the public's inability or unwillingness to demand candor in the political debates—has postponed serious consideration of tax policy issues that are fundamental to our nation's future economic well-being: First, is the current level of taxes adequate to finance government spending or is a substantially higher level of taxation inevitable? Second, is the current mix of taxes appropriate to the economic conditions that we face both domestically and internationally as we approach the twenty-first century? Finally, how can we raise the necessary revenues in a manner that is fair to the U.S. people, is reasonably simple to comply with, and, at the same time, facilitates the international competitiveness of our businesses, encourages savings and investment, and nurtures economic growth? Ultimately, accomplishing these often conflicting goals requires political action—courage even—and recent history inspires little confidence that Congress will enact the necessary changes.

Nearly 60 percent of the American people now think their tax system is basically unfair. Nearly 40 percent—Republicans and Democrats alike—favor a "complete overhaul" of the nation's tax system. These people are right. Our nation needs a new tax policy for the twenty-first century. The tax system of both federal and state governments has evolved almost haphazardly during the twentieth century, in the process expanding needless and wasteful compliance costs. Our current system of taxation may not have been a problem during the decades immediately following the Second World War, when, as one wag put it, "the United States had all the money there was,"[20] but today, such waste is demoralizing to the American people and debilitating to the American economy.

The ultimate question, of course, is whether our political process is capable of making a major improvement. Obviously we cannot ignore our history; we cannot start from scratch. Reviewing how we got to where we now are, setting forth the dilemmas that must be resolved given the political and economic conditions and tax laws we now face, and outlining an appropriate tax policy for the decades ahead are the basic tasks undertaken in this book.

While each person and company independently attempts to shed tax burdens, the citizenry at large demands that their local, state, and national governments provide goods and services, such as roads and bridges, retirement income and health insurance, education and national defense, all of which must be financed through taxation. This fundamental conflict—between the public's demand that the government provide a panoply of goods and services, subsidies, and transfers, on the one hand, and each person's desire to minimize their own taxes on the other—works its way through the political process to affect dramatically the shape and well-being of the country's economy as well as the details of the nation's tax laws and the government's expenditures.

The tax provisions in force today reflect no more than yesterday's political compromises, but the underlying structural and policy conflicts have changed little over time. A better understanding of the deficiencies of the current income tax and of the tax lawmaking process is the only inoculation against the snake oil salesmen. That's what I hope to provide here.

PART I

THE DECLINE

2

It's a Sin to Get a Mexican Divorce

It's your wedding day. Even friends and relatives who had hoped you would make a better match send gifts, smile, wish you the best. Your government, however, has something unexpected for you: an income tax increase just because you got married. It isn't right. But it happens. Today, about two-thirds of all married couples pay more income taxes than they would if they divorced.[1] If Joe and Jane are single and each has $20,000 of income they are both taxed at a 15 percent rate, but when they marry, part of their income is taxed at 28 percent and their total standard deduction is lower. Sometimes married couples pay a lot more income taxes; for very-high-income couples, $10,000–$15,000 more each year. What happened to family values?

This marriage tax doesn't apply to everyone, only couples where both spouses have about the same incomes. If you marry someone with a lot more or a lot less income than you, the couple may get a tax cut from filing a joint tax return. About one-third of married couples enjoy such a marriage gift.[2]

The tax law wasn't always like this. Until 1969, there was never a tax penalty for marriage. In fact, during the first thirty-five years of the income tax—from 1913 until 1948—the tax law tried to be marriage neutral. Married couples filed individual tax returns based upon their separate incomes. But some married couples soon found that they could reduce their total taxes by shifting investment income to the lower-earning spouse, an option the Supreme Court denied couples with only earned income. The ability of wealthy families to reduce their income taxes this way was an important landmark in instilling an unshakable belief in the citizenry that the arcane details of the income tax tend to work to the advantage of the well-off at the expense of the average wage earner.

The Supreme Court made the income tax more arbitrary and unfair by deciding that in those seven states where the property rights of a married couple were determined under a so-called community property regime—states located predominantly in the Southwest, from Louisiana to California—each spouse would be taxed individually on one-half of their community property income, regardless of which spouse actually earned the income. This meant that, for married couples in community property states, the husband and wife each paid the same tax as an unmarried person with one-half of the total income of the couple, but this tax-minimizing division simply was not possible in the other forty-one common-law states. Thus, prior to 1948, not only was a couple's federal income tax typically greater in common-law states than that of a married couple with the identical total income living in a community property state, but also the federal income taxes of married couples who had the same total incomes varied markedly in common-law states, depending upon how much income was earned by each spouse.

This bizarre state of affairs finally came to gall members of Congress. On the floor of the Senate, Senator John McClellan asked Senator William Knowland, Why is it that just because you live in California and I live in Arkansas, you pay "$646 less" every year than I pay? "My family could use that money just the same as your family could."[3] Senator Tom Connally of Texas, a community property state, suggested that if Senator McClellan was unhappy with the Arkansas situation, he should move to Texas. Which, of course, is just what some people did, especially those who lived in the border town of Texarkana, where people could move across the state line and save income taxes without even leaving town.

Needless to say, this absurd situation did not engender great respect for the integrity of the income tax. In 1941, the House Committee on Ways and Means proposed to eliminate the geographical variations in federal income taxes by taxing all married couples on their consolidated income in a manner identical to single persons who had the same amount of income. This proposal would have increased taxes for virtually all married couples and also would have introduced into the income tax for the first time a marriage penalty. The Ways and Means Committee denied that this would "result in any increase in the divorce rate" or "adversely affect the morals of American families." Nevertheless, the tax lawyer Randolph Paul, in his classic treatment of the income tax, described the 1941 House provision as "un-American," noting that its opponents viewed it as "striking at the institution of marriage, promoting celibacy, and attacking the family, by penalizing fidelity and rewarding perfidy."[4] This idea did not become law.

A number of state legislatures then started to move to community property laws to lower their residents' federal income taxes, but in 1948, Congress halted this stampede by adopting new joint-return provisions, which allowed married couples to combine their income and deductions on a joint return and to pay twice the tax that a single person would pay on one-half of the couple's total taxable income. This change was hailed for equalizing the tax treatment of married couples throughout the land, for treating equally couples with only earned income as well as couples with investment assets, and for reducing taxes for all married couples who did not have exactly equal incomes.

But this solution was not universally applauded. It meant that two single people often would pay significantly more tax than a married couple with the same total income, in some cases as much as

40 percent more. These people did not regard the income tax as at all fair.

The most effective advocate for single people, a successful Connecticut businesswoman, Vivien Kellems, who was described in her youth in the *New York World Telegram* as "an animated Dresden figurine," founded an organization she called War Widows of America, a group of single women who had never been married, they claimed, because the men they might have married were killed in World War II. Once she retired from her business in the 1960s, she began a relentless campaign against the higher taxes paid by single people. Ms. Kellems filed blank tax returns except for her name and Social Security number. She refused to turn over any books or records to the IRS and asked the IRS to return to her the excess taxes she had paid since 1948 because she was single, plus 6 percent interest. She had kept twenty years of tax records and her claim came to $73,000. She told the IRS: "You send me a check, and I will resume payment." Until then she "suspended" payment of her income taxes.

Ms. Kellems held a television news conference on the front lawn of Wilbur Mills's home. Mills was the chairman of the House Ways and Means Committee and was then often described as the second most powerful man in America, the president presumably being first. At the age of seventy-seven, Ms. Kellems threatened to haunt the Ways and Means Committee for the next forty-nine years if it failed to give single people justice. She said she picked forty-nine years because it took the National Women's Party that long to get the equal rights amendment passed by Congress.

Ms. Kellems told the House Ways and Means Committee that there were six million more single women than single men and asked, "Is it a reasonable classification to penalize these women because there aren't husbands enough to go around? What do you do if you can't get a husband? Should you be taxed for that?"[5] Vivien Kellems inspired thousands of Americans to mail teabags to their representatives in Congress and their senators to remind them of the Boston Tea Party as a way of protesting what she regarded as the excessive taxation of single people. She told her audiences: "If you don't drink tea, put coffee grounds in the envelope.

Something that will spill out and make a mess." Congressmen who supported her begged: "Please stop the teabags. I'm for you. You don't need to send any more teabags." She claimed to have received 22,000 letters from supporters.

Vivien Kellems recruited important allies in her endeavor to reduce taxes on single persons, including Ed Koch, then a congressman from New York, who championed legislation to reduce income taxes on single persons. Perhaps her most effective ally was the actress Gloria Swanson, a woman who had been married six times, having failed to take the advice of the title of the Cecil B. DeMille movie that had made her a star: *Don't Change Your Husband*. But her marriages had not gone well. She told the House Ways and Means Committee that she had been "single most of her life." Ms. Swanson and Ms. Kellems were an effective team protesting the unfairness of income taxes on single persons, and in 1969 Congress handed them a victory that continues to haunt the income tax today.

In 1969, Congress introduced into the tax law for the first time a tax penalty on marriage. Congress has since discovered that under a progressive-rate income tax some important segment of the American public will regard their tax burden as unfair. The essential difficulty is this: it is impossible for a progressive-rate income tax to neither encourage nor discourage marriage, meaning that people who marry should pay neither more nor less than they paid on the same income before they married, and also to tax all married couples who have the same total income equally. (For readers with no math phobia, a simple mathematical proof of this proposition is contained in the notes.[6])

During the period 1913–1948, the tax law attempted to be marriage neutral, but, as I have told, tax planning and differences in states' property laws created arbitrary tax differentials among married couples with the same total income. From 1948 to 1969, all married couples with the same total income paid the same total tax, but this feature of the law created a tax bonus for marriage and stimulated complaints from single persons. The 1969 legislation was an explicit attempt to compromise among these goals. In doing so it created chaos, penalizing some married couples (when husband's and wife's incomes are relatively equal) and advantaging others (when their incomes are quite unequal).

The initial economic impact of this new marriage penalty on the American public was small. In 1972 the Treasury estimated that fewer than 15 percent of married couples were disadvantaged by the marriage penalty while more than 85 percent enjoyed a tax reduction from filing joint returns.[7] The 1969 rate schedule imposed the greatest marriage penalty on upper-middle-income couples, reaching a maximum of about $4,500 a year when the husband and wife each had about $35,000 of income.[8] (A dollar then would be worth about $2 today.) Initially the marriage penalty had virtually no impact at the bottom or very top of the income scale, but both structural changes in the economy and subsequent actions of Congress soon conspired to extend the tax penalty on marriage.

Without doubt, the single greatest change in the nation's workforce in recent decades has been the dramatic entry of married women into the labor market. Today, nearly three-quarters of married women under age fifty-five are in the labor force.[9] The median income of these families is 40 percent higher than families with only one wage earner. For married women who entered the job market because it had become necessary for the economic well-being of their families, the income tax added a dose of bitter to their experience. The 1969 legislation and its progeny have given an ever-increasing number of married couples an arbitrary, capricious, and, they believe, unconstitutional income tax penalty to complain about.

All the while, Congress—completely out of touch with married people's growing anger—extended marriage penalties to segments of the population that previously had been unaffected. First, in the mid-1970s, Congress added and subsequently greatly expanded a refundable earned-income tax credit to reduce and in some cases eliminate the combined income and Social Security taxes of low-income workers. This provision sometimes imposes a very large marriage penalty on low-income workers. For example, in 1996 an individual who earned $10,000 and had two children was entitled to a tax credit of about $3,500; two such persons would receive a total of more than $7,000—so long as they didn't marry. However, if these two people married, they would lose more than $5,000 of their tax credits, a marriage penalty equal to more than one-fourth of their combined incomes.[10]

President Bill Clinton and the Democrats in Congress got together and changed the tax rate schedule to add a whopping marriage penalty at the top end of the income scale in 1993, in some cases $15,000 in additional taxes a year. It could take $1 million of wealth to produce this much after-tax money annually.[11] For many wealthy married couples, the best tax-planning response to the 1993 tax rate increase is divorce. In the late 1960s, Congress created a marriage tax penalty that gave young people a reason for living together without marrying that their parents could understand; in the 1990s, President Clinton may have given this same generation a reason for divorcing that their children could forgive. In response to these tax penalties on marriage, some Americans engaged in America's favorite indoor sport: tax minimization.[12]

David and Angela Boyter

David Boyter, a Defense Department physicist, and Angela Boyter, a federal procurement officer, married in Baltimore, Maryland, on April 2, 1966. They stayed married from 1966 through 1974, filing joint tax returns as a married couple. But in 1975, when a friend who had just gone through a traumatic divorce remarked at a dinner party, "at least my taxes will be lower," the Boyters' life changed.[13]

The income tax reduction from divorcing and paying taxes as single people would be more than enough to pay for both the Boyters' annual Caribbean vacation and a Haitian divorce.[14] At the Pratt Public Library in Baltimore, Angela Boyter found the names of seven Haitian attorneys, and took the lowest bid. On December 8, 1975, the Republic of Haiti granted the Boyters a divorce on the grounds of incompatibility of character. After a few more days of vacationing happily together in Haiti, they returned to Ellicott City, Maryland, and remarried there on January 9, 1976.

A year later, in November 1976, the Boyters traveled to Santo

Domingo in the Dominican Republic for another vacation and another divorce. Since Angela had been the complaining party in the Haitian proceedings, it was David's turn. The Dominican court granted the Boyters a second divorce decree, this time on the ground of "incompatibility of temperaments making life together unbearable."[15] On February 10, 1977, the incompatible and unflappable David and Angela once again remarried in Ellicott City, Maryland.

The media started using the Boyters' vacation-divorces to increase public awareness of the absurdity of the tax law. National papers including the *Wall Street Journal,* the *New York Times,* and, of course, the *National Enquirer* told their story. The Boyters appeared on more than seventy radio shows and on television talk shows in more than a half-dozen major cities. Their little pamphlet "Divorce for Fun and Profit" was in its fourth printing by 1980. Even the Internal Revenue Service heard about them and challenged their $3,000-a-year tax savings from filing taxes as single persons. The IRS claimed that, whatever their actual legal status, the Boyters were married under the Internal Revenue Code. This was peculiar since, in a rare moment of absolute clarity, the tax law provides that marital status depends only on whether a person is married on December 31 of the year.[16]

Nevertheless, the IRS challenged the tax validity of the Boyters' divorces in the United States Tax Court. The IRS attorney emphasized that, although their divorces were based on "incompatibility" of "character" and "temperaments," David and Angela stayed together in the same hotel rooms after their divorces. Angela and David both conceded under oath that their divorces had been purely tax-motivated, and, on cross-examination, Angela confessed that she and David had no intention of physically separating, separating their investments or other finances, or ever stopping living together.

In a strained effort to keep the Boyters' case within the bounds of prior precedents, the Tax Court judge concluded that David and Angela's divorces would not be recognized by the Maryland state courts, but he had no factual basis for such a finding. David Boyter remarked: "We were the only couple who were remarried in Tax

Court."[17] The Fourth Circuit Court of Appeals reversed this decision, noting that the Tax Court judge had no way to know Maryland's view without asking Maryland's courts actually to decide the legality of the divorces. But the court of appeals added that the divorce might be ignored under the tax law as a "sham."[18] After this decision, an increasingly confused David Boyter told the *Washington Post*, "Ask me if I am married or not and I will tell you I honestly don't know."[19] He added, "Corporations merge and diverge strictly for tax reasons and nobody questions it as a sham. Why should couples be treated differently?"[20]

But the Boyters did not sit idly by waiting to learn how much additional taxes, interest, and penalties the IRS might ultimately demand. They gave up their vacation-divorce-remarriage pattern to limit their debts to the IRS if they lost in litigation, and in November 1977 the Boyters divorced for the third time. This time they stayed divorced to preclude the IRS from challenging that divorce as a sham. In 1978, the IRS ruled that a couple who gets divorced for a variety of personal reasons, does not intend to remarry, and stays divorced, but lives together after the divorce, qualifies as two single people under the tax law.[21] The IRS apparently regards long-term living together as better public policy than divorces followed by remarriage. This led to the following exchange in August 1980 between Senator Robert Dole and the Boyters at a Senate Finance Committee hearing:

> SENATOR DOLE: "You are divorced now?"
> MR. BOYTER: "We are divorced now and have been for several years."
> SENATOR DOLE: "You live together, though?"
> MR. BOYTER: "That is right. The IRS told us that that was preferable to getting remarried every year and divorced."
> MRS. BOYTER: "My mother did not think so, but the IRS did."[22]

Despite their travails, David claimed that nothing the Congress or the courts could do would affect his and Angela's relationship with each other. Angela insisted, "We will stay single until the law is changed."

On the day in 1980 that would have been their fourteenth wedding anniversary, the Boyters, who made a total income of about $70,000 a year, told the Ways and Means Committee that they had saved more than $15,000 in taxes in the previous five years because of their divorces. They estimated that, even if they never got another salary raise, their divorces would save them more than $130,000 in taxes by the time they retired.[23] By this time, Angela had left her procurement officer job and had found her true calling as a certified public accountant.

The Boyters inspired Phyllis Pond, an Indiana legislator, to propose that married couples automatically be granted a twenty-four-hour legal separation on December 31 each year, which would expire one minute after midnight on January 1. She insisted that this was a serious legislative effort to solve the marriage penalty, not a ploy to spice up New Year's Eve.

Both Richard Cohen and Ellen Goodman, commentators for the *Washington Post,* recognized the Boyters in 1979 as "contemporary American heroes." Applauding their "quickie divorces to pay for their vacations," Cohen summed it up, "So here's to the Boyters, a little toast to them for standing up to the government, for fighting for fairness and the family. They were married once, but they're not any more. The government came between them."[24]

Vivien Kellems received similar recognition. The Raleigh, North Carolina, *News Observer* celebrated June 7, 1993, as Vivien Kellems Memorial Day: "A day to cheer Kellems, who protested what she considered unfair taxation."

Angela Boyter understood well both this kind of adoration and its implications. She told the Ways and Means Committee:

> In America today the fastest ways to become a national hero are to hit a home run in the World Series or to fight the IRS.
>
> In 1948 you convinced the single taxpayers that the system is unfair. In 1969 you added the two-earner families. If you continue adding complexities and favored groups to the tax code, you will eventually convince the

majority of the system's unfairness, and they will feel justified in making their own adjustments.

Needless to say, at that point we will no longer have
largely voluntary tax compliance.[25]

Conclusion

The married-single controversy, which has so plagued the income
tax throughout its entire history, teaches several important lessons,
lessons to which we shall return throughout this book. Most important, when a tax system departs dramatically from the fundamental values of the people it taxes, it cannot sustain public
support.

Barber Conable, then the ranking Republican on the House
Ways and Means Committee, admonished one married couple that
"to base all of your decisions on tax consequences is not necessarily to maintain the proper balance and perspective on what you are
doing."[26] But people like the Boyters are not wise enough to consider themselves lucky when the biggest problem with their marriage is additional taxes. And many couples who do marry postpone
their weddings from December to January to save at least one year's
marriage penalty. Never underestimate the imagination or the
doggedness of the American people in their willingness to engage
in tax-minimizing strategies. People routinely lose perspective when
it comes to saving taxes. People of other nations may be readier to
cheat outright, but America is a superpower in the game of creative
tax avoidance.

When people lose respect for a law, they will not obey it. Arbitrary and unfair tax distinctions—whether based on geographical location, marital status, or the kind of income people
make—instill disdain for the law and disrespect for those who write
it and who enforce it. The voluntary compliance of private citizens,
which is essential to enforce any tax statute, threatens to disappear.

Second, the tax law must respond to changes in society and
the economy. Even if Congress in 1969 viewed the marriage penalty

as a barely acceptable trade-off to reduce excessive burdens on single people, changes in the nation's economy and the workforce soon rendered it unacceptable. The dramatic increase in the number of working wives in the workplace and the narrowing gap between men's and women's earnings have made completely obsolete Congress's Ozzie and Harriet vision of the family—where the man works and the woman stays home—the only vision that could have justified the 1969 change. Nothing is gained by Congress denying the reality of the lives of the people it is supposed to represent.

Finally, the absence of a perfect, or even fully satisfactory, resolution to a difficult problem does not excuse the failure of political leadership and judgment. The impossibility of satisfying the genuine claims for equity of married couples and single persons in a progressive-rate income tax system does not absolve politicians of responsibility for the compromises they fashion. The public properly is not indifferent about whether the nation's income tax law encourages marriage or divorce. Politicians must be held accountable for failing to respond when they legislate contrary to the fundamental values of the American people. Both political parties bear responsibility for legislation expanding and extending marriage penalties. Token changes are simply not enough.[27]

Although the Boyters, like Vivien Kellems before them, told the Congress that a flat-rate system would eliminate the penalties for being single or married,[28] the marriage penalty is not responsible for the recent flurry of flat-tax proposals in the Congress. But, if Congress refuses to embrace other remedies to eliminate it, perhaps the marriage penalty alone justifies a flat-rate, or at least flatter-rate, income tax.

3

Chasing Chinchilla Coats
and Other Tax Shelter
Aerobics

The tax law has always contained
breaks for certain kinds of businesses or investments. These bless-
ings have fallen on real estate; oil, gas, and mineral businesses;
farming; movies; and purchasers of business equipment. Tax advantages for such investments have often been deliberately added
to the tax code to further one or another social or economic purpose: to kick-start a sluggish economy, to provide more housing, to
reduce the nation's dependence on foreign oil. In the 1970s, tax
advisers, investment bankers, and a motley cast of entrepreneurs
and promoters discovered that a little creativity, especially with the
use of partnerships, would allow them to market these tax breaks
throughout the land.

The growth in tax shelter investments from the mid-1970s to
the mid-1980s tells a tax-avoidance tale unprecedented in the his-

tory of the income tax. In 1981, the commissioner of internal revenue, Roscoe Egger, compared the IRS's battle against tax shelters to Mickey Mouse's battle against the multiplying mops in the "Sorcerer's Apprentice" segment of *Fantasia*. He said that every time the IRS cuts a mop in half, at least twice as many more come down the steps.[1]

In 1973, when the IRS initiated a tax shelter program, it focused on investments in four areas: oil and gas, real estate, movies, and farming. A decade later, the IRS commissioner accurately described tax shelters as "flaky schemes," "candidates for 'Let's Make a Deal,' " adding that "since 1973, every conceivable device, animal or property has become a candidate for a tax shelter."[2] In 1973, 400 tax shelter cases were being audited; by 1980 this number had risen to nearly 200,000 and by 1984 to 350,000. In 1983 tax shelter cases accounted for about one-seventh of the nation's entire tax understatements detected by the IRS.[3]

By the late 1970s, the vast majority of the public believed that "everybody else" was engaging in tax avoidance or outright tax evasion. Sixty-nine percent of respondents to a 1978 survey agreed that "most people who have a higher income than I do manage to get away with paying less than their fair share of taxes." By 1982, the pollster Lou Harris told the Senate Finance Committee that by an 86–7 majority, people agreed that "while most lower- and middle-income people now pay their tax by taking standard deductions, most higher-income people get out of paying much of their taxes by hiring clever tax accountants and lawyers who show them how to use loopholes in the tax law for tax shelters and other devices."[4]

The people were right. A 1983 congressional staff study estimated that nearly 40 percent of tax returns with income over $200,000 were reporting tax shelter losses, losses which reduced the total tax liability of those in the top tax bracket by more than 25 percent. In contrast, only 1/10th of 1 percent of taxpayers with incomes in the $10,000 to $20,000 range reported similar losses and these losses had a barely perceptible effect on their total taxes.[5]

Capital was running around the country like the Keystone Kops, looking for the most tax-favored investments. Much of the nation's innovative energies, entrepreneurial spirit, and marketing imagination had become concentrated in the creation, production, and selling of tax shelter investments. High-income individuals thought they had finally discovered the golden-egg goose. Unfortunately, it was the taxpaying middle class that was being plucked. Hardly any high-income people still believed it was better just to earn a dollar, pay fifty cents in taxes, and keep fifty cents than to throw the dollar at a tax shelter in the hopes of keeping it all.

In addition to virtually every doctor, dentist, and airline pilot in America, the tax shelter craze attracted many well-known people. William Casey, whose last job was as Ronald Reagan's director of Central Intelligence, claimed to have invented the tax shelter business in 1952, and he was a central player in the early days of tax shelter investing, having testified in Tax Court about how he arrived at a $5 million sales price for the syndication of a tri-rotor engine that he had paid $10,000 for a few months earlier.[6] The list of tax shelter investors spanned the political spectrum, attracting both the conservative losing Republican presidential candidate of 1964, Barry Goldwater, and the liberal Democratic loser of 1972, George McGovern. Tax shelters also attracted Ronald Reagan's attorney general, William French Smith; the U.S. postmaster general, Preston Tisch; *All in the Family* producer Norman Lear; numerous actors and actresses, including Barbra Streisand, Lorne Greene, Eddie Murphy, and Sydney Poitier; and a host of well-known athletes.[7] P. T. Barnum would have loved it.

How about a Chinchilla Coat?

Even I got calls from tax shelter promoters. My favorite was in 1977 from someone selling a chinchilla-farm tax shelter. Boy, did he have a deal for me! An investment that not only gave huge tax write-offs but also promised a chinchilla coat. For a mere $10,000 investment in his chinchilla breeding and rearing farm, I would receive not only $30,000 in tax deductions, but also a chinchilla coat "for the little woman." After he admitted that this deal didn't have any chinchilla coats in my size—something like a 52 extra large—I knew I wasn't going to join the nation's ever-increasing group of financially troubled family farmers.

I didn't put my money in chinchillas, but other people did. One of these was Howard Mager. Howard should have known better. He was a securities analyst, specializing in aerospace and electrical equipment companies, telling people which ones were likely to produce the best investment returns. Howard Mager's chinchilla investment demonstrates well how capable and intelligent people lost their bearings when offered irresistible tax savings.

Howard Mager invested $10,000 in chinchillas in 1976. Howard paid about three times what each chinchilla was worth. He bought too many beige chinchillas for starters, and none of his chinchillas had the four-generation pedigree necessary for a successful chinchilla breeding herd. Howard gave his money to people with no chinchilla knowledge or business experience, and he paid no attention to his chinchilla-breeding operation.

When the IRS challenged Howard's tax deductions and sent a chinchilla expert to examine Howard's chinchillas, the expert discovered that the tattooed numbers of the chinchillas did not match the numbers recorded for Howard's chinchillas. These chinchillas probably were sold more than once. Howard's chinchillas were never shown in competition, and no pelts from Howard's chinchillas or any of the progeny were ever sold. Howard did not even know how many chinchillas had been born to his breeding stock.

Why, then, did a smart guy like Howard so readily throw $10,000 at a flaky chinchilla-breeding operation? Simple. He thought he would save nearly $14,000 in taxes on his 1976 tax return. When you believe you're making an instantaneous 40 percent after-tax return by lowering your taxes, you don't worry too much about the underlying quality of the investment, even if you are a professional securities analyst.

The bad news for Howard was that the IRS discovered his chinchilla investment, and disallowed his $14,000 of tax savings. After Howard repaid the taxes due, plus more than seven years of interest, plus his lawyer's fees, he wished he had never heard of chinchillas. His original $10,000 was also gone.[8] But this was the tax shelter business.

The chinchilla-coat deal was simply an exotic variation of a standard farming tax shelter deal. Chinchillas were too small an animal for some people. Frank Goss, for example, the head of a ranching equipment firm in Fort Worth, Texas, started a buffalo farm as a tax shelter, but it didn't work out very well. Here's how Goss described the venture: "I bought this little ranchito in Tioga, Texas, and bought me a pair of buffalo, but my bull buffalo—I named him Billy of course—escaped and started cross-breeding with cattle. He wasn't supposed to do that, and the cattle didn't like it either. My advice for people looking for a tax shelter is to stay out of the buffalo business unless all they want is a good story."[9]

Tax shelters in cows, horses, trout, and even minks generally did better than chinchillas or buffaloes. Arabian horse tax shelters prompted Representative Marcy Kaptur of Ohio to complain that "the average American taxpayer should not have to subsidize wealthy individuals' speculation in Arabian horses." She lamented, "Our tax code should encourage productive investment in jobs and people, not tax shelters for the rich. I believe in investing in people before horses."[10]

A variety of bushes and trees also served well as tax shelters. When tax lawyer and professor Martin Ginsburg described to the Ways and Means Committee a tax shelter boom that had occurred in azaleas and rosebushes, he found it "difficult to believe the United States is in the throes of a rosebush crisis."[11] California's congressman Pete Stark expressed his disdain for jojoba-bean tax shelters: "We shouldn't be giving tax breaks to anything that takes three years to figure out its sex." Fruits and nuts—especially almonds and macadamia nuts—were particularly popular.

So were movies. Joe West of West Valley, Utah, tried to claim more than $10,000 in tax savings from a $400 investment in 1981 in a movie called *Bottom*. The next year he put in $10,000 and claimed more than $30,000 of additional tax deductions. By the time the IRS and the Tax Court were done with him, Joe had not only lost his $10,400, but also found himself owing the IRS more than $35,000 in taxes and penalties plus a substantial amount of interest.[12] Joe himself had hit bottom.

One of the most unseemly tax shelter deals married the tax law's incentives for charitable giving with the overvaluation common to the tax shelter craze. The Smithsonian Institution itself got involved with a group of people who bought semiprecious gemstones at wholesale, waited a short period of time, and then contributed them to the Smithsonian, taking charitable deductions for an inflated retail price.[13] In one case, opals purchased for $10,000 each were appraised for charitable purposes at $60,000 each. For a "donor" in a 50 percent tax bracket, this would mean a $30,000 tax savings from purchasing and giving away a $10,000 opal, tripling his money, not a bad return. Not enough, however, for everyone; some opals were overvalued by a factor of 50.[14]

The most outrageous charitable tax shelter involved buying copies of the Bible at wholesale and then contributing them to religious organizations for exaggerated tax deductions based upon a large multiple of retail. This was the American version of taking from Caesar, rendering a little to God, and pocketing the rest.

The Government Itself Enters the Tax Shelter Promotion Racket

Probably the most bizarre transactions during the tax shelter feeding frenzy occurred when government entities and private tax-exempt organizations tried to grab some tax shelter investors' money for themselves. They came up with the crazy, but lawful, idea of selling their assets to tax shelter partnerships, then leasing them back so that they could keep on using them. Bennington College sold and leased back its dormitories, the city of Atlanta its Civic Center. But the most remarkable tax shelter transactions involved sales to taxable corporations and high-income individuals of thirteen ships of the U.S. Navy's Rapid Development Force.

Here is the way the navy sale-leaseback deal worked. Having failed to convince the Congress to appropriate enough money to buy the ships it wanted, the Navy Department decided to "rent a navy."[15] Several contractors, including General Dynamics, the Maersk Line, Ltd., and Waterman Steamship Corporation, agreed either to construct new vessels or to convert existing vessels to meet the Navy's requirements and, once the construction was finished, to lease the ships to the navy for a twenty-five year period. A number of companies provided financing, including Bankers' Trust Co., Salomon Brothers, Household Finance Co., Beatrice Co., and General Foods. Both Salomon Brothers and Bankers' Trust asked the Internal Revenue Service for a specific ruling that these transactions entitled investors to deduct interest and accelerated depreciation on the ships. The depreciation deductions permitted the investors to write off the total costs of the ships in five years, even though the navy had agreed to pay rent for twenty-five years. The "investors" included companies like Phillip Morris Co., United Parcel Service, and others who were considered the "owners" of the boats for tax purposes, even though for national security reasons none of them was allowed to board "their" boats.

Ultimately the IRS issued a 143-page ruling blessing the deal.[16] As you might imagine, the legal gymnastics were spectacular. Nearly 100 pages of the IRS's ruling describes the financing and other arrangements, the leverage lease agreements, the assignment and assumption agreements, equity participation agreements, charters for the boats, indentures on the loans, mortgages on the ships, the lenders' security arrangements, credit assignments, trust agreements, insurance, and on and on.

This scheme decreased the Defense Department's annual expenditures because much of the money had been supplied through the back door of the U.S. Treasury in the form of tax breaks to the investors, but when all was said and done, it added $300 million, 12 percent, to the total cost of the boats. The navy even agreed to reimburse the contractors and investors for any anticipated tax benefits that were subsequently disallowed by the IRS and also to reimburse them for any legal expenses they incurred in combat with the IRS. The Navy Department had agreed to finance private lawsuits against the IRS. Your tax dollars at work!

Imagine the anger of the average hardworking family when they learned that $300 million of their taxes was being given to corporations and high-bracket individual investors in a navy rent-a-boat tax shelter leasing deal. The dining table conversation of that advertising "everycouple," Harry and Louise, would not have been fit for television, even in the nighttime hours. In 1984 Congress finally prohibited such deals.

Stemming the Tide, at Last

Congress finally halted the tax shelter phenomenon in the Tax Reform Act of 1986. But before it managed to do that, Congress had enacted more than half a dozen major tax revisions—in 1969, 1971, 1976, 1978, 1981, 1982, and 1984—which were supposed to "solve" the tax shelter problem. This legislative tinkering produced a remarkable number of new statutory provisions of unbounded complexity, but none of these provisions, either taken separately or all together, slowed the rising tide of tax shelter investments. As a congressional aide put it after learning that the 1982 legislation hadn't done the job: "Trying to control tax shelters is like stepping on Jell-O. It just squeezes out between your toes and the mess is worse than when you began."[17] Congress did not achieve success until the Tax Reform Act of 1986, when it enacted a limitation on "passive losses" that ended the ability of taxpayers to use losses from tax shelter investments to reduce taxes on their earned income, interest, and dividends.

The tax shelter era had come to an end. But in the meantime, untold dollars of potentially productive capital had been diverted to tax shelter investments, and a substantial segment of the American people had become addicted to tax-reduction schemes. More and more Americans had come to believe that the income tax was either completely out of control or deliberately rigged to favor the rich. Nearly two decades of tax shelters took a serious, perhaps ultimately even fatal, toll on people's respect for the fairness of the income tax.

The flood of tax shelter money stimulated overinvestment in unproductive assets. According to the Motion Picture Association, the number of movies released increased from 433 in 1982 to 520 in 1984, even though total theater revenues did not go up at all during that period. Observers of the motion picture scene described the movie industry as having "snorted up tax shelter money almost as fast as it has cocaine."[18]

The most devastating case of tax-driven overinvestment occurred in real estate. The 1981 tax law dramatically enhanced the tax shelter advantages of real estate investment, prompting a tax partner at the Price Waterhouse accounting firm to remark, "The syndication of real estate has replaced baseball as our national pastime."[19] One tax shelter partnership even syndicated the building where the IRS rented its Manhattan headquarters. The tax shelter phenomenon contributed to the real estate glut in the Southwest and to empty "see-through" office buildings nationwide, and tax shelters played an important role in precipitating and expanding the collapse of the savings and loan industry in the United States. In combination, the savings and loan and tax shelter excesses together involved so much "money for nothing" that many otherwise law-abiding people did a whole host of stupid things that landed many of them in jail.

It doesn't take a rocket scientist to know that a country that has designed and maintained a tax system that has inspired its nation's savings to chase after chinchilla coats, bad movies, rosebushes, and overvalued Bibles is seriously handicapping itself in global competition with other nations that are modernizing their steel and auto factories. When capital works as it should, it enhances the productivity of workers and makes a critical contribution to rising wages and an increasing standard of living. Enormous sums of tax shelter capital instead lined the pockets of lawyers, accountants, appraisers, investment bankers, syndicaters, promoters, and flimflam artists.

The adverse impact on our nation's economy was made worse by fiscal policy. While Congress was misdirecting the nation's private capital through the tax code, it also created a deficit-driven fiscal policy that in short order converted this country from the world's largest creditor nation to the world's largest debtor. Private U.S. capital was chasing chinchillas, and our government was borrowing from abroad to finance current consumption. How can it now come as a surprise that our national rate of savings and investment is a matter of deep economic concern? We have decades of very bad habits to overcome.

Tax shelters also caused a major shift in the role of tax lawyers and accountants. Virtually every tax shelter deal contained a lawyer's opinion that an investor had "a reasonable basis" for claiming on his tax return the tax deductions and tax credits offered by the deal. This so-called reasonable-basis opinion letter was careful not to guarantee any investor that the tax advantages claimed on the tax return would ultimately be upheld in court if they were challenged by the IRS, but instead served to ensure investors that they could avoid penalties for tax fraud.

The tax shelter promoters who bought these insurance policies had a purpose quite different from the one traditionally in mind between clients and their tax attorneys. Historically, when a client consulted a tax attorney, she wanted the attorney's best judgment about the tax risks of a transaction. Tax shelter promoters, however, wanted protection from penalties, not the lawyer's assessment of risk.

Tax lawyers were varied and creative in escaping any ultimate judgment about the tax benefits claimed. They sometimes assumed facts, thereby avoiding the independent diligent evaluation normally required when investments are sold to the public. Prestigious law firms favored an endless analysis of issues that failed to come to a conclusion, balancing arguments on both sides, but presenting no ultimate judgment about the likely outcome of the tax shelter if litigated. The bottom line was only that taxpayers had a "reasonable basis" for claiming the tax savings on their tax returns.

The notion that attorneys could advise their clients to take any position on a tax return for which there is a "reasonable basis" was the ethical standard adopted by the American Bar Association in 1965, but in the tax shelter era the reasonable-basis standard came to mean any basis at all. The Bar Association itself described the reasonable-basis standard as having been widely interpreted by lawyers to support "any colorable claim on a tax return to justify exploitation of the lottery of the audit selection process." My students, somewhat more colorfully and no less accurately, described the reasonable-basis standard as requiring only that an attorney could pass a "laugh-aloud test"; any argument that could be made without laughing aloud was viewed as satisfying the reasonable-basis requirement.

The tax bar, the accounting profession, and other tax-return preparers no longer hold the view—if they ever did—that filing a tax return should represent each taxpayer's best efforts at determining the actual tax due. Instead, they treat tax returns as an "opening bid," where every issue is resolved in favor of paying less taxes on the assumption that the taxpayer will not be audited or that, if audited, the IRS agent will either overlook or compromise on the issue.

In the late 1970s, in a bar in Scottsdale, Arizona, following a very hard-hitting speech by Assistant Attorney General for Taxation Carr Ferguson to the Tax Section of the American Bar Association on the ethical and legal responsibilities of tax advisers, I overhead a conversation at a neighboring table between a tax lawyer and his wife. The wife inquired about the meeting and her husband responded, "The assistant attorney general has just given an inspiring speech about how one should conduct his tax practice. He said that if you participate in a deal that is really a sham, you're getting pretty close to the line." Enough said.

Even with the advantage of hindsight, it is impossible to know for sure the extent to which Congress's incompetence in dealing with the tax shelter craze was due to interest-group pressure. But it has become harder and harder to believe that a majority of Congress is not in the hands of some special interests. Congress wrote the laws that created and maintained this spectacle and for a very long time failed to respond effectively to what had become very obvious problems. The 1986 act may have halted the public marketing of tax shelters, but it failed to restore public confidence in either the Congress or the income tax. The damage had been done.

4

Disappearing Dollars

This nation has known very few days that have turned American tax politics upside down, but June 6, 1978, was one of those days. On that day, by a vote of 65 to 35 percent, the people of California added to that state's constitution a measure known as Proposition 13. Proposition 13 had three results. Its immediate effect was to limit property taxes in California. It also shifted power from local governments to the state of California. Perhaps most important, it fired an unmistakable salvo in a tax rebellion whose influence is still felt today.

Proposition 13

Proposition 13 placed a ceiling on residential property taxes, taxes that had been escalating because of inflationary increases in the values of people's homes. For most Californians, increased taxes were the principal effect of the rapid increases in home values they had been experiencing. Homeowners could not profit from their increased values unless they were willing to sell their homes and leave California for less expensive climes, say the Midwest, a move that most Californians then considered unthinkable. Changing to another house in the same area typically required the homeowner to take all of the inflated price he received from selling his home and put it, and often a bit more, into the equally wildly inflated purchase price of the new residence. Californians joked, "I'll trade you my million-dollar dog for your million-dollar cat."

Inflation, however, was increasing government revenues. Local government coffers swelled as higher assessments of property values increased property taxes even if no one raised tax rates. The state viewed its homeowners as getting wealthier all the time and therefore able to pay more property taxes. But California homeowners knew the difference between inflationary paper wealth and real wealth they could spend. The increased property taxes left them with less money at the end of the day.

Similar things were happening throughout the country. Housing prices were not rising nearly so fast as in California, but with widespread inflation this phenomenon was spreading, and property taxes were rising across the country. Homeowners living on a fixed income—particularly retirees who traditionally vote in large numbers—were becoming especially angry.

In rejecting calls to be "responsible" by virtually all of their elected representatives and enacting Proposition 13, voters announced that tax politics hereafter would be something quite different. In one day at the ballot box, the people of California transformed raising taxes from a dangerous political suggestion into an act risking political suicide.

Bracket Creep

The same inflationary pressure was at work in the federal income tax, piling insult upon injury through the phenomenon of "bracket creep." When people's incomes went up just enough to keep pace with inflation, they were no better off. They had no increase in purchasing power. But the tax law acted as if they did, transferring a greater percentage of their earnings to the Treasury because the income tax brackets were not adjusted for inflation. Coupled with higher Social Security taxes on wages, this meant that workers whose nominal incomes had gone up, but whose purchasing power had not, were required to pay higher income and Social Security taxes to the federal government, higher property taxes to their local government, and higher prices for goods and services. They were keeping an ever-shrinking share of what they had earned or saved.

This bracket creep mugged middle-income taxpayers to a staggering extent. A family of four whose income went up from $15,000 to $16,500 in 1980 just to keep up with a 10 percent inflation rate had a 23 percent increase in federal taxes, from $1,243 to $1,530, having moved from the 18 percent tax bracket to the 21 percent bracket.[1] In 1970 a family earning $25,000 was in the 28 percent income tax bracket. By 1982, that family needed nearly $61,000 to maintain the same standard of living but that put them into the 49 percent tax bracket.[2] A couple of accountants found that a decade of bracket creep diminished the purchasing power of a person with a salary in the $30,000–$50,000 range, whose wage increases simply kept pace with inflation, by about 20 percent.[3]

By the end of the 1970s, nearly 80 percent of Americans were paying higher taxes because of bracket creep.[4] To get some sense of how many people were affected, consider this: In 1960, only 3 percent of income tax returns were taxed at a top rate of 30 percent or more; by 1981, as a result of bracket creep, more than one-third paid taxes at a 30 percent or higher rate.[5] Look at how much total income was taxed at higher tax rates. In 1964, only 8 percent of total income was taxed at a tax rate of 35 percent or above, and rates this high applied to only 1 percent of all tax returns.[6] By 1980, 31 percent of income was taxed at a tax rate of 35 percent or more and these rates affected more than 10 percent of returns. The fraction of tax returns that faced such high tax rates had multiplied by a factor of 10 during the period 1964–1980.

The tax revolt movement taking hold in the hearts and minds of the American people coincided with this inflation-induced increase in people's income tax burdens. Moreover, as more and more people moved into higher and higher marginal tax brackets, the potential market for tax shelter investments greatly expanded. Bracket creep was not only making people poorer and madder, it also sent them scurrying after tax shelters.

But Congress Loved It

As bad as this un-indexed tax system was for the American public, that's how good it was for Congress. Long ago, a French finance minister called taxation "the art of plucking the goose with the least amount of squawking," and for some time there was no better instrument of this art than bracket creep. Tax increases were automatic. For every 10 percent of inflation, federal revenues increased by 17 percent.[7] Each year's inflation took more and more money from the American people and moved it to the federal fisc, where Congress could redirect it, usually to different people. During the period 1972–1983, the consumer price index rose by 138 percent, more than it had increased in the entire period from the end of World War II until 1972. This gave the Congress an automatic increase in income tax revenues of nearly 235 percent during the same period, an additional $63 billion in taxes in the period 1978–1983 alone.

Congress was routinely obtaining ever-increasing funds for government spending even when it returned some portion of this windfall through tax reduction. Much of the increased spending involved transfer payments, particularly to the retired elderly through Social Security increases, which were indexed for inflation beginning in the 1970s, and through expansions of Medicare and Medicaid.

Increased revenues also permitted Congress to hand out tax reductions from time to time. Sometimes, as in 1975 and 1976, the tax reductions were targeted to low- and middle-income taxpayers, generally through increases in the standard deduction. In 1978 Congress adjusted the tax brackets to offset some of the adverse impact of bracket creep on upper-middle-class taxpayers. Congress also reduced corporate income taxes in 1978 through special tax credits for equipment purchases and reduced both corporate and capital-gains tax rates.

Some of the money was distributed quite narrowly. In 1976, for example, Congress gave special tax breaks to the railroads, airlines, and the merchant marines. Russell Long, the chairman of the Senate Finance Committee, would remark at these tax-reduction occasions, "Remember tomorrow we spread the joy!"[8] It was purely accidental if the money went back to the people from whom it came.

The politics of bracket creep were glorious for the politicians. They never had to legislate a tax increase in order to obtain ever-increasing revenues; all they had to do was sit back and wait for the money to flow in. They could then distribute this largesse to their constituents as they pleased. Given this political Nirvana, it is miraculous that bracket creep ever was eliminated.

In 1981, President Reagan proposed an across-the-board 30 percent cut in income tax rates as his key legislative initiative, a proposal that sparked a bidding war as congressional Democrats and Republicans competed to see who could give away more in tax reductions. Neither Reagan himself nor the House of Representatives proposed eliminating bracket creep, preferring instead such expensive items as unlimited IRA deductions for individuals and extremely generous depreciation allowances for corporations.

But by the time the 1981 tax bill was considered on the Senate floor, indexing the income tax to eliminate bracket creep had become impossible to resist. Senator Bill Armstrong of Colorado introduced an amendment to index the income tax brackets, the standard deduction, and personal exemptions. He wanted not only to end the unfairness of automatic tax increases due to inflation, but also to halt the automatic flow of increasing tax dollars in the hopes of controlling federal spending.[9] Although Jim Baker, Ronald Reagan's premier vote counter, was confident that Senator

Armstrong's effort would fail, indexing passed by a vote of 57 to 40.[10]

The indexing provisions do not affect all taxpayers equally. Because the earned-income tax credit, applicable only to low-income wage earners, and the standard deduction and personal exemptions are indexed as well as the tax rate brackets, indexing has had the greatest impact for lower- and middle-income families. Since high-income families do not typically claim the standard deduction and are not eligible for personal exemptions, they would suffer the smallest percentage tax increase if indexing were repealed.

Under the 1981 law, however, tax indexing did not go into effect until 1985, and in 1983 and 1984 there were serious political attempts to repeal or postpone indexing. This movement attracted some conservatives concerned with mounting deficits and a rapidly growing national debt, but was spearheaded by politicians who recognized that tax indexing took away their ability to appear magnanimous by enacting periodic tax reductions and also demanded that they make voters unhappy by either cutting spending or enacting explicit tax increases. This attempt to repeal indexing failed, in part because Congress knew indexing was right as a matter of principle, but mostly because having once enacted tax indexing, not enough votes could be mustered to turn back.

The delay of indexing from 1981 to 1985 added to people's skepticism regarding politicians' promises of tax relief. Having been told in 1981 that Congress had eliminated bracket creep, people continued to face its adverse effects until 1985. By the time indexing actually reduced income tax withholding in January 1985, new Social Security tax increases, which had been legislated in 1983, offset much of the benefit for most wage earners. Rather than finding their withholding and total federal tax bite decreasing, many wage earners saw little or no net increase in their after-tax wages.

In addition, as we all now know, Congress did not either cut spending or raise sufficient revenues to pay for the spending they were voting. As a result, deficits and our national debt mounted. The amount of revenues lost to the federal government through tax indexing has been enormous. The cumulative national debt would have probably been more than $500 billion lower had indexing not been enacted.[11] Indeed, the revenue effects of indexing are so substantial that reducing indexing by only 1/2 of 1 percent of the inflation increase in every year would produce more than $10 billion in revenues each year.

Stated Dollar Thresholds

The 1981 tax legislation indexed the tax rate brackets, the earned-income tax credit, personal exemptions, and the standard deduction. Congress has also indexed a variety of other tax provisions stated in specific dollar amounts. These include, for example, the income level where high-income people's taxes are increased through a "phaseout" of itemized deductions, and the income level where personal exemptions are eliminated.

In other instances, however, specific dollar amounts in the income tax are not adjusted for inflation. Home mortgage interest deductions, for example, are allowed on up to $1 million of borrowing to purchase a home and for $100,000 of home equity indebtedness, amounts which are not indexed. Inflation therefore reduces over time the real amount of home mortgage indebtedness that qualifies for the interest deduction. Even at the current relatively low rate of inflation, if Congress does not index or otherwise increase them, these limits, which were enacted in 1987, will only be half as great by the year 2000; the $1 million limitation will be worth approximately $500,000 and the $100,000 limitation worth $50,000 in 1987 dollars.[12]

There are many additional provisions of this sort, including, for example, a $3,000 limitation on deductions for capital losses on the sale of stock and other assets (which if indexed would be $12,000 today[13]), the credit for child-care expenses, and the floor for income taxation of Social Security benefits, the latter two of which affect large numbers of people each year.[14] In each of these instances, the failure to index the stated dollar amount for inflation increases the government's tax take.

Inflation and
the Mismeasurement of Capital Income

Inflation also distorts the income tax's measurement of income from capital. In inflationary times, net income is mismeasured for tax purposes whenever dollar amounts spent in an earlier year are netted against amounts received in a later year. The best-known case is in determining amounts of capital gain or loss. Assets are frequently sold in years subsequent to when they were purchased, but the income tax measures capital gain or loss simply by offsetting the amount received on sale with the amount spent for the asset's purchase. No adjustment is made to the earlier year's purchase price to reflect inflation that occurred during the period while the asset was held. This means that capital gains are often, at least in part, not "real" gains because they merely reflect the inflationary rise in general prices. In such cases, they do not add to an individual's purchasing power. The extent of mismeasurement of gains and losses that occurs depends on the rate of inflation and how long the asset is held. Taxation of inflationary gains inspires periodic calls for indexation of the purchase price of assets or a special lower tax rate for capital gains.

An indexing provision for capital gains did pass the House of Representatives in 1989, but was not ultimately enacted. This indexing rule would have required very difficult recordkeeping and many additional mathematical computations. To see why this is so, just consider the different inflation adjustments that would be necessary with a stock or mutual fund that automatically reinvests each quarter's dividends in purchases of new shares. Different inflation adjustments would be required for each quarter's purchases. A host of special rules would also be necessary for investments through entities such as partnerships or mutual funds. Indexing provisions would add such a great complexity to the income tax that many thoughtful experts vastly prefer the arbitrariness of some special tax rate for capital gains.

Inflation also sometimes overstates income from sales of in-

59

ventories by comparing purchase prices of earlier years to sales prices of subsequent years and mismeasures capital income whenever depreciation deductions are allowed. Depreciation allows the cost of an asset purchased in one year to be taken as a deduction against income earned during a number of future years. Failure to adjust depreciation for inflation during the period the asset is held causes an overstatement of the real income generated by the asset. This problem commonly occurs with rental income and other business income generated by real estate or equipment. The tax law has addressed this problem from time to time by giving rapid depreciation write-offs or special tax credits for purchases of certain kinds of assets, particularly equipment. Many other special tax write-offs have been enacted to benefit income from important categories of assets, including natural-resources exploration and development, and real estate, including housing. Each of these favors has been defended by their supporters as a partial offset to the potential overtaxation that might otherwise occur because of inflation.

The ad hoc congressional tinkering in response to these problems has been arbitrary and unfair, creating large disparities in income taxes both across different industries and among different companies in the same industry depending on their investments and their financing and accounting practices. Equal amounts of income have been taxed at very different rates and resources have been channeled toward tax-advantaged activities. In the mid-1980s, for example, average corporate tax rates were widely disparate; they ranged from a low of *minus* 20 percent for the water transportation industry to a high of 37 percent for water companies, sanitary supply companies, and certain other utilities.[15] Companies selling goods at wholesale were subject to a corporate income tax of less than 8.5 percent while retailers paid tax at about a 23.5 percent rate.[16] The 1986 act tried to level somewhat this playing field.

Inflation Also Enhanced
Tax-Saving Opportunities

Probably the most debilitating breakdown of the income tax in connection with inflation has involved the tax treatment of debt. In sharp contrast to the increased tax burdens imposed on ordinary workers through bracket creep, the tax law's treatment of debt in inflationary times has provided enormous tax-saving opportunities for corporations and individuals with borrowing power.

The income tax mismeasures both interest income and interest expense when inflation occurs because interest (unadjusted for inflation) is typically deductible by the payer and taxed to the recipient, while principal (also unadjusted for inflation) is neither deductible by the payer nor taxed to the recipient. Thus, whenever borrowing occurs, the income of both lenders and borrowers is mismeasured. Interest income and interest expense are both overstated in inflationary periods because interest rates include an inflation premium intended to compensate lenders for an anticipated decline in the purchasing power of their loans. Greater rates of inflation produce higher interest payments and larger distortions. Lenders who are subject to income tax tend to be overtaxed because some of their interest income represents a payment of principal rather than interest, and borrowers tend to be undertaxed because their deductible interest expense includes not only real interest, which should be deductible, but also an inflation premium, which should not be.

If lenders and borrowers were subject to identical tax rates, these effects would precisely cancel each other, and the overtaxation of lenders would exactly offset the undertaxation of borrowers. But this does not happen. The current income tax provides great incentives for undertaxed assets to be held by people and companies subject to the highest marginal tax rates and for overtaxed assets (such as loans that produce taxable interest) to be held by low-bracket taxpayers, foreigners, and tax-exempt entities.[17] A huge amount of loans in the United States are made by tax-exempt entities, such as pension funds and university endowment funds, and although the taxable corporations to which they lend the money can deduct the inflated amount of interest, the offsetting overstated interest income does not produce any additional tax. Even taxable lenders, such as banks and insurance companies, historically have been able to shelter much of their interest income through special tax breaks. In 1981 the taxes saved from interest deductions exceeded the taxes paid on interest income by $61 billion, nearly one-seventh of total corporate and individual income taxes that year, a gigantic tax stimulus to borrowing.[18]

Consider some of the consequences. During the 1970s and 1980s there were large tax incentives to buy real estate with borrowed money. Inflation increased the value of the real estate, but no income tax was due until the property was sold. In the meanwhile, the owners could deduct their inflationary interest payments against income that would otherwise have been taxed. This occurred with all sorts of real estate, and when the inflated values ultimately tumbled, those who made the loans and ultimately the federal government that insured them were left holding the bag.

Of course, not everyone could play this game. A young farmer who did not have enough income to use large interest deductions would be outbid for his family's farmland by a large corporation or a partnership of high-income individuals who had plenty of income to shelter. Some farmers who overextended their borrowing in an effort to compete ended up in bankruptcy court when commodity prices fell in the early 1980s.[19]

There were even ways for some people to take advantage of the income tax treatment of debt without taking any financial risk. You could go to a bank, borrow $2,000, say at an 8 percent interest rate, and leave the money there in an IRA account that paid 6 percent interest. The bank liked this transaction. It got a 2 percent spread on a paper transaction without any money ever leaving the bank. But why would you pay 8 percent interest to make only 6 percent? Because the tax law let you deduct the 8 percent you paid without taxing the 6 percent you made. If, for example, you had income that otherwise would have been taxed at a 50 percent rate, which you sheltered by the interest deduction, the deductible interest really cost you only 4 percent after-tax. Like the bank, you made 2 percent without putting up any money or taking any financial risk. Where did the government get the money to make you and the bank so happy? From some other sucker's taxes, of course. If you don't have enough income to use the interest deductions or if your tax rate isn't high enough to more than offset the higher interest rate on the loan, this deal isn't for you. You have to have enough income to qualify for these kinds of tax breaks.

Fortunately, the $2,000 annual limit on amounts that could be put into an IRA put a ceiling on the total amount the Treasury contributed to this paper shuffle, but, even so, the tax revenues lost from the 1981 extension of IRA eligibility vastly exceeded the amounts predicted.[20] And IRAs were not the only such opportunity. Some people can do the same thing with their pension or 401(k) plans, and for substantially greater amounts. Borrowing to buy certain tax-favored life insurance products is another option. You can use home mortgage borrowing to finance a variety of tax-favored investments. Of course, you have to have borrowing power to play this game.

The tax law's deduction for interest also has encouraged corporations to borrow to finance their investments rather than issuing new equity. In the 1980s corporations' borrowings to finance repurchases of shares increased so greatly that by 1990 over one-quarter of total corporate interest payments went to finance such repurchases.[21] Money was just being moved around to take advantage of the tax rules.

A new market for junk bonds also developed to finance leveraged buyouts of companies with enough cash flow to cover the interest payments. In effect, the U.S. government was helping to finance such acquisitions through the tax law.[22] By 1990 net corporate interest payments were nearly 20 percent of their total cash flow, a post–World War II high.[23] As corporate borrowing increases, the risks of bankruptcies in times of economic distress grow.

The combination of rapid depreciation write-offs and increased corporate interest deductions in the early 1980s threatened to wipe out entirely the corporate income tax as a source of federal revenues. The corporate tax, which had provided 20–30 percent of total federal revenues in the 1950s and 1960s, dropped below 10 percent of the total in the early 1980s and is now about 12.5 percent.

The kinds of transactions I have described here have resulted in an enormous number of limitations on interest deductions and many so-called anti-abuse rules, which have significantly increased the tax law's complexity. Some of these are described in the next chapter. In addition to their complexity, these provisions have had the effect of increasing the advantages of tax breaks to persons wealthy enough to liquidate other assets instead of borrowing to finance tax-favored investments.

The income tax has inspired transactions that otherwise make no economic sense and has rewarded excessive borrowing by giving tax breaks that themselves have to be financed by the government either issuing more debt or taxing hardworking people. Congress has completely failed to address, even in a piecemeal fashion, the problems that inflation poses for the taxation of debt.[24] This particular reluctance undoubtedly reflects the political reality that undertaxed borrowers are far more numerous than overtaxed lenders in every legislative district in the land. Since virtually every individual and corporation in our society has ignored Polonius's admonition to refrain from both borrowing and lending, an incorrect tax burden has been imposed on virtually every taxpayer.

Congress's failure to adopt any systematic solutions to the mismeasurement of capital income due to inflation has resulted in an income tax that is incapable of properly measuring the income of asset owners, debtors, or creditors, but the prospect for enactment of a comprehensive tax-indexing scheme is slim. Partial indexing schemes, particularly for capital gains, continue to be advanced in the Congress, but there remains great resistance to the idea because of its complexity. No politician has any will to advance indexing for debt, which not only would be enormously complicated, but, more important, would increase taxes of homeowners by denying deductions for a portion of their home mortgage interest—an idea widely regarded as political suicide.

Inflation Makes
Income Tax Timing Issues More Important

The final important effect of inflation on the income tax is to magnify greatly the significance of timing issues. High interest rates, which are typically correlated with high inflation, in combination with high effective tax rates, which were themselves for many people a product of inflation, raised substantially the tax stakes of the timing of deductions and income. Many of the tax shelter transactions of the 1970s and 1980s were designed simply to accelerate deductions to earlier taxable years and postpone income to later taxable years.

For a long time, Congress regarded income tax timing issues as trivial, and routinely described its decisions to accelerate deductions or defer income as *"only* a matter of timing." The distinction between life and death, however, also is *"only* a matter of timing." A great deal of the complexity added to the income tax in the 1980s and 1990s reflects Congress's ongoing attempts to deal more systematically with income tax timing issues.

Conclusion

There are several lessons from the interaction of the income tax with inflation during recent decades. First is the lesson of unintended consequences. Certainly Senator Armstrong and his supporters underestimated the Congress's unwillingness to cut spending even if faced with diminished revenues. Ronald Reagan often described the Congress as wedded to that old tax and spend, tax and spend. After the 1981 tax cut legislation, a more accurate description of Congress would have been "borrow and spend, borrow and spend." One can only speculate whether those who greatly expanded the 1981 tax cut, in part through indexing tax rates, would have proceeded more cautiously and made different trade-offs if they had known how difficult it would be to reduce federal spending.

Indexing the income tax brackets, personal exemptions, the standard deduction, and the earned-income tax credit was undoubtedly proper in principle and laudable in practice. If Congress is to be faulted for enacting indexing in 1981, it is only because it did so by adding it to a large tax cut rather than facing up to the difficult choices that would have been required if income tax indexing had to compete with other tax-reduction measures. Ronald Reagan was committed to the so-called Kemp-Roth across-the-board reduction in tax rates and the Congress, at the behest of large businesses, had become committed to a very large increase in depreciation allowances and reinstatement of an investment tax credit for purchases of business equipment. So indexing's only real chance was as an add-on, with a few years' delay to keep the five-year revenue loss within an acceptable range.[25] Congress has a long history of unwillingness to face up to difficult choices.

Congress's failure to enact structural indexing of assets and debt as part of the 1986 tax reform, coupled with the relatively low rates of inflation that we have experienced in recent years, no doubt makes such comprehensive indexing of capital income a dead letter for the foreseeable future. And given the complexities that would be added by indexing capital gains and debt, one is hard-pressed to complain that this is the wrong result. Nevertheless, the mismeasurement of income under an un-indexed income tax is serious and for many families and businesses can produce very substantial understatements or overstatements of tax liability. Future ad hoc legislative responses, such as reduced capital-gains rates as assets are held for longer periods of time, seem inevitable. Some of these ideas may well resurrect tax shelter opportunities; others will simply create new arbitrary differentials in tax burdens.

Inflation therefore continues to pose a major barrier to a fair and economically efficient income tax. In substantial part, this explains the search for alternatives to the income tax, and particularly the renewed fascination with taxing consumption rather than income. A consumption tax, whether in the common form of a retail sales or a value-added tax or a more exotic variation like the "flat" tax on wages, does not raise similar problems of having to deal with inflation.

Finally, the failure of Congress to act sooner to eliminate bracket creep was a major factor in the decline of public confidence in government and, more particularly, in the income tax itself. In addition to pushing money in directions common sense would never have let it go and expanding greatly the market for tax shelters, the higher tax rates inflation produced created particular despair for married women who entered the labor market only to discover how little additional income their wages produced for their family after they paid their taxes and the additional expenses of working. There is no evidence that the enactment of indexing in 1981 has been effective in restoring public confidence in the income tax. This decline of confidence may not be reversed without radical surgery.

5

Dad Is Not at
the Dining Room Table
Anymore

People who work hard, play by the rules, stay married, borrow as little as possible, and put what little money they can save into traditional savings vehicles, such as savings accounts or mutual funds, instead of chasing after tax shelters have another good reason to despise the income tax. They face overwhelming tax complexity. Let's visit one middle-class couple to see how the income tax can drive people crazy.

Joe and Jane Six-Pack

As the television show *Dragnet* prefaced every story, the names have been changed to protect the innocent: I call these people Joe and

Jane Six-Pack. Joe and Jane have a combined income of about $50,000.

Jane is a self-employed physical therapist. Other than the 15 percent fee she pays an agency for patient referrals, Jane has few expenses connected with her work. She buys uniforms to wear on the job and occasionally purchases medical or physical therapy equipment. She drives the family car from her house to her patients' homes and sometimes to an equipment supply company or the hospital. She pays $600 a month in child-care expenses for her young daughter, Jenny. Jane uses one room of their house exclusively as an office for keeping medical records of her patients, maintaining her billing records, paying her agency's fees, and communicating by telephone with the agency, doctors, nurses, and her patients.

Joe works for the local television cable company. He drives a company truck, which he uses during the day to call on customers for cable installations or repairs and which his employer allows him to take home at night and drive to work in the mornings. His employer generally reimburses Joe's job-related expenses, except for a few technical repair books that he buys from time to time and his subscription to the local television cable company's monthly magazine.

Joe and Jane do not have many investments other than the house they own, a house they purchased years ago for $65,000 and on which they still have a mortgage of $50,000. It is a large house near the local community college, and Joe and Jane rent out one room to a student for $100 a month. The student has limited kitchen privileges, but Joe and Jane always try to find a student likely to live mostly on restaurant or junk food. In exchange for the low rent, the student spends a couple of hours a day reading to Joe's retired mother, who also lives in a room of their house. Joe's mother lives off her Social Security income and contributes $2,000 of this amount each year to help cover household expenses.

Jane pays her neighbor Susan $40 a week to come one morning each week to clean their house, although Jane never knows what day Susan will appear. Jane also pays her seventeen-year-old next-door neighbor Allison $20 a week to walk the family's twelve-year-old beagle, once in the morning and once in the evening.

The Six-Packs are a hardworking middle-class American couple trying to get ahead. For people like them, filling out a tax return should not be trial by fire; nor should it require an expensive trip to a tax-return preparer. But I'm afraid it will; let's look at some of their tax questions.

Let's Start with Some Softballs

The tax law allows people to deduct all their "ordinary and necessary" business expenses, so Jane can deduct her fees to the agency. Equipment costs usually must be deducted over several years through depreciation allowances, but a special provision, which Jane qualifies for, allows her to deduct her small amount of equipment purchases each year.[1]

Congress in 1986 enacted a "simplification" measure—which conveniently also raised substantial additional taxes—that disallows "miscellaneous itemized deductions" that do not exceed 2 percent of income. For the Six-Packs, this provision could disallow up to $1,000 of otherwise allowable deductions, but it does not apply at all to Jane's business expenses because she is self-employed, not an employee.

Child Care

The Six-Packs would not have to pay $600 a month in child-care expenses if they both did not have jobs. But the income tax has always been parsimonious, denying deductions for common inevitable additional expenses, such as commuting and child care, that are required to earn a second income, a stark contrast to the tax law's historical generosity regarding deductions for such things as business travel, meals, and entertainment, executive perks of the workaday world to which few women were admitted.

In 1954, Congress enacted a deduction for up to $600 of child-care expenses in limited circumstances. This deduction was later replaced by a child-care tax credit. Today the maximum tax credit allowable for the care of one child is $480, which covers less than one month of the Six-Packs' child-care expenses. For families with more than one child, the maximum credit is twice as great, $960, no matter how many children there are. The dollar amount of the child-care credit is not automatically increased for inflation so its real value declines over time.

To obtain this stingy tax credit, one must meet a long list of requirements, far too complex to be detailed here. For example, the expense must be "incurred to enable the taxpayer to be gainfully employed." A leading tax law treatise says that this may make it necessary to psychoanalyze the working parents to determine whether they hired a babysitter in order to work or worked in order to hire a babysitter.[2] Many of the rules make no sense; my favorite insists that if the child is cared for at a "dependent care center," payments qualify for the child-care tax credit only if the "center complies with all applicable laws and regulations" of the state or local government. The tax law offers no clue as to how people are supposed to know this. Why shouldn't the state and local governments who write the laws and regulations applicable to child-care centers enforce these laws? The Six-Packs, of course, routinely ignore this provision.

Work Clothing

Thanks to the efforts of a private duty nurse, Helen Krusko Harsaghy, Jane can deduct the costs of her uniforms and the costs of laundering them. Ms. Harsaghy in 1943 won a Tax Court contest over $8.75 in additional taxes the IRS said were due when it denied her deductions of $217.44 for the costs of purchasing eight nursing uniforms, three pairs of shoes, six caps, and thirty stockings and laundering same. (Both tax rates and the value of the dollar were different then.) The Tax Court concluded that the uniforms weren't suitable for wear off the job, observing: "Women outside the nursing profession would hardly consider a nurse's uniform and accessories as incorporating such qualities as would make them suitable for any purpose, much less general and continued wear."[3]

Ozzie and Harriet Nelson, America's most beloved couple, deducted nearly $40,000 in clothing expenses for filming *The Adventures of Ozzie and Harriet*. Following its usual practice, the IRS insisted that the costs of the clothes that the Nelson family wore on their shows were not deductible because the clothes were "suitable for personal wear." The Tax Court, however, concluded that since Ozzie had never worn these clothes off the TV show's set (except once when he used a heavy sweater to go to a football game) their costs were deductible.[4]

Not everyone fares so well. Sandra Pevsner, the manager of the Sakowitz Yves St. Laurent Rive Gauche Boutique in Dallas, Texas, surely deserved a clothing deduction, but she didn't get one. Her boutique sells women's clothes and accessories designed only by Yves St. Laurent, a creator of high-fashion apparel. The store's dresses cost $800 or $900 in 1978, and several customers spent as much as $20,000 a year there.

Ms. Pevsner's employer required her to wear Yves St. Laurent clothes when she was at work so that whenever a customer complimented her clothes, Ms. Pevsner could remark that they were Yves St. Laurent. She wore these fancy clothes only at work and on the way there, at fashion shows the boutique sponsored, and to boutique business meetings. She never wore her YSL apparel outside of work because she could not afford such expensive clothing, nor was she the sort of person to wear such high-fashion apparel. The IRS disallowed Ms. Pevsner's deductions for the clothing, and the court of appeals agreed, deciding a deduction required an objective finding that the clothing was not adaptable to general use as ordinary streetwear.[5] Sandra Pevsner could have used Ozzie Nelson's judge.

Despite the extensive litigation over clothing deductions, Jane can rest easy; her uniforms are deductible. Accessories, on the other hand, are less certain. Carol Steiner, an airline stewardess, tested the limits by deducting not only her uniforms, but also the costs of her watch, luggage, sunglasses, cosmetics, handbag, shoes, boots, and gloves, but these deductions were disallowed.[6] Nurse Helen Harsaghy, in contrast, won deduction of her white shoes and stockings. The Six-Packs will just have to decide how aggressive a tax return they want to file.

It could be worse. In Australia work clothing must be registered with the Register of Approved Occupational Clothing to qualify for a tax deduction. That sounds like a joke, but it's not.

Home Office Deductions

Can Jane deduct her home office? Liberace deducted his. The flamboyant pianist's wholly owned corporation purchased for him an extraordinarily expensive home on which it spent $300,000 for repairs and decorations. Liberace stored his extravagant wardrobe, seven pianos, an organ, and countless candelabra in the house. The corporation deducted nearly $154,000 for his business use of his home over a three-year period. Finding no clear path to a "right" answer, the Tax Court split this baby and allowed half of the claimed deductions.[7]

During the 1970s, many more people started taking deductions for home offices. People who had full-time jobs but did some work at home, such as schoolteachers who graded papers at home, often deducted a portion of their housing expenses. The key IRS loss occurred in litigation against one of its own lawyers, Steve Bodzin, who claimed that the office the IRS provided to him was inadequate to do his job and that he had to use an office in his home to perform satisfactorily. He won his case, opening doors for others.[8] In response, Congress in 1976 enacted stringent rules allowing home office deductions only when the home office is the taxpayer's "principal place of business," but this only served to challenge creative tax planners.

By 1992, the outcomes and legal tests in home office deduction cases were so varied and inconsistent that the Supreme Court decided to resolve the conflicts in a case involving Nader E. Soliman, an anesthesiologist, who had deducted the costs of a spare bedroom that he used exclusively as a home office. He spent two to three hours every day there, contacting patients, surgeons, and hospitals by telephone, maintaining his billing and patient records, studying medical journals and books, and preparing for treatments and presentations to colleagues. None of the hospitals with which he worked provided him any space for these chores. Nevertheless, the Supreme Court disallowed his home office deductions, concluding that in order for a home office to qualify as the principal place of business, it must be the place where goods or services are rendered.[9] So, for the moment at least, the expenses of Jane's home office are not deductible since she does not provide physical therapy services there.

But Jane should not despair. Lower courts will certainly soon chip away at the Supreme Court's moment of clarity, and the ink was hardly dry on the *Soliman* decision before a number of key members of Congress moved to liberalize this test.

Joe's Company Truck

Since the costs of commuting to and from work are not deductible expenses, the IRS tries to tax employees' use of an employer's vehicle for commuting so that people cannot get around this rule by having their employer provide a vehicle for them to commute in. This requires Joe to value his commuting use of the company truck based on the standard IRS mileage allowance for the business use of personal vehicles, now about 30 cents a mile. Many people would ignore the requirement to report the value of commuting if their employer failed to include the amount on the annual W-2 form, which it also sends to the IRS. But Joe says "that would be wrong."

Jane may deduct her costs of driving between patients' houses and between their houses and the hospital, doctors' offices, clinics, or equipment supply stores, but she cannot deduct the costs of her first commute of the day or coming home in the evening. She can use either the IRS standard mileage allowance or compute her actual pro rata automobile expenses.

Renting a Room in the House

Jane and Joe rent out a room of their home, a common transaction that produces excessive tax complexity to no good purpose. For most people, after extensive calculations the rules generally serve to disallow a part of otherwise deductible home mortgage interest and property taxes. The rules that arrive at this arbitrary result are so daunting that many people simply refuse to report such rental income to the IRS. Getting this one right can be a very tedious and inexact task.

For the Six-Packs, even knowing the proper amount of rental income to report is difficult since they charge a below-market rent in exchange for their tenant spending time with Joe's mother. The law requires them to increase their $100-a-month rental income by the value of the services rendered by the tenant. At the minimum wage, this would be about $200 more a month, for a total rent of about $3,600 a year.

Joe and Jane must then divide their house into two tax pieces, the personal residence piece and the rental piece, and allocate all deductible expenses between the two pieces. If their allocable deductions exceed their rent, the tax loss attributable to the rental unit is not deductible. Worse yet, the allocable portion of home mortgage interest and property taxes, which are normally deductible anyway, must be used first to offset their rental income.[10]

State income tax rules frequently vary significantly from the federal rules for an issue like this, so Joe and Jane may have to keep two separate sets of books and records, one for the state and one for the feds. No wonder most people just ignore the gobbledygook. But Joe says "that would be wrong."

Interest Deductions

Although Jane and Joe face other serious contenders for the title, the provisions that now win the foolish-complexity prize involve deductions for interest expenses. The tax law used to allow individuals who itemized their deductions to deduct interest paid on borrowing regardless of how they used the borrowed funds. Today, however, whether an interest deduction is allowed or not depends on what the money borrowed is used for and whether the loan is secured by a home mortgage. The rules are horrendously complicated. For example, there are limitations on deductions for interest on money borrowed for investment purposes, interest on loans to buy or hold tax-exempt bonds and certain insurance contracts, interest paid in connection with real estate construction, interest paid to hold bonds acquired at a discount, and interest paid on borrowing from retirement plans. Of course, since money can be used for any purpose, it is folly to require people to attempt to trace the funds they borrow to particular uses. Futility, however, is no bar to this legislation. The law now distinguishes at least seventeen categories of interest expense with separate rules for each.

In 1986 Congress decided that, although it would be political suicide to deny interest deductions for home mortgages, it should eliminate deductions for interest on credit card and other personal borrowings. This has inspired many homeowners to recast their automobile, consumer, educational, credit card, and other debts into home equity loans or home equity lines of credit. Joe has a small account with a stockbroker, and when Joe feels strongly about an investment, as he did about Nike stock when Michael Jordan returned to basketball, he sometimes buys stock on margin in this account. Doing so, however, subjects the interest to the investment interest limitations, which Joe could avoid if he financed his stock purchases with a home equity loan. Joe is reluctant to do this. He fears that hard times would put not only his credit rating but also his home at risk.

Since Congress eliminated the interest deduction for car loans, the automobile industry has restructured the way it finances automobiles. Rather than simply selling people automobiles and having them borrow the money to finance their purchases as before, automobile companies now lease automobiles, providing financing for these leases themselves or through some financial institution. By shifting to leasing rather than selling many of their cars, automobile companies not only deduct their financing costs (since interest paid by a business remains fully deductible), but also obtain deductions for depreciation, which are not allowable to consumers. In the process automobile makers may have expanded their market for new cars because people turn in their leased cars more frequently and switch to new cars more often.

It is surprising that Congress failed to anticipate the substantial changes in people's behavior that occurred. Economic studies indicate that the primary effect of the 1986 change has been shuffling other consumer debt into home mortgage debt with little impact on overall borrowing. One study estimates that such debt restructuring reduced the potential revenue increase from this change by almost one-half.[11] Congress could have been far more effective and much less complicated by simply enacting a dollar limit on the amount of interest people are allowed to deduct.[12]

Dependency Exemptions

At one time or another everyone claims someone as a dependent or is claimed as a dependent by their parents. So knowing whether Joe's mother qualifies as his dependent can't be hard, right? Wrong.

To claim a dependency exemption, the dependent must either be a relative or reside in the claimant's household and cannot earn more than that year's level of the personal exemption, today about $2,700. The requirement that will tell us whether the Six-Packs can claim an exemption for Joe's mother is that the taxpayer must provide more than one-half of the dependent's support. In order to satisfy it, Joe and Jane must know how much Joe's mother spends during the year not only for housing but also for such things as clothing, food, and medical expenses. Much controversy has occurred over what counts as support and what does not, including such things as church contributions, music and dancing lessons, medical and life insurance premiums, entertainment, haircuts, pet care, vacations, babysitting costs and other child care, school lunches, summer camps, toys, wedding expenses, and income taxes.

There also often are questions about how to count amounts received by the "dependent" from a third party. Joe's mother's Medicare benefits, for example, do not count as contributions to her own support, but her Social Security does. We do not have enough facts to know whether Joe can claim his mother as a dependent or not. Joe may not have enough facts either.

The law could be made much simpler by allowing a dependency exemption for all persons who reside in the household who earn less than the exemption amount. But, so far, Congress has rejected this idea; it's too simple.

Nanny-Tax Nuances

Jane pays her friend Susan $40 a week to clean her house and her neighbor Allison $20 a week to walk the family dog. Jane read about both Zoë Baird, President Clinton's first nominee to the post of attorney general, and Bobby Ray Inman, his choice for secretary of defense, who were accused of failing to pay Social Security tax obligations for household workers, and, although she has neither aspirations nor expectations for public office, Jane doesn't want to be "Zoë'ed." Unfortunately, Jane's tax obligations are not at all clear, although you can be sure the IRS will claim that she owes the employer's share of Social Security taxes for both Susan and Allison since she pays each of these women more than $1,000 a year.

The obligation to pay Social Security taxes on full-time employees is clear, and denying tax scofflaws high government office is probably appropriate, even though this particular legal requirement has been widely ignored. But some people may have been disqualified from public office for not paying taxes they did not owe, and others may have paid taxes they may not legally owe.

From 1950 until 1994, the tax law had provided that an employer's Social Security tax obligation applied to anyone who paid a domestic employee more than $50 a quarter.[13] The requirement was originally enacted for the admirable purpose of providing Social Security retirement and disability benefits to domestic employees. In 1950, however, 17 cents would buy what a dollar does today, the minimum wage was 75 cents an hour, and babysitters earned 50 cents an hour or less. By limiting the requirement to employers who paid at least $50 of wages a quarter and requiring "regularity of employment," casual and irregular providers of household services were exempt. At the minimum wage, in 1950 you had to work nearly 70 hours a quarter to make $50; you had to babysit or walk dogs about 100 hours. Susan works only about 48 hours a quarter in cleaning the Six-Packs' house and Allison walks the dog for a total of about 60 hours, but they both earn more than the $1,000 annual minimum.

The IRS described its expansive view of this legal requirement at a congressional hearing. Butlers, cooks, housekeepers, babysitters, gardeners, and "handymen" are all covered. If you pay someone to clean your co-op because your mother is coming, or to walk your dog or sit your cat, those are domestic services. The IRS says that if you haven't filed the required returns, there is no statute of limitations, but as an administrative indulgence, the IRS usually demands payment for only six back years.

The IRS admits, however, that the requirement to pay Social Security taxes applies only for your "employees," and that a test involving twenty factors applies to distinguish "employees" from "independent contractors." The IRS claims that "in almost all cases, workers who perform these services will be employees of the person in whose home they are performed."

But this twenty-part test is not nearly as clear as the IRS suggests; its application is inconsistent, its results uncertain. In 1994 the House Government Operations Committee called the twenty factors "an inadequate guide to compliance with tax and other laws," describing misclassification of workers as a "pervasive and serious problem." The IRS is currently in controversies with many giant corporations and many small businesses about whether certain people are or are not their "employees." The Treasury Department admits that applying the test "does not yield clear, consistent or satisfactory answers, and reasonable persons may differ as to the correct classification."

Whether a person is an employee or an independent contractor depends on such factors as whether the person performing the services is paid by time or by the job; whether the hours of work are flexible; whether the relationship is a continuing one; whether the person is free to provide services to others or to hire assistants; whether the services must be rendered personally; whether the payer can control how the results are achieved or whether the service provider is responsible only for results; and who supplies the tools. A tax lawyer might advise people like the Six-Packs to change babysitters frequently, pay by the job, insist that your neighbor's kid open a "lawnmowing business," and make your dogwalker bring her own pooper-scooper. This shambles confirms Will Rogers's adage that when Congress makes a joke, it's a law.

Whether or not the Six-Packs owe Social Security taxes for the house cleaner and dogwalker therefore cannot be known with any degree of confidence. The tax law simply does not tell people who want to be honest and upstanding citizens, but not dupes, what is required of them. Congress knows well the problem but has offered no solution. Meanwhile, the IRS is conducting thousands of audits, but concentrating mostly on companies like IBM, rather than fighting with families like the Six-Packs.[14]

Dad Is Not at
the Dining Room Table Anymore

Jane and Joe's host of tax questions shows how difficult it is for many ordinary citizens to figure out and pay the taxes that are due. The more carefully and honestly they address questions like these, the more confused, frustrated, and angry they become. So what do people like the Six-Packs and millions of others like them do?

One of my most vivid childhood memories is of my father sitting at our dining room table in the spring, surrounded by piles of paper. Dad took over the dining room table every year around the ides of March and maintained his papers—if not his position—there until April 15 each year. At a certain age, I came to learn that this annual ritual was my father's way of calculating how much tax he owed to the federal government and the state of Georgia. This, along with voting, was how he expressed his citizenship. This ritual was not altogether pleasing to my mother.

Until his very old age, when he was no longer mentally capable, nothing could keep my father from this tradition. After his health failed, my mother sent their tax information to me to prepare their tax return. In each of the first three years thereafter, when teaching my course in federal income taxation to law students at Yale, I realized that I had made an error on my mother's return. Each time I suggested that Mom could obtain an additional refund by filing an amended return, which I prepared for her. My mother erroneously regarded this as a signal of my astuteness, not incompetence. She was thrilled, but I knew better. I soon turned these matters over to an accountant, who now prepares both her tax returns and mine.

My father-in-law still takes over his dining room table to prepare his own return, but virtually everyone else I know has turned either to a computer program or to a paid tax-return preparer. More than half of all income tax returns filed now are signed by paid tax-return preparers. Four decades ago, this number was less than 20 percent. This is how H & R Block grew from two brothers with calculators into a multibillion-dollar company.

H & R Block

Who is the one person in America who likes the income tax just the way it is? Henry Bloch, of course. Henry Bloch has lived the American dream.[15] In 1955, he borrowed $5,000 from his aunt and started a one-man company to provide bookkeeping services to small businesses. At his mother's insistence, Henry took his brother Richard into the business. Forty years later, in 1995, H & R Block, which is still headquartered in Kansas City, Missouri, prepared and filed over 13 million tax returns, 12 percent of all individual tax returns filed that year, nearly one-fourth of those filed with the help of a paid tax-return preparer.

The public's response to a $100 ad in the *Kansas City Star* in

1955 led Henry and Richard to shift their business from general bookkeeping to tax-return preparation. That year Henry and Richard prepared about 2,700 individual tax returns, made $25,000, and realized they were on to something. Today, H & R Block has more than 9,000 offices worldwide, employs nearly 90,000 people during the tax-filing season, and earns about $200 million on nearly $2 billion of total revenues, half of which comes from their tax-return preparation business. The average cost of having H & R Block file a federal tax return is $55 with additional fees due for state returns and if they supply a loan in advance of a person's receiving a tax refund. In 1956, for $5 (the equivalent of $30 today) they prepared both the federal and a state tax return.

Following a practice usually associated with drug dealers, H & R Block says the first one is free; it offers new high school graduates and any elderly person their first tax-return preparation free. Why? Because the second one is not free, or the third, the fourth, the fifth, etc. Henry Bloch says that business grows steadily through repeat customers. "Make them happy the first time," he says, "and they will come back forever."

The majority of H & R Block's clientele are low- and middle-income people with total income of $35,000 or less. Many of the tax returns that bear H & R Block's stamp are the simplest short-form returns, barely over a half page long. It's the thirty-three pages of small-print instructions that drive these people to H & R Block. A postcard-size tax return is little help when it takes a book of instructions to fill out the postcard.

Second place to H & R Block is a very long distance away. Jackson-Hewitt Tax Service claims that honor with nearly $20 million of revenues and just under 1,000 offices in thirty-seven states. It does about 1 percent of the volume and revenues of H & R Block.

Self-Help Tax-Return Preparation

Although half the people now use paid tax-return preparers in filling out their income tax returns each year, the other half of returns still are self-prepared. This keeps book publishers and computer software companies happy. The most famous, long-standing, and successful book is J. K. Lasser's *Your Income Tax*. But there are a host of competitors. They fill up a complete shelf in my local bookstore.

A new market has also recently developed for tax-return computer software programs, which people use to figure out their tax liability on their own personal computers. More than 2 million people used these tax-preparation computer programs in 1995, making this a rapidly growing phenomenon.[16] The best-seller is TurboTax, produced by the company Intuit, the Menlo Park, California, publisher which also owns the dominant personal finance program, Quicken. These programs cost about $35 each, and they determine a person's tax liability by asking a series of questions, then performing the required mathematical calculations and printing out the required tax forms and schedules.

The bad news is that you have to be able to answer the questions. But this is also true when you go to a tax-return preparer. You also need a new computer program each year because the tax law changes that often, through either legislation or annual adjustments for inflation. My colleagues who use TurboTax said it took them three days to do their tax returns in 1996.

How Well Do
Tax-Return Preparers Do?

H & R Block and the other companies that prepare tax returns all take pride in how well their preparers are trained. But the question lingers: Do tax preparers get it right?

In March or April every year, newspapers and magazines test the tax-return-preparation industry. They create hypothetical families and ask a number of tax-return preparers to compute the tax they owe. *Money* magazine, the quiz kingpin, runs a story every year, often with a headline like "The Pros Flunk Our New Tax Test."[17] Sometimes journalists ask the IRS the same questions, and feign great surprise when the IRS does no better, and often worse, than the tax-return preparers.

Sometimes the variations in preparers' answers are stunningly large. *Money* magazine, for example, one year asked fifty preparers to compute a tax owed by a hypothetical family with a total salary of about $56,000, plus some pension plan distributions. The correct amount was about $23,400. Eleven of the fifty preparers, less than one-fourth, got very close to that answer. Neither a lot of time nor a lot of cash guaranteed a correct result. The fees of those preparers who got it right ranged from $325 to $2,500, and they took from four to twenty hours to do the job. Four of the preparers who made the largest mistakes charged more than $1,500, and two of them worked on the tax return for at least twenty hours.

The preparers' determinations of the income tax due ranged from $12,500 to nearly $36,000, a low equal to about half the right amount and a high about one and a half times the tax owed. On average, the preparers' answers were more than $1,500 less than the tax actually due, which, in addition to the complexity of the tax law, helps explain why so many people flock to tax-return preparers. They tend to resolve their doubts in your favor.

The issues that stumped most of these experts were the treatment of a lump-sum distribution from a pension plan before age sixty-five and more common issues involving such things as interest deductions and dependents. Having visited the Six-Packs, we should not be surprised about that.

Conclusion

The American people face overwhelming income tax complexity, even in common and ordinary circumstances, complexity that has driven people to spend enormous amounts of time and money on books, computerized tax-return programs, and tax-return preparers. In the process, respect for and public approval of both the income tax and the people who enact and enforce it has diminished. Complexity may be unavoidable for high-income families with multiple trusts and varied investments around the world and inevitable for multinational corporations, but not for people like the Six-Packs.

The lack of conformity between the federal income tax and state and local income taxes adds significant additional complexities and expense for many people. Unfortunately, only a handful of states have so closely conformed their income taxes to the federal tax to require only a few additional calculations. Many individuals are now required to file income tax returns in more than one state, and a large number of businesses in America operate across state lines. Greater conformity to eliminate wasteful costs of tax compliance is long overdue.

Congress is far too willing to accept unnecessary complexities for everyone, even for large multinational corporations. The 1993 tax return for Mobil Corporation, the oil company, totaled 6,300 pages and weighed 76 pounds. Mobil estimated that it cost the company $10 million to prepare each year's federal income tax return and required a year's work for fifty-seven people. This is not right. Some of these people should be making or selling goods or performing services people value.

Worse yet, the tax law applies basically the same income tax rules to businesses whether they are large or small. As a result the tax compliance costs of small businesses are disproportionately and unacceptably large.

Even people with incomes lower than the Six-Packs are not spared tax complexity. In 1975 a new earned-income tax credit (EITC) was enacted in order to provide tax relief to low-income workers with children and to improve people's incentives to work rather than collect welfare. Even though it applies to people who earn low wages, this credit is extraordinarily complex. The IRS has historically uncovered more errors with the earned-income tax credit than with any other item on the individual income tax return, recently on as many as 35–40 percent of tax returns claiming it. Some of these errors may be due to intentionally excessive claims, but the complexity of the rules that govern eligibility for this credit produces large numbers of mistakes even for people trying to get it right.

The reasons the tax law is so complex are well illustrated by the 1990 legislation. It added three new supplemental tax credits to the EITC, one which applied to households with more than one child, another to households with children who were under one year old, and a third to households who purchased health insurance for a child. The health insurance addition was added at the behest of Lloyd Bentsen, then the Democratic chairman of the Senate Finance Committee. The credit for households with newly born children—the "wee tots" credit—was added at the insistence of the Bush administration to please a group of conservative Republicans. Congress compromised, as it so often does, by accepting both proposals instead of neither, worrying not at all about people's inability to comprehend or comply with the provision. These particular filigrees were repealed in 1993, but great complexity remains. When political compromises are being fashioned, tax simplification typically is a bystander.

Although it is hard to believe from this chapter, no one is opposed to tax simplification; everyone is for it. It is an apple-pie issue. The difficulty is that simplification rarely has any effective political constituency.

In the 1980s and the first half of the 1990s, the search for revenues to narrow deficits led to frequent tax law changes. In the 1950s, 1960s, and 1970s, there were at most two or three major tax bills each decade. In sharp contrast, in the 1980s Congress enacted nine major tax bills that together contained more than 8,000 pages of statutory changes. The 1990s may surpass this record. Changing the tax law each year makes tax compliance more burdensome and costly for the citizenry and tax enforcement more difficult for the IRS. Constant revision of the tax law also makes business and investment decisions much more risky, another source of anger at both the tax law and Congress.

The costs of tax compliance for American businesses and families are excessive, and these expenditures of time and money do not contribute one whit to the long-term success of the American economy. In virtually every country in the industrial world, the costs of compliance imposed on the citizenry are four to five times as great as the administrative costs of the tax collection authority.

In the United States, that number is substantially higher. Congress must begin to reduce these real economic costs, which are having a serious adverse impact on the U.S. economy, costs that can only be lowered through a major simplification of the tax system.

To limit complexity requires a willingness by Congress to enact law that is arbitrary—arbitrary, but relatively simple, such as the law that now limits deductions for business meals and entertainment expenses to 50 percent of their costs. American businesses—even small businesses—can multiply by 0.5.

Recently Edwin Cohen, a distinguished tax attorney and former undersecretary of the Treasury, told of how he began the practice of tax law in July of 1936. The senior tax partner of the prestigious law firm where he worked asked that he read the relevant tax law. Between the day he began work, Tuesday, July 7, 1936, and the following Friday morning, this young lawyer read the 100 pages of the income, estate, and gift tax law—the Revenue Act of 1936—from beginning to end twice. The following week, he read once all of the income tax regulations then in effect, a total of about 400 pages.[18]

As I have said, in the decade 1981–1990 alone, more than 8,000 pages of statutory amendments were enacted to the Internal Revenue Code. The income tax regulations now take up six volumes of small print, more than half a shelf of office space. This does not even begin to count the additional volumes of cases, IRS rulings, international tax treaties, and legislative histories. The advent of CD-ROM promises to reduce the space these materials require, but not their opacity.

Even in far simpler times, people complained about income tax complexity. Consider the following lament from a 1926 law review article entitled "Is It Not Time to Simplify the Income Tax?"

> The Revenue Act of 1926 is permeated with special provisions, ifs, ands, buts, provisos, parenthetical expressions, and cross references. It defies understanding. Its spirit is smothered in words and it wilts the spirit of anyone who tries to read and understand.[19]

Today, when Congress talks about income tax simplification, people may well be reminded of Emerson's comments regarding an acquaintance: "The louder he talked of his honor, the faster we counted our spoons."

6

Have We Become
a Nation of Tax Cheaters?

Americans don't cheat on taxes; that's an Italian or Spanish phenomenon, or so American myth insists. IRS commissioners have always claimed that our nation enjoys the highest level of "voluntary" tax compliance in the world. The behavior of American taxpayers supposedly is the "envy of the world."[1]

A Conversation with a Waitress

But how uncommon is this attitude expressed in a National Public Radio interview with a New York waitress, a waitress who remained anonymous for obvious reasons?

WAITRESS: "You know, I have nothing against the government, they need the money too."

NPR REPORTER: "That is a waitress, she works here in New York City, at a not very nice restaurant. She told me that she does not report any of her tips at tax time. The Treasury Department meanwhile, in Washington, has estimated that up to 84 percent of tip income has gone unreported . . ."

I asked my waitress what was her salary. How much did she make?

WAITRESS: "I get a buck fifty-five an hour."

REPORTER: "A buck fifty-five an hour, on the understanding that's not really what you are getting?"

WAITRESS: "Oh no, you think I'd work for $1.55 an hour?"

REPORTER: "You don't look like the kind of person who'd work for $1.55 an hour. (ha, ha.) What do you do with the cash when they give it to you?"

WAITRESS: "I put it in the bank, what else am I going to do with it?"

REPORTER: "Well do you have any fear that little you, a waitress somewhere in the city of New York, would be noticed by the Internal Revenue Service and caught?"

WAITRESS: "I bank the money, I don't spend it very much."

REPORTER: "But there it is. It's on file. Your deposit slips are there, they know that you've earned it which they wouldn't know if you didn't put it in the bank."

WAITRESS: "That's true, I don't know."

REPORTER: "My waitress is not unusual. Congress found that restaurant workers believe the possibility of an audit is so remote that they have become fearless."[2]

A Conversation with a Commissioner

The same month of that interview, in March 1984, Ronald Reagan's commissioner of internal revenue, Roscoe Egger, admitted that tax compliance had gotten worse: "Clearly there's a trend away from compliance. . . . There's definitely a continuation of the downtrend that started 20 years ago . . . I think there's a belief on the part of some taxpayers that they won't get caught." But then Egger added, "Even though we're talking about downtrends, you're still talking about compliance in the 90 percentile level."

This nation, to be sure, has not yet experienced the blatant tax cheating that goes on in some countries, but a downtrend to 90 percent? The IRS commissioner was putting on a happy face.

A recent survey by Louis Harris and Associates, appropriately done for the Boy Scouts of America, found that only 65 percent of the men questioned believe it is absolutely wrong to cheat on one's taxes. There is far more claimed honesty among older than young men: 78 percent of men age sixty-five and over agreed it is absolutely wrong not to declare all income, but only 58 percent of those age twenty-five to twenty-nine expressed this view. The report "doesn't say great things for the ethics and morality of our society," said Humphrey Taylor, chief executive of Louis Harris and Associates.[3]

IRS commissioner Egger viewed the decline in tax compliance as "a reflection of the whole national mind-set, the relationship between individuals and institutions," and placed no blame on either the tax law or the IRS's enforcement of it.[4] But this is too easy. Individuals have become disenchanted with many institutions, government institutions foremost among them. But blame also lies in an income tax that stimulated investments in chinchilla farms, took ever-increasing shares of inflated dollars, still encourages divorce, and drives people mad by mindless complexities.

The IRS also shares responsibility. While the IRS wants to be even-handed and thoughtful in administering the tax law, often it overreaches. Consider this widely publicized incident: Gary D. Keefer, a twelve-year-old, had his life savings of $10.35 seized by the IRS to settle a tax debt owed by his parents. Gary's parents apparently were delinquent on a $200 monthly overdue tax bill, and Gary's account was seized because his mother's Social Security number was on it. A number of similar cases were reported, but Gary fought back. His first salvo was a letter to President Reagan, stating: "Greetings from Virginia. I regret to inform you that there is once again trouble in the colonies." Reagan did not answer, but after many phone calls, the IRS returned Gary's $10.35. Gary called the IRS action "highway robbery" and "operating above the law." The IRS subsequently announced that it will no longer ask banks to seize accounts with balances under $100 and will freeze temporarily—rather than seize—any accounts that bear a name in addition to the delinquent taxpayer. Bless the children.

A footnote to this story. Sympathizers with Gary, including patrons of the New Paradise Lounge in Madison, Wisconsin, sent him checks for $10.35 and his account grew. Gary said, "The IRS is going to want to tax all of that as income. A piggy bank is awfully inviting, considering they can just go into your account and take it again."

I myself have had difficulties with the IRS. Shortly after moving to Connecticut, I was audited. In response to a question about deductions for medical expenses, I presented the IRS revenue agent canceled checks and evidence that the expenses had not been reimbursed by insurance. "Not enough," the agent said. "I need a letter from your doctor indicating dates of treatment, etc."

"What!" I replied, trying to remain calm. "Why do you need more?"

The agent turned smugly to the table behind his desk and patted the Internal Revenue Code benignly. "It's in this book; we just have to go by this book," he said.

I had not identified my line of work, and I then felt a surge of adrenaline. The agent had patted a book I knew something about. Cloaking my voice now with sugar and innocence, I asked, "Could I just see what it says?"

The agent promptly flipped the tax code open to contemporaneous recordkeeping requirements for travel and entertainment expenses but pointed only to the language requiring recordkeeping. Almost leaping from my seat, I pointed out that this statute was limited to travel and entertainment expenses and did not anywhere mention medical expenses. Undaunted, the revenue agent replied, "It may say 'travel and entertainment,' but it means everything."

I then hired an accountant who charged me several thousand dollars to obtain a "no change" letter from the IRS. Encounters like these, along with things like the IRS's unwillingness to be bound by its own answers to telephone inquiries and its inability to provide taxpayers prompt and correct information about their accounts, have aroused anti-IRS sentiments throughout the land, sentiments that politicians of all stripes would like to turn to their own political advantage.

Two-Tier Tax Enforcement

What we now have is a two-tier system of tax enforcement. Low- and middle-income taxpayers who receive only wages, interest, and dividend income and take the standard deduction or itemize, claiming only home mortgage interest and state and local tax deductions, have virtually no opportunities not to comply with tax requirements. Their employers withhold income tax on their wages and file a W-2 form with the IRS reporting the amount of wages; their banks and others who pay them interest and dividends report the amounts to the IRS on Form 1099. The IRS now matches 100 percent of those reports with individuals' tax returns. Their state reports any tax refunds and their home mortgage lender reports their home mortgage interest. These people's "voluntary" compliance rates are very high; any IRS commissioner would be proud. On the other hand, people who are self-employed, who run businesses where cash frequently changes hands, or who have investment transactions not routinely reported to the IRS have considerable opportunities to cheat.

A major shift in IRS tax enforcement strategy occurred beginning in the 1970s, a foolish move from which the IRS probably will never recover. In the 1980s, the IRS, along with other nondefense government agencies, became hostage to the limited-government philosophy of the Reagan administration and simply was not funded at a level high enough to assure proper administration of the tax laws.[5] Amidst reports of accelerating increases in the total amount of taxes unreported and unpaid, the IRS allowed the coverage of tax audits to fall dramatically. Six percent of tax returns were audited in 1965. In 1976, the IRS audited only 2.5 percent of all returns, and by 1982, audit coverage was down to 1.5 percent. After that, the audit rate fell below 1 percent, and until 1995 the IRS audited only about 1 million of the more than 100 million tax returns individuals file every year. In 1995, the IRS said it had audited 1.9 million returns.

A substantial source of unreported income from legal activities apparently involves capital gains. One IRS estimate claims that capital-gains underreporting accounts for about seven percent of the total unreported income of individuals, but this number, like all noncompliance estimates, may be far off base.[6] Substantial capital gains noncompliance, however, is consistent with the view of both the IRS and independent experts that the overwhelming share of noncompliance with respect to legal income involves business income and property income of high-income taxpayers.[7] Capital-gains reporting requirements, enacted in 1982, which require brokers to report the proceeds from the sales of stocks and commodities, apparently have had some positive effects in addressing this underreporting problem, since before they were instituted the IRS thought capital gains accounted for about 11 percent of the tax gap. But much noncompliance regarding capital gains often does not involve securities or commodities covered by information reports, but instead real estate, exchanges of assets, and sales of collectibles, such as coins, antiques, precious metals, and works of art, which are not covered.

The large underreporting attributable to capital gains offers a striking counterpoint to the optimistic belief that lower tax rates will stimulate tax compliance. For the period 1981–1986, a top rate of 20 percent applied to capital gains in contrast to the maximum 50 percent rate that applied to ordinary income. Nevertheless, during this period underreporting of capital-gains income remained very high. In fact, the IRS estimated that capital-gains compliance increased between 1985 and 1988, when the tax rate was increased from 20 percent to 28 percent.[8] Opportunity to understate taxes, not the rate of taxation, seems to be the principal determinant of noncompliance. People who do not now report capital-gains or cash income are not likely to change simply because tax rates are reduced, at least not until they are reduced to zero.

The IRS has also long believed that tax compliance is 15–20 percent lower for people with non-corporate business income, such as farms or other small businesses, than for people without such business income. Indeed, the IRS now believes that unreported business income accounts for two-thirds of all unreported income of individuals.[9] In 1978, the audit rate for non-corporate business tax returns with more than $25,000 of income was 7 percent; a decade later it had dropped to about 2 percent, where it has remained. The IRS has estimated that there are at least one-half million self-employed people making over $25,000 a year who do not even file federal income tax returns, costing the Treasury an estimated $7 billion a year in lost revenues.[10]

The total number of corporations audited declined almost as precipitously as individuals, from a total of nearly 150,000 in 1977 to less than 40,000 in 1988, where it has remained. The audit rate of small corporations has dropped from about 8 percent in 1978 to about 1 percent today, and the proportion of companies of substantial size that are audited, those with assets of more than $50 million, has declined as well. The audit rate of corporations with more than $100 million of assets has declined from about 80 percent to around 50 percent.[11]

But the very largest corporations are audited annually. IRS agents have offices at corporate headquarters. When they finish auditing one year's tax return, they simply move on to the next. For these companies, the tax compliance game is quite different. Their tax returns are so large and complex that even a highly trained team of IRS revenue agents cannot review every detail, cannot check every questionable reporting position. Thus, the audit lottery for these companies does not turn on the probability of an audit; they know they will be audited. Rather it turns on the likelihood that the revenue agents auditing the return will discover and respond effectively to aggressive reporting tactics. The more of these there are, the more trouble for the agent. The goal of the corporate executives responsible for the return is to pay the lowest amount of tax while avoiding tax penalties. Given the high stakes and high-priced tax advice and return preparation talent available to corporations, the IRS is typically overmatched.

Even estate tax audits have declined, to 14.2 percent of returns in 1994, the lowest level in a decade. In 1988, nearly a quarter of these returns were audited. Only half of the returns for estates valued at $5 million or more are audited.

In the past two decades, the IRS engaged in an experiment, attempting to put an economic theory of law enforcement into practice. Economic theory regards tax underreporting, along with other economic crimes, as simply a rational individual calculation, based on a simple cost-benefit calculation of the probabilities of detection and levels of punishment. This view regards a person's morality or attitude about the obligations of citizenship as irrelevant to tax-return filing practices. Tax enforcement shifted in three directions in a test of this economic theory. Audit rates and criminal prosecutions for tax crimes, where no other criminal activity was involved, were allowed to decline. This lowering of the likelihood of detection was supposed to be offset by two other changes, which were supposed to stem the rising tide of noncompliance.

First, additional information reporting by banks, brokers, and other third parties and matching of these reports to tax returns was instituted to increase the possibilities of detection, at least in some cases, and penalties for failures to file information returns were increased.[12] Large restaurants, for example, are now required to report credit card tips of waiters and waitresses, but that requirement probably has had little effect on restaurant workers whose tips are paid in cash.

One information-reporting requirement added in 1986 required people to include on their tax returns Social Security numbers of all dependents over age two. This caused 7 million dependents to disappear from the tax rolls. More than 75,000 families lost more than four dependents each between 1986 and 1987. Obviously not all of these "children" suddenly grew up and left their parents' homes.

Second, those taxpayers who were unlucky enough to be caught were punished more severely, through more frequent and increased civil penalties for tax understatements and jail time for those convicted of tax crimes. Beginning in 1981, Congress increased existing penalties and added new penalties for substantial understatements of tax liabilities, for the filing of frivolous returns, and for failure to file returns.[13] Criminal penalties were also increased.[14] Interest on tax understatements was increased and required to be compounded daily.[15]

Although specific estimates should be viewed cautiously, a pattern of increasing civil penalties during the 1980s is indisputable. While an increase of up to 200 percent might be explained by inflation, the rough data suggest that the total net amount of penalties on individuals increased five-fold from less than $700 million in 1979 to nearly $3.5 billion in 1995. Tax-understatement penalties, negligence penalties, and fraud penalties for individuals increased tenfold, from just over $40 million in 1978 to nearly $400 million a decade later. Penalties assessed for substantial understatements of tax rose by a factor of 65, from $1.75 million in 1985 to $114.5 million in 1988; as an average amount of penalty per individual return examined, this was an increase from about $22 to $375.[16]

The dramatic increase in third-party information reporting and in the IRS's ability to match such information to tax returns and the new and increased penalties enacted in the 1980s clearly improved some people's compliance with the tax laws. Information reports give people readily usable data about their incomes, making it easier to complete an accurate tax return. In addition, whenever the discrepancy between the self-reported tax-return information and the information reported by third parties is above a certain threshold, the IRS sends taxpayers an automatic notice that taxes are due. The IRS sometimes has claimed this compensates for the decline in individual audit rates. However, information matching and audits are far from perfect substitutes. Audits are necessary to detect underreporting of much investment and business income and overstatements of business expenses and deductions. Recently, despite the relatively low level of audits, the IRS has estimated that audits produce about $1.50 of additional revenue for every $1.00 produced through document matching.[17]

For many people the fear of an audit is the only effective stimulus to comply with the tax law. The "ripple" effect of audits on taxpayer compliance—the effect on collections from taxpayers, whether or not personally audited, who might have reported less taxes due in response to the decreased likelihood of audit—is extremely important. There is much evidence that taxpayers do respond to the nature of the tax audit lottery confronting them, and, despite the additional information reporting and enhanced penalties added in the 1980s, the audit rate was allowed to fall too far. Regardless of the benefits of other compliance measures, it was foolhardy for Congress and the IRS to permit the substantial decline in audit rates that has occurred. An increase in audits in 1995 prompted proposals within Congress to decrease the IRS's audit capacity, but this is just imprudent political pandering to anti-IRS attitudes.

Criminal Tax Enforcement

The ability of the IRS to focus its resources to improve tax compliance was also thwarted by congressionally mandated diversions of IRS personnel and resources away from tax enforcement to other chores, such as collecting unpaid child support and delinquent educational loans. Most important has been a shift in IRS law enforcement resources to develop cases against narcotics dealers and to prosecute non-tax federal financial crimes, most frequently violations of the Bank Secrecy Act and money-laundering statutes. This non-tax law enforcement effort has been sufficiently large to raise serious questions concerning the continuing ability of the IRS to engage in criminal tax enforcement adequately enough to fulfill its primary mission of assuring maximum compliance with federal tax laws.

Consider this imaginary group photograph. What do the following people have in common?

> Al Capone, former gangster; William Campbell, a United States judge for forty-eight years who had previously been involved with the prosecution of Al Capone; Mickey Cohen, former gangster; Robert B. Anderson, former secretary of the Treasury; Joseph D. Nunan, Jr., former commissioner of internal revenue; Dave Beck, former

president of the Teamsters Union; Chuck Berry, rock and roll star; Albert Nippon, fashion designer; Mario Biaggi, former congressman and, as of 1989, the most decorated New York City policeman; Spiro Agnew, former vice-president of the United States; Dana Kirk, former basketball coach at Memphis State University; Robert Huttenbeck, former chancellor at the University of California at Santa Barbara; Victor Posner, millionaire industrialist; Harry Reems, co-star of the porn classic *Deep Throat;* Heidi Fleiss, the Hollywood madam; Leona Helmsley, the "Queen" of the Helmsley Hotel chain; Moses Annenberg, founder of *TV Guide;* Pete Rose, former baseball player and manager; Darryl Strawberry, Willie McCovey, and Duke Snider, other baseball players; and Webster Hubbell, associate attorney general in the Clinton administration.

What these people have in common is that they all were convicted of a tax crime.

This list spans more than five decades of criminal tax enforcement, a period that was characterized by prosecutions of highly visible individuals, some of whom had violated only tax laws, while others had violated other laws along with their tax crimes. Indeed, robbers, embezzlers, drug dealers, and other criminals rarely report their ill-gotten gains to the IRS; the violation of criminal tax statutes has long been a natural handmaiden of the commission of other crimes.

Although the share of the IRS's budget devoted to criminal enforcement has remained relatively constant throughout the past two decades, at between 5 and 6 percent of its total budget, the increasing role of the IRS in enforcing non-tax federal crimes, in combination with the declining audit rate, has changed the sources of IRS criminal prosecutions. The number of criminal investigations as a percentage of returns filed has fallen by about two-thirds. Since the late 1980s, non-tax criminal cases have accounted for more than half of all IRS criminal prosecutions. While the kinds of financial skills located in the IRS's criminal investigation division have an important, often even crucial, role to play in the drug enforcement effort, the tax compliance function of the IRS's criminal process should not be shortchanged as a result.

The IRS policy of fewer investigations coupled with harsher civil and criminal penalties of those investigated raises serious fairness issues. Is it fair to combat widespread noncompliance through stiffer penalties on fewer offenders? Is it fair for ordinary people with uncomplicated tax situations reported on W-2 or 1099 forms to have almost 100 percent of their returns checked while only a handful of business and high-income returns are audited?

People who come in contact with the IRS are often penalized for honest mistakes or disagreements with the IRS about how the law applies. In combination with the IRS's cumbersome process for resolving disputes, the current system makes them angry. For large numbers of other people, given the extremely low likelihood of an audit, the income tax is a game that favors those who underreport. The current system of tax enforcement makes such people bolder. People with the greatest opportunities to understate their tax liabilities have become the boldest. It is wishful thinking to believe the compliance problem will be solved merely by lowering tax rates or modifying the tax base without addressing the structural issues of detection and punishment.

The most rapidly expanding tax fraud scheme has been electronic filing of false tax returns claiming refunds. The IRS estimated that such claims totaled $3.4 million in California alone in 1992, up tenfold from less than $300,000 a year earlier.[18] Electronic filing fraud was a particularly easy mark then because the IRS did not even check Social Security numbers on such returns before authorizing tax refunds. By 1995, however, billions of dollars were leaking this way and the IRS started delaying refunds for as long as eight weeks while it matched Social Security numbers to taxpayers' names. The IRS found that the most frequently used false Social Security number was 111-11-1111, closely followed by 123-45-6789. In a masterful understatement, Jennie Stathis, the director of Tax Policy and Administration for the General Accounting Office, observed, "[The IRS] should be checking all social security numbers and they should have been doing it a long time ago."[19]

I Protest!

Most people are like the Six-Packs. They try their best to figure out how much they owe and to pay it. Many even pay a tax-return preparer to help them. But when so many people regard the tax system as hopelessly complex and rigged to favor corporations and wealthy people, tax compliance inevitably takes a hit. The anti-tax movement has spawned a boom in the number of so-called tax protesters, people who simply refuse to pay taxes. Sometimes they just don't file returns; sometimes they claim an excessive number of personal exemptions or claim the income tax to be unconstitutional. There are many variations. People of moderate means may not have opportunities for tax avoidance, but they sure can protest.

The IRS estimated that the number of tax-protest returns more than quintupled between 1978 and 1983 from 7,000 returns to more than 35,000.[20] Some of these people are protesting in the long tradition of David Thoreau, who refused to pay taxes to support the Mexican-American War, or William Penn, the Quaker founder of Pennsylvania, who in 1711 urged "true Christians" not to pay taxes to carry on war contrary to their own conscience. But the vast majority of tax protesters today are seeking monetary, not spiritual, salvation.

Many tax-protester claims are coupled with constitutional and statutory challenges to the tax law that have routinely been rejected by the courts and now guarantee penalties for filing frivolous claims. Among the favorite assertions are that the ratification of the Sixteenth Amendment permitting an income tax is invalid; that Federal Reserve notes are not money, so wages are not income; that paying taxes is voluntary, not compelled; that the tax law is unconstitutionally vague; and that filing a tax return violates the Fifth Amendment privilege against self-incrimination and the Fourth Amendment protection against unreasonable searches and seizures.[21]

Among the most common of these diverse claims is the practice of hiding behind some "religion" or "church" that miraculously came on the scene to bless the protester's notion that paying the hated tax would itself be sinful. More than half the tax-protester returns each year involve false church schemes. The most popular involved the Universal Life Church, whose members worship no particular god but instead are committed to the pursuit of happiness, which this church's doctrine insists requires money. For a fee, this Modesto, California, church provided kits that supposedly would permit thousands of dollars of tax-deductible contributions to oneself. Sergeant Robert F. Fowler, a thirteen-year veteran of the Prince George's Maryland Police Force, for example, claimed more than $15,000 of such deductions in 1981. His "contributions" funded his home mortgage payments, lawn service and trash removal, video equipment, a power mower, furniture, a microwave oven, a Ford van, and vacation "retreats" for himself and his family.[22] He was found guilty of filing false tax returns.

On June 25, 1984, then–U.S. attorney Rudolph Guiliani indicted nine people for ordaining ministers in the Life Science Church. Ministers of this church took a "vow of poverty" and a 100 percent charitable contribution for payments to themselves. The promoters apparently grossed $10 million from their sales of ministries during the period 1979–1981 and attracted 150 New York City police officers to their "ministry." Mr. Guiliani also announced that an additional 550 city police officers and 300 other city employees, including firefighters, sanitary workers, and transit personnel, had engaged in similar activities by joining the Life Science Church, the Freedom Church of Revelation, or the Universal Life Church. New York City's police commissioner, Benjamin Ward, claimed the police officers might not have realized that the scam was illegal, expressing unusual sympathy for such behavior by describing them as "more victims than offenders," because the Life Science Church promoters had a "convincing sales pitch."[23] The award for the most offended "church" member goes to Dean Harvey Hicks, an aerospace engineer who lobbed thirteen mortar shells at a Fresno, California, IRS office and tried to blow up three other IRS facilities in Los Angeles after the IRS denied him an $8,000 deduction for a "contribution" to the Universal Life Church.

New York City continues to harbor tax protesters. In July 1996, the Justice Department arrested fifteen New York City police officers for tax evasion and revealed that at least six hundred city employees were suspected of participating in a tax-evasion scheme. Nothing very complicated was involved. Workers simply declared dozens of exemptions on their withholding forms so that little or no money was deducted from their paychecks. Some claimed as many as ninety-nine dependents. They did not pay any federal taxes and did not submit tax returns. Some wrote letters to the IRS claiming "I am not within a 'state' of the 'U.S.' nor am I a 'person' nor 'individual' nor 'taxpayer' as those terms are defined" in the federal tax code. "I am outside the scope of the Internal Revenue Code."[24]

Rudolph Guiliani, then mayor of New York, said that these tax protesters were motivated more by greed than principle. "This isn't ideological," the mayor said. "This is pure out-and-out cheating. This is a way of cheating and not paying your taxes by people who are sworn to uphold the Constitution of the United States." The mayor added that any W-4 forms with ten or more exemptions would subsequently be flagged for further inquiry.[25]

Tax protesters have not limited their activities to avoiding their own taxes. Instead, following a path once traveled in the early 1970s by President Richard Nixon, who maintained a widely publicized "enemies list," they have tried to sic the IRS on people who have caused them difficulties. Rocco Del Monaco, Sr., of Fort Lauderdale, Florida, for example, filed false 1099 forms claiming to have paid large sums of "non-employee compensation" to officials of a bank which had foreclosed on his mortgage and to officials of the local power company and city officials.[26] The Justice Department has labeled this a fast-growing tax-protester scheme, designed to "annoy" and "impede" the IRS, harass government employees, and disrupt the administration of the tax laws.[27]

In July 1995, the *New York Times* reported that Irwin A. Schiff, a famous tax protester, who has long insisted that paying taxes is voluntary and has logged jail time for his efforts, now is finding increased public acceptance of his views. The *Times* quotes Mr. Schiff as saying, "Ten or 15 years ago I was called a Communist. People who called in would say if you don't like America, leave it. Tomorrow I will be on nationwide radio for three hours telling people the same things and I won't get one negative call." The *Times* reports that he didn't.[28] No one knows how large the tax-protest movement actually is.

Sadly, our highest government officials, our presidents, have also been far from perfect role models in inspiring ordinary citizens to obey the tax law. President Clinton, when he was governor of Arkansas, deducted $2 a pair in 1986 for old underwear he contributed to Goodwill and $15 for his long johns. Energetic reporters discovered the top price for used underwear in Little Rock thrift shops to be less than $1, typically much less. Joe Cheslow of the Union Rescue Mission in Little Rock said, "I don't think people want that too much." President Clinton also deducted $100 for a used brown sports jacket and $75 for a "gabardine suit," described in a burst of candor as having "ripped pants." Imagine what Jackie Onassis could have claimed for her discarded frocks. The Clintons also apparently deducted substantial amounts of interest that someone else paid in connection with their famous Whitewater land investment. An audit of their tax returns by *Money* magazine suggested that the Clintons understated their taxes by nearly $6,500 and owed the IRS more than $45,000 of back taxes and interest.[29]

But the Clintons were pikers compared to President Richard Nixon, who left office, according to a congressional staff investigation, having understated his taxes for the years 1969–1972 by nearly $445,000. The major cause of this tax understatement was a charitable gift of Nixon's papers, which was claimed as a deduction by backdating the time of the gift.[30]

When this is the way the nation's presidents sometimes behave, who can be outraged, or even surprised, when ordinary citizens claim a little extra in charitable deductions, perhaps by pretending that they put $5 in the church collection plate each week—or perhaps $200 at Easter, the one day they went to church, to make up for past absences?

Conclusion

While no one can be sure exactly how much, the government clearly loses large amounts of revenue each year from unreported income and overstated deductions. Conservative estimates suggest that unreported taxable income has averaged about 15 percent of total taxable income in recent years. The IRS has estimated that the "income tax gap" created by revenues lost from legal sources of income totaled nearly $100 billion from individuals alone. Corporate noncompliance adds to this amount.[31] Large estimates are also advanced for income tax evasion in the illegal sector of the economy. Many proponents of restructuring the tax system claim that significant reductions of tax rates or the replacement of income taxation with consumption taxation will produce far fewer compliance problems, but there is little evidence to support these claims.

The Pollyannaish notion that compliance problems will disappear if we lower tax rates or shift from an income to a consumption tax does not withstand even cursory analysis.[32] Because taxpayer morale is important, tax simplification may be a more promising course. Using several kinds of taxes also has compliance advantages. A drug dealer who evades income taxes will pay sales taxes when he spends his illegal earnings.

The tax compliance problem is different from other "crimes" because of the important and confounding roles played by a variety of third parties. These include attorneys and accountants who advise clients on tax matters and thus often insulate them from criminal and civil penalties; bankers, brokers, and others who accumulate considerable information about their customers' financial affairs; appraisers who are often paid to estimate values that have important tax consequences; and tax shelter promoters and tax protesters who have inspired many citizens to be aggressive in reducing taxes and sometimes to engage in fraudulent tax-reduction activities. Improvements in tax enforcement and compliance have recently focused on the role of these third parties by increasing their reporting requirements and penalties. Additional innovations in this regard may be a necessary step in improving tax compliance.

Effective tax enforcement depends upon the efficacy of withholding, third-party information gathering and reporting, the ability of the IRS to match third-party information with individual returns, and IRS modernization of its computers and its employees' capacity to deal with them. Increased services to help taxpayers file returns must accompany restoration of a higher level of tax audits. Making the tax law easier to comply with by making it much less complicated would greatly help the IRS and taxpayers alike.

Filling out a tax return continues to be the most common form of participation in our governmental process. More people file tax returns every year than vote in presidential elections every four years. Tax compliance necessarily falters when the act of filing a tax return is a time of anger and frustration. As filing a tax return becomes just another occasion for making a selfish economic calculation rather than an expression of the responsibility of citizenship, the tax system itself is at risk. Interposing a tax-return preparer, particularly an aggressive one, further distances the citizen from his or her government. The culture of the IRS also must change so that, rather than regarding itself simply as a collection agency, it recognizes its crucial role as the main bridge between the people and their national government. The IRS must stop penalizing people who do their best but still make honest mistakes.

Voluntary compliance has declined. Of this, there can be no doubt. The future looks bleak; the younger generation is more prone to cheat than the older. The crucial question is whether the tax system and its administration can be reconfigured to halt, or even reverse, this trend. Ultimately, the trend toward lower income tax compliance must be attributed at least partially to the decline in the public's respect for the income tax. Some of that, of course, can be attributed to people's disdain for what their money is being spent for, the widespread view that much government spending is wasteful. But the failures of income tax policy itself—many of which have been described in the preceding chapters—must shoulder much of the blame. A fair, straightforward, simple tax system will command greater support both politically and at filing time than one riddled with inequities and weighted down with complexities. The critical test is whether our elected officials have the vision and the will to enact new policies into law. Before looking to specific policy ideas, however, let us visit the sausage factory.

PART II

———

THE SAUSAGE
FACTORY

7

A Visit to
the Sausage Factory

As every schoolchild knows—or at least as all schoolchildren once knew—in the beginning, at the time of the American Revolution, some wag labeled taxation without representation tyranny. Of course, neither Thomas Jefferson nor Alexander Hamilton nor their compatriots had yet experienced the pleasure of seeing taxation with representation—the U.S. Congress at work on the tax law. That is something else altogether—not quite tyranny, but far from a thing of beauty. The rules that I lamented in previous chapters did not enter the tax code by magic; Congress put them there.

Although 1978, when Proposition 13 was enacted, was the year that transformed the retail politics of taxation—the relationship between the American people and their tax laws—tax politics within Congress had come unglued four years earlier in 1974. That year the Ways and Means Committee chairman, Wilbur Mills of Arkansas, fell from power and major "reforms" of the tax legislative process were put in place.

A Tidal Wave Goodbye

At 2:00 A.M. on October 9, 1974, police stopped Wilbur Mills for speeding near the tidal pools adjacent to the Washington Mall. An Argentine striptease dancer, whose stage name, Fanne Foxe, is the only name we know, jumped from the car into a tidal pool. Mills's face was reported to be very red and adorned with numerous scratches. Nevertheless, Mills easily won reelection in November of 1974, but on November 30 he appeared on stage in Boston with Ms. Foxe to congratulate her on a striptease performance he had particularly admired. On December 3, he entered Bethesda Naval Hospital and two days later the House Democratic caucus stripped the Ways and Means Committee of its power to determine the committee assignments of House Democrats, a major source of Mills's power. Mills's alcoholism, which these incidents brought to the public's attention, abruptly ended his congressional power and slowly terminated his public career. Mills promptly stepped down from his Ways and Means chairmanship and did not seek reelection to Congress in 1976.

This created a black hole in the tax legislative process from which it is yet to recover. Mills's successor as Ways and Means chairman, Al Ulman of Oregon, became the first such chairman ever defeated for reelection. He narrowly lost on November 4, 1980, after twenty-four years in Congress, shortly after he had proposed a value-added tax for the nation. Although some claim this is not why he was defeated, Ulman's picture, hanging in the Ways and Means Committee room along with the other committee chairmen, serves as a constant reminder to committee members that it doesn't pay to be too farsighted in advancing new taxes, even if you believe it is for the public good.

Al Ulman's successor, Dan Rostenkowski of Chicago, became

the second Ways and Means Committee chairman defeated for re-election. Rostenkowski was voted out of office in 1994 after having been indicted for a variety of misuses of his public office for private benefit. He subsequently pled guilty to a number of these charges and began serving a seventeen-month sentence on July 24, 1995. Rostenkowski's experience teaches a different, perhaps even more important, lesson.

A critical shift in power and leadership over tax matters was not the only change occasioned by Mills's demise. Like nature, Congress abhors a vacuum, especially a power vacuum, and the abrupt termination of Wilbur Mills's career was soon followed by a major dispersion of power and staff expansion. Before looking forward at these far-reaching changes, however, let us glance backwards to Mills's final major legislative achievement, the Tax Reform Act of 1969, the most significant post–World War II peacetime tax legislation up to that time—the last tax legislation enacted during a year that the federal budget was not experiencing a deficit. Both the tax system and the political context for tax revision were quite different then.

The Tax Reform Act of 1969

The 1969 legislation began with an extraordinary moment in tax politics. Joseph Barr, who served as secretary of the Treasury for less than a month at the close of the Johnson administration, announced in January 1969 that 155 taxpayers with adjusted gross incomes of $200,000 or more had paid no income tax in 1966.[1] This announcement generated a spontaneous outpouring of public outrage about the income tax. The fact that even this small number of high-income people were able to pay no tax violated the public's sense of fair play, the view that everyone who can afford it should help finance public obligations. Congress in 1969 received more letters about these high-income taxpayers than any other subject, even though a very controversial war was raging in Vietnam. As a direct result, Congress introduced a new "minimum tax" into the law, a provision which would become a key element in future tax legislation. Both the incoming Nixon administration and the Congress produced major tax reform proposals that year.

In 1969 most people still prepared their own tax returns, and the national tax shelter industry had not yet made an appearance. Political leadership on tax matters resided in the House Ways and Means Committee—principally with Chairman Mills. The House Ways and Means Committee had no subcommittees, further concentrating power in the chairman. Each day during the committee's deliberations, Chairman Mills would announce a "consensus" on the tax revisions at issue. Committee votes simply were not taken.[2]

In fact, during consideration of three tax bills during the period 1969–1971, Wilbur Mills took only one vote: on a proposal by President Nixon to reduce business taxes by allowing more rapid depreciation deductions for purchasers of equipment. He lost by one vote, 13 to 12, when a relatively junior Democrat, Sam Gibbons of Tampa, Florida (who was himself to serve briefly as chairman more than two decades later in 1994 after Dan Rostenkowski was indicted for misuse of public office), joined all the Republicans on the committee to support the Nixon proposal, arguing, "Let's give Nixon what he wants; this plan will never work." Mills was not amused.

At that time, decisions of both the Ways and Means and Senate Finance Committees were made in relative privacy. The committees' sessions for writing legislation were closed not only to the public but also to individual members' staffs. Virtually all of the staff work on tax matters for both the House Ways and Means and Senate Finance Committees was performed by the nonpartisan staff of the Joint Committee on Taxation. Amendments were generally not permitted on the House floor.

The Ways and Means Committee Democrats also served as the House Democrats "Committee on Committees," thereby controlling the committee assignments of all the Democratic members of the House. This made it potentially very costly for an outsider to cross Mr. Mills. A city dweller, for example, might in short order find himself serving on the Agriculture Committee. Needless to add, the Ways and Means Committee's bill typically became the bill passed by the House of Representatives.

The Senate Finance Committee, under the leadership of Russell Long of Louisiana, operated quite differently, voting constantly, but with no vote binding until the final version of the bill was voted out of the committee to the Senate floor. In September 1969, the Senate Finance Committee took a vote on average once every thirty seconds to produce its version of what was to become the Tax Reform Act of 1969. This prompted Fred Harris, senator from Oklahoma, to whisper to his committee colleague Abe Ribicoff, senator from Connecticut, that this act surely proved Bismarck right when he remarked, "No one should ever see how law or sausage is made."

Then, as now, consideration of tax legislation on the Senate floor was something of a circus with unlimited amendments permitted. In those days, one of the favorite Senate sports was to pass amendments, knowing that they would be discarded in the final bill as a result of the conference between the House and Senate. For example, in virtually every year during the sixties, the Senate passed an amendment permitting an extra personal exemption for persons with disabilities, knowing full well that the provision would be killed by the House-Senate conference. The senators, of course, could then tell their constituents that they had gotten the proposal through the Senate, but that their unfeeling colleagues in the House of Representatives had eliminated it.

There were lobbyists twenty-five years ago, to be sure, but they were barred from the deliberations of the House, Senate, and Conference Committees. This enabled their supporters to claim to have fought the good fight on their behalf but to no avail, without a lot of wasted energy or posturing during the actual committee deliberations. C-Span didn't come into existence until 1981. A "PAC" was a group of cool cats who hung out with Frank Sinatra.

Lobbying techniques were far less sophisticated then. Only a few large companies had full-time Washington lobbyists, relying instead on their trade associations to make their case with the legislature. Groups that are extremely powerful in the legislative process today, such as the American Association of Retired Persons and the National Federation of Independent Businesses (which claims more than half a million members), were far less sophisticated in their lobbying techniques. For example, intensive lobbying on the 1969 Tax Act was done on behalf of private charitable foundations, which were fighting regulatory provisions that would require them to distribute a specified minimum amount of funds each year, limit their relationship to certain businesses, and impose a low-rate tax to fund IRS monitoring of the newly enacted regulatory scheme. No one in Congress or the administration had proposed that this tax exceed 2 percent, but when the foundations were done with their lobbying, Congress enacted a 4 percent levy.

Of course, the very small number of legislators who could actually influence tax legislation in Wilbur Mills's Congress was the greatest impediment to successful lobbying strategies. If Mills wasn't convinced, there wasn't much more to be done.

Even at that time, during what was a relatively golden period of congressional decision-making, taxation with representation was terribly messy. Everybody is for tax reform, at least in principle. No one is against simplifying the tax laws, producing greater equity among taxpayers, and promoting economic efficiency and growth. But these general goals are far easier to embrace than specific legislation. The capacity of Congress to deal with major tax reform legislation has long been subject to criticism. The Tax Reform Act of 1969, quite a successful piece of legislation, for example, prompted syndicated columnist Joseph Kraft to remark: "It is now clear that taxes are too complicated and sensitive a matter to be decided in detail by the Congress. . . . The Congress in fiscal matters is a dinosaur—huge body and tiny brain."[3] Since then, Congress has become a more gargantuan body, but no larger of brain.

Adding Players to the Game

Ironically, the congressional process for writing tax legislation became more diffuse and cumbersome as Congress was endeavoring to take greater control over the federal budget process. During 1972 and 1973 Richard Nixon blamed Congress for continuing deficits and refused to spend billions of dollars of appropriated funds when he disagreed with congressional policies. In 1974 Congress attempted to wrest control of the federal budget from the president and completely revised its processes for enacting budget legislation.

One goal was to have spending and tax details conform to aggregate budget goals for expenditures and revenues. Budget committees were established in both the House and Senate and a new Congressional Budget Office was created to serve the new budget committees. Each year these committees propose a budget resolution, which then is taken up by the House and Senate and ultimately becomes a Joint Budget Resolution specifying the amounts to be spent for various categories of expenditure and the amount of revenue to be raised. This budget resolution now typically instructs the tax-writing committees to produce legislation meeting certain revenue targets and, if so, both the House Ways and Means Committee and Senate Finance Committee are bound to comply. If a legislative proposal fails to do so, any member can raise a point of order in objection, and such objections can only be overridden by special supermajority voting rules. In the 1980s and 1990s these budget rules were further constrained by the so-called Gramm-Rudman legislation and the Budget Enforcement Acts of 1990 and 1993, making meeting specific revenue targets the dominant goal of tax lawmaking.

These revisions of the congressional budget process have had a major impact on the tax legislation process. They have made even more critical the role of staff economists' revenue estimates in shaping new tax law and have transferred important power that had long resided in the tax-writing committees to the new budget committees. Beginning in the 1980s massive tax bills have been routinely incorporated in mammoth "Omnibus Budget Reconciliation Acts."

Most important, power has become diffuse. The 1970s marked the beginning of a great expansion of the number of people—particularly congressional staff—involved in the tax lawmaking process. Tax specialists have taken positions as minority and majority staff to the tax-writing committees and to individual members of the tax-writing committees, in the process diminishing substantially the influence of the staff of the Joint Committee on Taxation.

That committee, which had maintained its nonpartisan character largely because only three persons had served as chief of staff in its first fifty years from 1926 to 1976, had seven different staff chiefs during the period 1977–1995, three in the 1991–1995 period alone. That staff now apparently changes leaders routinely depending upon which party controls the Congress.

Do not underestimate the effects of staff proliferation. In the spring of 1990, I attended a meeting among key staff people to try to simplify the earned-income tax credit, an important source of funds to low-income workers, which was so complex that many eligible families failed to claim the credit while many others claimed credits that they were not entitled to. About forty staffers attended the meeting, overflowing the Senate Finance Committee's conference room. In 1969, a similar meeting would have required only four staff people, who in short order would have agreed upon a solution which the House and Senate committees almost certainly would have accepted. Even if these forty people had appeared there that day to work toward a common solution, which they did not, agreement on a proper solution would have been difficult to attain. Perhaps it is just coincidence that the earned-income tax credit which emerged in the 1990 act was more complex than ever and once again in 1993—I'm sure not for the last time—underwent a "simplification." Somehow I don't think so.

Beginning in the 1970s, power also shifted away from the House Ways and Means Committee to both the House and Senate Budget Committees and to the Senate Finance Committee. In addition, the leadership of both the Democratic and Republican Parties responded to the new public status of tax legislation by taking a more active and more partisan role. Public pressure to enact tax reforms—as opposed to tax reductions or tax increases on someone else—seems to have all but disappeared.

The 1970s were also a time for specific "reforms" of the tax decision-making process itself. The Ways and Means Committee was stripped of its power to appoint Democrats to other committees and was forced to appoint subcommittees. Subcommittees further dispersed the power to set the agenda, added more staff, and also added occasions for more hearings.

As campaign contributions from special interests have taken on increased importance, subcommittee chairmanships have become coveted positions. Elizabeth Drew tells of a fundraising party sponsored by a Washington law firm for the liberal Democrat Fortney ("Pete") Stark of California shortly after he had become chairman of the Ways and Means Committee's Select Revenue Subcommittee in September 1981. She describes that subcommittee as the place to seek "special tax provisions" for a "particular client," "little technical amendments" that "won't cost the Treasury much." Ms. Drew reports that this subcommittee has been "referred to on Capitol Hill as 'Santa's Workshop.' "[4]

"Public interest" tax reform proponents, such as Common Cause and Ralph Nader, also insisted on opening up the then-closed process of enacting tax legislation. This opened sessions for writing tax legislation to the public and permitted somewhat greater opportunities for tax bill amendments on the floor of the House. Contrary to the reformers' Pollyannaish predictions, however, open hearings contributed principally to more active surveillance and participation by those with narrow tax objectives, people more interested in taking money out of the public pot than putting it in. Committee deliberations open to the public are routinely well attended by representatives of groups with a special financial interest in the outcome. The halls of Congress are now filled with lobbyists whose purpose is to deplete the public fisc. This is why the area outside the House Ways and Means and Senate Finance Committee rooms is known as "Gucci Gulch." Public participation in the political process was not advanced by opening up the tax-writing process. Joe Six-Pack and his friends simply cannot afford to be present at open markup sessions on tax bills. And no public interest group depending on private donations can hope to amass the resources and clout of profitable financial interests. After he left Congress, Dan Rostenkowski said that moving the Ways and Means Committee into closed executive sessions was crucial to enactment of the 1986 Tax Reform Act:

> It's not that you want to ignore the public. It's just that the lobbyists, the pressure groups, the trade associa-

tions—they all have their pet projects. If you put together something in public, the members are looking over at the lobbyists and the lobbyists are giving the "yes" and "no" signs.[5]

Reforms in congressional practices have thus served to strengthen rather than weaken the sway of those advancing their own narrow financial interests. In short, there is ample cause for despair.

Conclusion

Substantively, federal tax legislation of the 1970s was most notable for what failed to happen. In 1974, 1975, and 1976 various proposals that would have eliminated people's ability to offset unrelated income with tax shelter losses were not enacted, thereby creating conditions that nurtured the tax shelter frenzy of the decade to follow. As Chapter 3 has told, not until the 1986 Tax Reform Act was this situation halted.

In his 1976 campaign Jimmy Carter had called the income tax a "disgrace to the human race" and urged a "major overhaul." President Carter's Treasury Department developed an extensive proposal for revision of the income tax that would have reduced the top rate from 70 to 50 percent and expanded the tax base by limiting deductions and expanding taxable income—the kind of change that was proposed by Ronald Reagan in 1985 and ultimately enacted in 1986. Al Ulman, then the Ways and Means chairman, told the Carter administration that Congress would not be amenable to such a far-reaching proposal, and Carter abandoned his plan, recommending instead only minor changes in the income tax. The 1978 legislation was far from the major overhaul Carter had promised; it was barely an oil change and lubrication. The 1978 legislation is known principally for reducing capital-gains taxes at the behest of Jim Jones, a Ways and Means Democrat from Oklahoma, who was subsequently rewarded with the chairmanship of the American Stock Exchange.

As I have remarked earlier, the key tax enactment of the 1970s did not occur in Congress, but rather at voting machines across California in June 1978 where the people changed the future of American tax policy at both the state and federal levels. Within the next five years, by the end of 1983, Proposition 13 had been imitated in twenty states, where new tax or spending limitations were enacted either by the legislature alone or through public referendums or initiatives. Even the people of Massachusetts voted to shed the label "Taxachusetts" by limiting the ability of their legislature to increase taxes.

At the federal level, Proposition 13 transformed tax policy into a key aspect of presidential politics. In 1980 Ronald Reagan, who had supported Proposition 13 in California, swept into the presidency promising an across-the-board income tax cut that became the centerpiece of his domestic policy in his first term. In 1984 Walter Mondale challenged Reagan for the presidency announcing proudly in his speech accepting the Democratic Party's nomination that he was the presidential candidate who would be candid about the need to raise taxes. He was not heard from after that until Bill Clinton appointed him as ambassador to Japan a decade later. Almost to the day of the ten-year anniversary of the enactment of Proposition 13, George Bush sought the presidency of the United States uttering in the summer of 1988 the only phrase of his that the American people remembered: "Read my lips: no new taxes!" Political pundits claim that breaking this pledge in the Deficit Reduction Act of 1990, rather than his general lack of interest in domestic policy issues, was Bush's political undoing in the 1992 election.

George Bush's successor, Bill Clinton, won both the Democratic nomination and the presidency in 1992 promising a tax cut for the beleaguered middle class, which he had defined in his campaign to include about 90 percent of the American people. As Chapter 10 tells, in 1993 he abandoned—or "postponed"—this pledge, advancing instead a new tax on energy consumption, which Congress did not accept, and a handful of other tax increases, which were enacted in the Budget Act of 1993. In 1994 candidates for governors of many states, including George Pataki in New York,

John Rowland in Connecticut, and Christine Whitman in New Jersey, won election by promising large tax cuts. People who had supported major tax increases routinely lost, most notably the incumbent New Jersey governor, Jim Florio. In 1996, Bob Dole decided that proposing a 15 percent across-the-board tax cut of his own might both rouse new support and remind America of Clinton's broken tax promise.

The anti-tax movement, which made its first effective political statement in 1978's Proposition 13, remains a powerful national political force today, almost twenty years later, and shows no signs of abating. Confirmation of this fact comes during every presidential and congressional campaign, where politicians routinely promise tax cuts, often for everyone, and annually at the state level. Today, all politicians want to embrace tax cuts; all fear political reprisals for suggesting tax increases.

8

Rosie Scenario
Becomes the Belle of
the Ball

P aying far too little homage to the breakup of the Soviet empire or Madonna becoming a rock star, one commentator labeled the 1980s the "Tax Decade."[1] In terms of output, this would be incontestable; Congress enacted nine major tax laws between 1981 and 1990, 8,000 pages of statutory changes amending more than 8,250 subsections of the Internal Revenue Code.

The key income tax changes were in 1981 and 1986. The 1981 tax reduction was the highlight of Ronald Reagan's first term, and the 1986 Tax Reform Act was the major domestic policy achievement of his presidency. Together, they were intended to repair and reconstruct the income tax by dramatically lowering and flattening income tax rates, simplifying the tax, having it interfere less with private economic decisions, and making it more congenial to economic growth.

The "reformed" income tax of the 1980s, however, delivered far less than promised. The tax cuts of 1981, which Congress expanded substantially beyond what President Reagan asked for, raised too little revenue to finance the spending that Congress voted, and the 1986 act was explicitly designed to produce no increased revenues. The combination of spending and revenues in the 1980s led to a dramatic expansion of federal borrowing, quadrupling the federal debt from $1 trillion in 1980 to $4 trillion in 1990. Fiscal conservatives, led by Senate Majority Leader Bob Dole, enacted tax-increase legislation in 1982 and 1984, and tax increases to narrow deficits became the dominant policy goal of tax legislation for nearly a decade after 1986. The 1982 tax increase provided the occasion for Newt Gingrich, then a member of the House Republican leadership, to label Bob Dole "the tax collector for the Welfare State." Dole's Republican Senate colleague, and briefly his rival for the 1996 presidential nomination, Phil Gramm of Texas well described the difficulty: "Balancing the budget is like going to Heaven. Everybody wants to do it, they just don't want to do what you have to do to make the trip."[2]

Congress's revenue-raising tax changes reversed some of the key policies of the 1981 and 1986 tax laws, but both of these laws had serious shortcomings of their own. The 1981 act went too far, the 1986 act not far enough.

Reagan and Rosty Have a Bidding War

In 1980, Ronald Reagan ran for president, promising an across-the-board cut in income tax rates, and the 1981 Tax Act more than fulfilled this promise. Once the Democrats in Congress realized that there was no way to defeat this popular president's popular tax cut, they joined in by upping the ante, adding additional expensive tax reductions of their own. When Congress's Christmas giving ended, everybody was getting a tax cut and virtually everybody was happy.

Corporations were happy, particularly large capital-intensive corporations. The corporate tax burden on income from new investments had essentially been eliminated, largely as a result of reinstatement of a tax credit for part of the costs of equipment purchases and a speedup in depreciation write-offs of both equipment and buildings. The 1981 legislation significantly reduced the role of corporate income tax as a source of federal revenues, bringing it down to less than 9 percent of total revenues, compared to about 15 percent in the 1970s and 20–25 percent in the 1960s. The 1981 act produced great differences in tax burdens for businesses in different industries and for different companies in the same industry, depending on how much new plant and equipment they were buying and how much they relied on debt financing.

The real estate industry was happy. The National Association of Realtors PAC had contributed $1.6 million to the congressional elections of 1980 and was the largest PAC spender in 1982, giving $2.3 million.[3] A decade earlier, in 1970, it had contributed $6,700.[4] The 1981 act increased tax write-offs for real estate, which were expected to cost tens of billions in lost tax revenues over the next five years. Real estate investments were so favorably treated that overbuilding became commonplace, leading to virtually empty "see-through" office buildings and shopping centers throughout the land.

Independent oil producers, whose campaign contributions were actively sought by both Democrats and Republicans in Congress, were happy.[5] They, too, got several billion dollars of tax breaks in 1981 and, unlike some others, were spared reversals in 1982.

Financial institutions were happy. The savings and loan industry helped Congress create a new tax-favored savings vehicle, the "All-Savers Certificate," but this product attracted few takers and soon was terminated. Banks, mutual funds, and other financial institutions were greatly helped by the extension of IRA eligibility to everyone. This cost the government far more revenue than had been anticipated, with the mistaken revenue estimators insisting that their enormous mistake was due to their failure to anticipate the successful mass marketing of IRAs by the banks and brokers.

Corporate executives benefited from more favorable income tax treatment of stock options. In addition, the top tax rate on dividends, interest, and other investment income was reduced from 70 percent to 50 percent and the top capital-gains tax rate was decreased from 28 percent to 20 percent. Cuts in tax rates for everyone else were phased in over the next three years, although for many middle-income people this benefit was largely offset by increases in Social Security taxes enacted in 1983.

As Chapter 4 describes, the most significant enduring feature of the 1981 Tax Act was tax indexing, the elimination of "creeping" tax rate increases automatically caused by inflation. As I have told, as a political matter, inflation adjustments to the personal exemption, standard deduction, and rate brackets, enacted in 1981 to take effect in 1985, eliminated the routine escalation of revenues that previously had enabled Congress to vote tax cuts and created instead a revenue plateau, requiring Congress to enact explicit tax increases to boost revenues.

Buy a Tax Break

Only one aspect of the 1981 Tax Act raised the public's hackles. This was a provision the law called "safe-harbor leasing," but reporters labeled "buy a tax break." This law allowed companies that did not owe any income taxes nevertheless to capture some of the 1981 business tax cuts. The straightforward means of aiding such companies would have been for the government simply to write them checks for any tax savings they could not otherwise use, but this would have smacked of "corporate welfare," so Congress's solution was to let companies that couldn't use the tax write-offs themselves sell their tax reductions to companies that could use them. The companies buying the tax breaks would simply write checks to the selling companies instead of paying taxes to the government. Of course, the buyers would pay the sellers something less than $100 million for $100 million of tax savings; otherwise they would gain nothing from the transaction.

To consummate these "buy-a-tax-break" deals, a document

called a "lease" was required. This enabled lawyers, brokers, and investment bankers also to share in the government's largesse and accounts for the name "safe-harbor leasing." The Treasury Department originally estimated that this brilliant idea would cost about $18 billion of revenue in five years, but it mistook how creative companies could be in garnering these benefits. In 1982 it upped this estimate to nearly $30 billion. After that, it quit reestimating.

Utilities, railroads, airlines, automobile manufacturers, and other companies saved taxes. Ford sold its 1981 tax breaks to IBM; Chrysler sold to G.E.; both deals involved over $100 million of tax deductions. General Electric was the champion buyer of tax breaks. In 1979, it had paid more than $400 million in taxes; in 1980, nearly $350 million. In 1981, it had pre-tax earnings of $2.67 billion and got a net tax refund of about $100 million. Talk about corporate welfare. In addition to its Chrysler deal, G.E. bought nearly $1.5 billion of tax deductions from at least nine different companies, including Pan American Airlines, Phelps Dodge, Cleveland Electric, and Commonwealth Edison.

The transaction that finally brought safe-harbor leasing down was a sale of tax breaks from Occidental Petroleum to Marsh and McClennan, an insurance company. Occidental Petroleum was a profitable company that owed no U.S. taxes because most of its profits were earned abroad. As a result of foreign tax credits for oil royalties and taxes paid to foreign governments and special U.S. tax breaks for oil and gas drilling and production, Occidental's U.S. tax liability had been wiped out. Not only that; it had $100 million or so in excess deductions available to sell—a tax savings of more than $30 million—which Marsh and McClennan bought.

This sell-a-deduction scheme was so easy to understand that even cartoonists could capture it. A Buffalo, New York, tax lawyer, Diane Bennett, suggested that two-worker families should be able to "lease" a welfare family to get the tax exemptions for their children.[6] My favorite idea was to allow the 99 percent of people whose wealth is too low to pay estate taxes to sell the unused portions of their $600,000 lifetime estate tax exemptions to rich people who could use them. At the top estate tax rate, these exemptions would be worth about $300,000 each. This would then end the spectacle of the government having to write checks directly to needy people, a perfect welfare reform. Possibilities for "leasing" tax breaks are unlimited.

In 1982, Congress restricted, but did not eliminate, safe-harbor leasing. In 1986, it finally was eliminated, but by then corporate attitudes toward the income tax had changed forever. Corporate managers had come to regard their tax departments as another potential profit center. They could increase their returns to shareholders by producing a better product, by selling more goods or services, or by saving taxes. Often saving taxes was easier.

Rosie Scenario Becomes
the Belle of the Ball

Debate still rages over the consequences of the 1981 act, both for the economy generally and as a catalyst to federal deficits. But there can be no question that Congress went too far. It enacted a host of misguided tax breaks confident that economic growth would be so stimulated by this legislation as to cure any adverse side effects. Much of the optimism was generated by Ronald Reagan himself, but he got an important assist from a new girl on the block, Rosie Scenario.

David Stockman, Reagan's budget director, in his book *The Triumph of Politics,* tells how Rosie took center stage in 1981 and stayed there. Her task was to help forecast economic growth, inflation, and the other key economic variables, such as corporate profits and interest rates, which together determine the size of total government revenues and spending and therefore predict the deficit. Rosie was relentlessly upbeat. She helped the Reagan administration forecast high and continuous economic growth, which kept estimates of tax revenues high and predictions of certain government expenditures, such as for unemployment compensation, low. Rosie also predicted low inflation, which held down the expected Social Security benefit payments, as well as other major government expenditures, such as those for Medicare, military and civilian government pay raises, and interest on the public debt.

In combining these optimistic forecasts of growth and inflation, Rosie wasn't bothered at all by the fact that in order to squeeze inflation down to an acceptable level, Paul Volker, the chairman of the Federal Reserve, and his colleagues would have to tighten the money supply and, in the process, squeeze the potential for immediate economic growth out of the economy. Needless to say, Rosie failed to predict the rather deep recession of the early 1980s. Nothing could darken the tint of her rose-colored glasses.

The Reagan administration found these optimistic forecasts congenial and generally refused to moderate increases in defense spending or to propose any tax increases. The administration then was frequently surprised by the size of the federal deficit and the rapidly accumulating national debt. In 1985, the *Washington Post* suggested that David Stockman's forthcoming book should be titled "How Rosie Scenario Fell Off Her Trojan Horse When I, Too, Stopped to Feed at the Public Trough."[7]

The Social Security Amendments of 1983

In 1983, projections of Social Security tax revenues and outlays made clear that within a few years taxes would not be adequate to pay benefits, but no one wanted to take the political heat for either cutting Social Security benefits or increasing taxes. Enter a "bi-partisan commission," headed by Alan Greenspan, who would later be rewarded with the chairmanship of the Federal Reserve. The Greenspan Commission offered crucial political cover to both Congress and the administration, and the commission's proposals ultimately were accepted by the Reagan administration and both political parties in the Congress.

The 1983 Social Security amendments accelerated into the 1980s a series of payroll tax increases adopted in 1977 that had been scheduled to go into effect in 1990, brought federal civilian employees and most state and local government employees into the Social Security system, increased the Social Security retirement age slowly from sixty-five to sixty-seven, and subjected one-half of Social Security benefits to income taxation for recipients with income above a certain level. The Social Security tax rate increased in the 1980s from about 12.25 percent to 15.3 percent of wages. The 1983 changes increased Social Security tax revenues by more than $20 billion annually by the late 1980s, and the combined 1977 and 1983 changes together produced additional tax revenues of about $85 billion a year by 1990, mostly from low- and middle-income workers. The Social Security tax hikes significantly increased the tax burdens of the working middle class, and contributed substantially to the ability of Bill Clinton to characterize the tax policies of Presidents Reagan and Bush as favoring the rich and disadvantaging the middle class. They also, I think, presage a long battle between the elderly, who collect the benefits, and younger workers, who pay the taxes.

The Truth about Tax Reform

The Tax Reform Act of 1986 was widely heralded as the most important tax legislation since the income tax was extended to the masses during the Second World War. One analyst for Washington's Brookings Institution described it as "The Impossible Dream Comes True," but surely that tells more about the author's dreams than about the 1986 Tax Act. Reading the glorifications of the 1986 act following its enactment was like watching a Tennessee Williams play: you know there is something very wrong, but nobody's talking about it. We should be surprised that nobody even asked President Reagan "Are you sure?" when he described the 1986 Tax Act as "the best anti-poverty measure, the best pro-family measure and the best job-creation measure ever to come out of the Congress of the United States." Wrong. Wrong. Wrong. Zero for three, Mr. President.

The 1986 act was a product of an uneasy marriage of two contrary ideological and political camps. Conventional Democratic tax reformers—who were interested in improving tax equity by expanding the income tax base by eliminating or cutting back on deductions and treating income the same for tax purposes regardless of its source—joined together with Republican supply-siders and deregulators—who were interested in enacting lower tax rates "to get government off the backs" of the American people and businesses. Many Republicans viewed eliminating or reducing tax incentives as an essential element of deregulation of the American economy. By 1986, reducing the size of government and deregulating the national economy had become an article of faith within the Reagan administration and within the Republican Party generally. Restricting the government's role in influencing private economic decision-making argues strongly for expanding the tax base and lowering tax rates. Although the goal of greater neutrality in affecting economic decisions has long been claimed for tax revision legislation, the 1986 tax reform seems genuinely to have been designed in substantial part to serve deregulation, an unconventional tax policy idea. A massive reduction of tax rates had also long been Republican supply-siders' dream.

In response to the growing public antipathy toward the income tax, many "tax reform" bills had been introduced in Congress in the early 1980s. In his 1984 State of the Union speech President Reagan instructed the Treasury to prepare a "plan for action to simplify the entire tax code so all taxpayers, big and small, are treated more fairly."

A number of proposals—principally by academics, but also by some members of Congress—called for replacing the income tax with consumption taxes. But both Republicans' and Democrats' leading proposals were to reduce and "flatten" the income tax rate and expand the definition of taxable income by eliminating tax exclusions and deductions. The tax reform proposals that President Reagan submitted to Congress on May 29, 1985, took this tack, which ultimately was accepted in the 1986 Tax Reform Act.

Probably the most remarkable thing about the 1986 legislation is that it happened.[8] Support for the idea of income tax reform was bipartisan, but tepid. Conventional wisdom holds that major tax legislation cannot be enacted unless three forces coalesce: presidential initiative, enthusiasm from the tax-writing committees' chairmen, and strong vocal public support. The latter two were missing. So much for conventional wisdom. How on earth was this tax reform enacted?

To begin with, Ronald Reagan and his Republican colleagues became surprising leaders of a tax reform movement. Ronald Reagan once described the progressive income tax as having come "direct from Karl Marx," who, according to Reagan, "designed it as the prime essential of a socialist state."[9] Yet President Reagan made tax revision the highest domestic priority of his second term, attempted with many cross-country trips and public speeches to foment public support, and, by going personally to Congress at a critical moment, rescued the bill from destruction by the House Republicans. In sharp contrast, despite many efforts to convince him to do so, Walter Mondale refused to embrace tax reform in his 1984 presidential campaign, emphasizing instead the need to increase taxes to combat deficits.

President Reagan's key congressional ally ultimately proved to be Senator Robert Packwood of Oregon, then the Republican chairman of the Senate Finance Committee, who later became notorious for other activities. Packwood had so often praised the prior tax code and urged new loopholes that the *New Republic* had dubbed him "Senator Hackwood." He seemed to share a very limited ambition for tax reform with Dan Rostenkowski, the Democratic chairman of the Ways and Means Committee, who had led the 1981 tax-reduction bidding war and, prior to 1986, had demonstrated little substantive interest in the tax law. Rostenkowski later said he regarded the 1986 act as his opportunity to "prove that I could be Chairman of the Ways and Means Committee."[10] Neither Packwood nor Rostenkowski wanted to be the man who murdered tax reform.

Congressional ennui mirrored the public's lack of interest. Unlike 1969, for example, when letters on tax reform flooded Congress, the 1986 tax reform faced public silence. Although everyone supports tax simplification and reform in the abstract, no groundswell of support for the president's proposals emerged. On June 25, 1986, the day after the Senate passed the tax reform bill by a 97–3 vote, the *New York Times* reported that less than one-third of the American public believed that the Senate bill would either produce a fairer tax system or reduce their taxes.

That this tax reform actually occurred was due to a split in business interests. Some businesses, such as service and high-technology businesses, enjoyed a substantial tax reduction from the 1986 act principally because of the lowering of the top corporate rate from 46 percent to 34 percent. Others faced a significant tax increase because special industry-specific tax breaks were repealed or, more generally, because depreciation allowances were reduced and the investment tax credit was terminated. Such differences caused the business community to split politically over the trade-off between enacting a lower corporate tax rate and keeping incentive provisions with a higher rate. Some major corporations fought the tax reform every step of the way, but others, including IBM, General Motors, Sara Lee, and Proctor and Gamble, played a strong supportive role.[11]

Even with this important political advantage, however, enactment of tax reform was touch-and-go. The key turning point apparently was a two-pitchers-of-beer lunch at a Capitol Hill watering hole, the Irish Times, between Finance Committee Chairman Bob Packwood and his key staff aide Bill Diefenderfer.[12] At this lunch, Packwood became determined to seek a major reduction in tax rates, setting as his goal a top rate of 25 percent, much lower than the 35 percent rate of the House bill. To get the top rate nearly that low, considerably more expansion of the income tax base was required than had previously been seriously considered by the Finance Committee. Ultimately, Packwood and his colleagues achieved a top rate of 28 percent, the lowest since the presidency of Calvin Coolidge, when Andrew Mellon was secretary of the Treasury. Ironically, it took Packwood's "two-pitcher" lunch to attack, even partially, tax deductions for what Jimmy Carter a decade earlier had labeled the three-martini business meal.

The 1986 tax reform clearly was a major improvement in the income tax, but it had serious shortcomings. Although the principal mission of the 1986 act was more equal treatment of people similarly situated, it did not fulfill its goal of tax fairness. On the positive side, its greatest achievements were cutting off avenues for high-income families to achieve lower tax rates by shifting assets within the family or to trusts and ending their ability to use tax shelters to eliminate taxes on earnings or investment income. On the other hand, many avenues for tax-favored investment income remained in place, including such things as tax-exempt state and local bond interest and tax-deferred annuities. Tax exclusions for fringe benefits were hardly touched, so that important tax differences continue to turn on a worker's mix of cash wages and tax-free fringes. The tax advantages of owning a home rather than renting were enhanced by new interest deduction rules. A variety of incentive provisions were continued, promoting, for example, investments in low-income housing and rehabilitation of historic buildings. Many families were granted a tax cut when a child turned fourteen; this new distinction was no doubt enacted to offset somewhat the burdens of having adolescents in the house. Finally, as I describe below, this legislation gave special tax benefits to particular companies or individuals while denying them to others similarly situated.

There can be little argument that the 1986 act failed as a simplification measure. Although an increase in the standard deduction allowed many lower- and middle-income people to avoid the computations and recordkeeping necessary to itemize deductions, staggering new complexities were introduced. Compromise is the root of tax complexity and the 1986 act reflected an unending series of political compromises. Rather than simply eliminating or ratifying provisions of dubious merit, Congress often either reduced their benefits or imposed new limitations on their use. One example, the new rules for interest deductions, was described in Chapter 5. The 1986 "minimum-tax" provisions introduced three separate methods of calculating income, each subject to its own rate schedule, not only tripling the complexity but also ensuring that people with identical economic incomes pay different amounts of tax.

Congress also refused in 1986 to address the remaining fundamental problems of the income tax base caused by inflation.

While this may have been reasonable at the low rates of inflation that existed in 1985 and 1986, it seems likely to haunt both tax-payers and Congress in the future.

Perhaps most important, the massive 1986 act failed even to begin to address the dominant economic issue of its time—the size of the federal deficit. In the decade that followed, this contributed to its own undoing, although the constraint of revenue neutrality in 1986 enabled the act to go forward. By insisting on revenue neutrality, both the Reagan administration and the congressional leadership were able to demand that amendments to the tax bill could be offered only if any revenue losses were offset by revenue gains. As one senator remarked during the Finance Committee's deliberations, an important business constituent felt far less enthusiasm for an amendment that would have restored a 100, rather than 50, percent deduction for business entertainment expenses when that change was explicitly coupled with an increase of 1 percent in the corporate tax rate. Senators themselves behaved quite differently in this novel environment; to pay Peter, they had to be explicit about how they intended to rob Paul.

Tax reform started out not only revenue neutral, but also distributionally neutral; that is, the key political players urged that this tax reform not become an occasion for significant shifts in the distribution of income tax burdens among people with different levels of income. By the time the 1986 tax reform finally made its way through Congress, however, any pure effort at distributional neutrality was abandoned.[13] Corporate taxes were raised somewhat from their very low levels of the early 1980s to finance individual income tax reductions for middle- and lower-income people. But the 1986 act never became an occasion for any important shift in the distribution of income taxes across income classes. The singular distributional achievement of this legislation was the widely heralded removal of 6 million poverty-level families from the income tax rolls. But as one experienced tax hand quickly pointed out, these were the same 6 million people whom Congress originally removed from the tax rolls in 1969, and again from time to time throughout the 1970s, and who nevertheless kept finding themselves paying income taxes because of inflationary increases in their level of taxable income.

A tax act forged from a concerted effort to be *neutral* in terms of both total federal revenues and the distribution of the tax burden simply will not have massive economic effects on the American economy, no matter what the politicians, the journalists, or some economists would have you believe. This tax bill therefore neither revitalized American productivity, as some of its admirers hoped, nor destroyed it, as many of its detractors warned. The best economic estimates after its enactment suggest that the 1986 act significantly affected the timing of transactions to take advantage of favorable provisions that the act was phasing out and might have spurred perhaps a 1 percent increase in total hours worked, a genuine benefit, but far from a new American revolution.[14]

The most important thing about the 1986 act was that it reflected a political decision by both Republicans and Democrats to retain and strengthen the income tax rather than to heed the calls of economists and some politicians to replace it with a value-added tax or some other form of consumption tax. The failure, however, of the 1986 act to adopt and maintain a coherent vision of tax equity, coupled with its complexity, has made it unstable. Congress did not in 1986 agree to clear principles that could serve as a basis for resisting change.

The ink was hardly dry on the 1986 act before divorce proceedings started. Some Democrats, notably Speaker of the House Jim Wright of Texas, started talking immediately about delaying the rate reductions scheduled to go into effect in 1988 as a way to reduce the federal deficit. But that did not happen, and the majority of Democrats were not prepared politically to push immediately for an income tax rate increase. The only Democrat who "stood up" for tax increases in the 1988 presidential campaign, Bruce Babbitt, former governor of Arizona, was promptly given his exit pass from the presidential race. The debacle of Walter Mondale's tax-increase strategy was far too fresh for a repeat. But the Budget Act of 1990 edged the top income tax rate up to 31 percent, and in 1993 Bill Clinton and congressional Democrats ratcheted the top rate to about 40 percent.

On the other side, supply-siders and other Republicans instantly expressed concerns about the effect of the provisions of the 1986 Tax Reform Act on savings and investment and began readying new tax-incentive ideas and trying to resurrect old ones. The most notable effort in this regard was the tireless pursuit of the Bush administration for a tax rate reduction for capital gains.

A decade of legislative retreats from the vision of low-rate uniform taxation of all sources of income, which had inspired the 1986 legislation, undermined that tax reform's potential to reverse the decline of public support for the income tax and to solidify its central place in this nation's tax system. If anything, the income tax is now more precarious than ever.

The way that congressional leaders garnered enough votes to pass the 1986 Tax Reform Act also contributed to the public's distaste for the tax lawmaking process. At the very moment that Congress was attempting to achieve greater tax fairness and neutrality by removing a host of special tax breaks from the law, it engaged in an unprecedented vote-buying, horse-trading spectacle. The political currency of the day was "rifle-shot transition rules," which gave special tax breaks to a single person or company, disguised in technical general language amending the tax code.

One rifle-shot provision provided that the new rule that disallowed charitable deductions in connection with obtaining football or basketball tickets from a college or university would not apply to the University of Texas or Louisiana State University.[15] The statute, of course, never mentioned these two universities by name, instead requiring in one case that the qualifying institution "was mandated by a State Constitution in 1876" and in the other that it "was established by state legislation in March 1881 and opened its campus on September 15, 1883." In this case, the targeted relief was too tempting for other football and basketball schools not to try to expand, and in 1988 the tax law was changed to allow anyone an 80 percent deduction for charitable contributions that make the donor eligible to obtain athletic tickets.[16]

The practice of Congress enacting such special tax rules is ancient. Russell Long of Louisiana, the longtime chairman of the Senate Finance Committee, who was no doubt responsible for the LSU exception, in 1969 had secured a special tax benefit for the New Orleans radio station WWL, which was then owned by Loyola University. When the statutory exception was drafted in general terms, carving out an exception for a business owned by a religious order carried on before May 27, 1959, under a license issued by a federal regulatory agency, the drafters of this provision began each subsection of the relevant tax law with the radio station's call letters. Reading letters down the statute instead of words across reveals that it applies only to WWL.[17]

One of the earliest special tax exceptions, known as the Philadelphia Nun provision, was enacted in 1924 to benefit only Mother Katherine Drexel. Contrary to the general practice, this rule allowed Mother Drexel full deduction of amounts she had diverted from a large family trust to create a network of schools for Native Americans and African-Americans. Mother Drexel died at the age of ninety-six in 1955 and on November 21, 1988, she was beatified by Pope John Paul II in a mass at St. Peter's, putting her one step away from sainthood.

None of the beneficiaries of the special tax breaks of the 1986 act seem likely to become saints, or even to get close, and the number and size of the changes targeted by the 1986 act were unprecedented. On the House side, Dan Rostenkowski handed out more than $5 billion of such rewards, principally to favored projects or constituents of Ways and Means Committee members or of other important House heavyweights. To mention but a few examples, transition "relief" was given to the Metropolitan Transit Authority of New York, the Meadowlands sports facility in New Jersey, the Miami Dolphins' football stadium, and a new headquarters for Merrill Lynch. Rostenkowski's hometown electric company, Commonwealth Edison, got one of the largest special tax cuts, worth about $200 million.[18]

On the Senate side, Bob Packwood and his Senate Finance Committee colleagues rewarded 174 taxpayers, also with about $5 billion of tax relief. Continuing the sports theme, and as always protecting Louisiana, the New Orleans Superdome was a winner. So were many large corporations, including General Motors (described in the statute as "an automobile manufacturer incorporated in Delaware on October 13, 1916"), RCA, Pan American Airlines, Avon, MCI, General Mills, and one of Lloyd Bentsen's favorite Texas newspapers, the *Houston Chronicle*.[19] So much for a level playing field.

The $10 billion to $15 billion of special tax breaks contained in the 1986 tax legislation was regarded within Congress as an evil necessary to secure a majority vote for the massive tax reform legislation. But these specific tax breaks were widely publicized and the American people had to wonder what the House and Senate sponsors of these narrowly targeted changes got in return. We know many of them received substantial campaign contributions from beneficiaries of special tax relief. The 1986 act, therefore, restored public confidence in neither Congress nor the income tax.

9

The Madness
of Two Georges

The first year of a president's term is supposed to be a honeymoon with the American people and the Congress. Instead, 1989 marked the beginning of a war between the Bush administration and Democratic leaders in Congress. Perhaps this occurred because the congressional Democrats refused to acknowledge that the presidency had changed hands. They insisted on calling it the Reagan-Bush presidency. In sharp contrast, the Republicans in Congress knew well that there had been a shift in the nation's executive, and many of those, particularly the activists in the conservative wing of the House, did not like it. Some honeymoon.

Shortly after his inauguration, George Bush started pressing for his premier domestic policy proposal, restoration of a lower tax rate for capital gains. Ronald Reagan had also called for a capital-gains tax cut in his final State of the Union address in 1988, but for George Bush lowering capital-gains taxes was an obsession. Soon after Bush became president, George Mitchell of Maine, the majority leader of the Senate, discovered that no greater pleasure could be had than denying President Bush fulfillment of this desire. A less than irresistible president had run into an immovable force.

The Debate over Capital Gains

Probably no income tax issue has been as much debated as the taxation of capital gains. Certainly no issue better reflects the tension between traditional Democratic tax reformers and Republican supply-siders than their conflicting passions over capital-gains taxation. Since 1921, capital gains have been taxed at a top rate substantially lower than that applicable either to earned income or to other kinds of investment income. During the period from 1942 until 1969, capital gains had been taxed at a top rate of 25 percent while the top rate on other income had ranged as high as 91 percent. Eliminating or narrowing that gap had long been a priority of Democratic tax reformers and during the period 1969–1977 they enjoyed considerable success. Under the 1976 tax law, for example, the capital-gains rate could be as high as 49.9 percent compared to a 50 percent maximum rate on earned income (and a 70 percent rate on unearned income).

President Carter's Treasury Department in 1978 developed proposals for equal taxation of capital gains and other income at a maximum rate of 50 percent, but Congress took the opposite course. The Revenue Act of 1978 kept the maximum rate on ordinary investment income at 70 percent while lowering the capital-gains rate to 28 percent in an effort to encourage investment.

President Reagan's 1981 tax cut dropped the highest income tax rate to 50 percent and also reduced the top capital-gains rate to 20 percent. The 1986 act reversed course again by taxing capital gains and ordinary income alike, but, under that legislation, the average tax rate never exceeded 28 percent. In his 1988 presidential campaign George Bush urged that the top rate for capital gains be reduced to 15 percent, and he made a cut in capital-gains taxes his highest domestic legislative priority in 1989.

After months of bitter negotiations with Congress, however, on November 2, 1989, President Bush agreed to postpone enactment of a capital-gains tax cut in exchange for "clean" budget legislation and a necessary increase in the federal government's debt limit. When George Bush called on Congress to postpone a capital-gains tax cut and promptly to enact a budget bill, he surprised many of his key allies in Congress. Bush retreated, however, only because the capital-gains tax cut proponents in the Senate could not muster the 60 votes necessary to shut off a Democratic filibuster. Knowing that he had achieved an important political victory, George Mitchell described himself and his fellow House and Senate Democrats as "heartened" by the "apparent" change in Bush's demand that any budget bill include a capital-gains tax reduction. George Bush emphasized that he would continue to push for a capital-gains tax reduction.

Newt Gingrich of Georgia, then the House minority whip, was right when he announced "this is not the end of the game," but he proved badly mistaken in describing Mitchell's success in precluding a 1989 Senate floor vote on capital gains as only a "Pyrrhic victory."[1] George Mitchell's 1989 victory ultimately proved far more than Pyrrhic. The two Georges were at loggerheads, and there they would remain until they both left government service in the 1990s.

A Silver Bullet
or a Middle-Class Shaft?

For reasons that remain mysterious to me, capital-gains taxation is unique in tax policy debates. No other issue arouses such vigorous and immutable passions on both sides. Proponents of lower capital-gains tax rates regard them as a silver bullet for the economy, a cure-all for our economic blues. If only the capital-gains tax were lowered, advocates proclaim, new investments would multiply, gobs of new venture capital would come out of hiding, technological advances would accelerate, economic growth would soar, and the world would be safe for democracy. With similar but contrary hyperbole, opponents of a special tax rate for capital gains insist that only rich people would benefit, tax shelters would again flourish throughout the land, the added tax complexity would immobilize America, and any remaining tax justice would evaporate. The capital-gains opponents admit only one economic consequence from a reduction in capital-gains taxes: that the rich would become richer. This is not the place for an extensive excavation of these arguments, which have filled volumes in the tax literature, but the claims on both sides seem grounded more in fantasy—in dreams and nightmares—than on solid empirical economic evidence.

The reason why opponents of capital-gains tax cuts claim that an across-the-board reduction in capital-gains taxes benefits the rich is that most capital-gain income accrues to the wealthiest people in our society, even though nearly one-half of all families do have a capital gain at some time during their lifetime.[2] But the truth is that, no matter what the capital-gains tax rate, wealthy people, who have a sizable portfolio of stocks, bonds, and other capital assets, have always enjoyed great discretion about when to pay capital-gains taxes or even whether to pay them. This occurs because they control the timing of their sales of assets and thereby the timing of the payment of capital-gains tax. People like Bill Gates can postpone taxes on most of their capital gains by not selling their assets. If they need cash, they can borrow against assets that have appreciated in value, rather than selling them, and avoid capital-gains taxes. People who have assets with both capital gains and capital losses in their portfolios, a common occurrence among the wealthy, can avoid or postpone capital-gains taxes by timing their sales of the loss assets.

This discretion was buttressed by a gambit that emerged in the 1990s, which enabled very rich people with large unrealized capital gains to diversify their portfolios without paying capital-gains taxes. Bankers Trust Company advertised "Get rid of the risk, not the stock," directed to people with stock worth $2 million or with $10 million or more in assets.[3] The target group was corporate executives who hold large blocks of stock in their own companies. The deal—a so-called equity swap—involved a contractual arrangement, usually with a bank, to exchange the cash flows from specified investments for a period of time, usually three to five years.

One of the people who entered into such an equity swap with Bankers Trust was A. Lorne Weil, the chairman of Autotote Company, a successful supplier of gambling equipment to racetracks and state lotteries. Mr. Weil, who owned 500,000 shares of Autotote stock, agreed to pay Bankers Trust over the next five years the dividends and any gains on this stock, valued at $13.4 million, and, in exchange, Bankers Trust agreed to pay him the income from an alternative $13.4-million portfolio of investments less its fees. Bankers Trust will also pay Mr. Weil for any decline in the value of the Autotote stock. Mr. Weil will continue to vote the stock. He reported no sale and therefore no gain to the IRS.[4]

But such good things do not last forever. Especially when they are tax loopholes widely advertised in newspapers. The IRS issued regulations that were designed to close this particular arrangement down effective May 1, 1995, and in January 1996 President Clinton proposed legislation to close this and some related capital-gains loopholes.

Finally, if assets can be held until a person's death, all capital gains that have occurred during the person's lifetime are forever exempted from income tax. Michael Kinsley has dubbed this the "angel of death loophole."[5] It costs the Treasury about $5 billion a year in lost revenues.

The opportunities for high-income taxpayers to defer and avoid capital-gains taxes make high rates of capital-gains taxation nonproductive. Eliminating the flexibility of such people to time their sales or to avoid capital-gains taxes by holding assets until death by taxing gains on assets as the gains accrue, whether or not the asset is sold, has long been a dead letter politically.

One key question in setting the capital-gains tax rate is this: Given the great flexibility many people have in selling or holding appreciated assets, what rate of capital-gains taxation maximizes the government's revenue? Although one cannot be certain about the precise level of the revenue-maximizing tax rate for capital gains, much recent economic evidence suggests that it currently lies somewhere between 19 and 28 percent. Treasury Department economists have believed this rate to be about 20 percent, while key congressional staff economists have regarded it as closer to 28 percent. Perhaps the 25 percent top rate in effect during the 1940s, 1950s, and 1960s was a pretty good approximation. Indeed, the 28 percent top rate applicable to both ordinary income and capital gains under the 1986 Tax Reform Act was derived from what Congress viewed as a maximum realistic rate on capital gains. When the top tax rates on ordinary income were increased above that level in both the 1990 and 1993 Budget Acts, the maximum capital-gains rate was retained at 28 percent in order not to lose revenues.

The case for a rate lower than the revenue-maximizing rate is advanced with the claim that lowering capital-gains taxes will increase savings and investment and spur economic growth. A commission headed by Jack Kemp, for example, in 1996 urged a zero tax rate for capital gains on the ground that this tax cut would make an important contribution to economic growth. This view, however, seems more an act of faith than a reading of solid economic evidence. A recent comprehensive and even-handed survey of all the empirical economic studies of the likely effects of capital-gains tax cuts describes "considerable uncertainty in attempting to determine the effects of capital gains tax cuts on saving, investment and growth" and concludes that "its effect on domestic investment and growth is likely to be quite muted," that "it is rather unlikely that [such a cut] will result in a significant increase in economic growth."[6]

Even the most touted goal of a capital-gains tax cut—stimulating risky investments in start-up companies and new business ventures—seems likely to be fulfilled far less often than true believers in capital-gains tax cuts suggest. This is because pension funds, funds of charitable organizations such as universities and private foundations, foreign investors, and foreign corporations, which typically supply most of the start-up capital for new ventures, are not taxed on capital gains and therefore are not sensitive to the capital-gains tax rate. Debt finance, which is not generally affected by capital-gains taxation, also accounts for a substantial proportion of new firms' start-up capital. Individuals who supply capital for risky new ventures may care more about the ability to deduct fully any losses they incur than about the tax rate that will apply to any gains they receive when they sell their stock in the future. One reasonable estimate suggests that no more than 20 percent of start-up firms' capital is affected at all by the capital-gains tax rate.[7]

Making a convincing case for a capital-gains tax rate either higher or lower than that which maximizes government revenues is, in my view, impossible. Choosing any capital-gains rate other than that which maximizes revenues necessarily will require the revenues lost to be made up through higher taxes elsewhere or increased government borrowing, either of which may themselves cause economic losses or inequities. On the other hand, choosing the revenue-maximizing capital-gains rate permits a reduction in the government's budget deficit or in taxes on labor and capital, either of which might contribute to an increase in savings.[8] But neither the staunch proponents nor the steadfast opponents of lower capital-gains tax rates have been able to agree simply to set the capital-gains tax rate at the economists' best estimate of the revenue-maximizing level, perhaps as determined by a bipartisan panel of experts. How could they reach such an agreement when each side regards the nation's future as turning on this tax policy issue?

Conclusion

In 1991 and 1992 proponents of capital-gains tax cuts came close to precipitating a constitutional crisis between the legislative and executive branches over capital gains. Frustrated with George Mitchell's continuing successes in blocking George Bush's efforts to get a capital-gains tax reduction through the Congress, passionate capital-gains tax cut advocates urged the Bush administration to issue regulations exempting from tax any capital gains due to inflation.

The National Taxpayer's Union Foundation and the National Chamber Foundation, an offshoot of the National Chamber of

Commerce, commissioned a legal analysis of the question whether such an inflation adjustment could be ordered by the president or the Treasury without legislation by Congress. This legal analysis, principally authored by Charles Cooper, who had served as an assistant attorney general in the Reagan administration, concluded that, although the income tax law had provided throughout its entire history that the determination of the "cost" of an asset for determining the taxable gain or loss on sale is the amount paid for the asset by the taxpayer—its purchase price—Treasury nevertheless had the legal power to revise the definition of cost to mean cost increased by inflationary price increases.[9] The general counsel of the Treasury Department, the chief counsel of the Internal Revenue Service, lawyers in the White House counsel's office, and Justice Department attorneys all disagreed, concluding that such a regulation would not be upheld by the courts. Many capital-gains tax cut proponents, however, cared far more about George Bush fulfilling his campaign promises of capital-gains tax cuts than about the legality of the regulations, and they urged President Bush and his Treasury secretary to issue such regulations even if they would fail in the courts. Ultimately, the Bush administration decided not to attempt to introduce such indexing without congressional approval, approval it never got.

After 1989, George Bush would have only one other realistic opportunity to fulfill his wish for a capital-gains tax cut—another failure—although he would continue to urge such reductions in his State of the Union addresses. This occasion was the Budget Act of 1990, the most costly political exercise in George Bush's presidency.

One Sunday night, toward the very end of the budget negotiations, the Bush administration had one last opportunity to fulfill its capital-gains tax cut wish. George Mitchell offered a capital-gains cut in exchange for a 32 percent top income tax rate and hinted that he might settle for 31 percent. But President Bush's chief of staff, John Sununu, was convinced that the political fallout to George Bush would be minimal so long as the top rate did not exceed 30 percent. The Republicans counteroffered at a 29.9 percent top rate, which was quickly rejected, and capital-gains tax cuts once again moved to the cutting room floor. A special deduction for purchases of stock in certain small and middle-size companies emerged for a while as a capital-gains alternative, but it found no friends. Before all was said and done, George Mitchell would get his tax rate increase to 31 percent and George Bush would have two more State of the Union addresses to call for a cut in capital-gains taxes, but as a practical political possibility, broad capital-gains tax reductions were dead at least until 1997.

In 1995, House Republicans passed a capital-gains tax cut as part of their Contract with America, but it got bogged down in the negotiations over the budget. Equally predictably, notwithstanding Bill Clinton's claim to be amenable to some cut in capital-gains taxes, congressional Democrats used the capital-gains tax cut as a key exhibit in their claims that Republicans wanted to cut spending for the poor to finance tax cuts for the rich. The two Georges had both left their political offices, but the capital-gains dispute rages on. Religious wars are hard to stop.

10

Sin Looks Pretty Good
When the Alternative
Is Taxes

During the decade following the
1986 Tax Reform Act, other industrial nations, with the exception
of France, imitated the United States by enacting tax legislation to
expand their individual and corporate income tax bases and to reduce their tax rates, although these changes varied enormously in
their details.[1] Having led the world in this direction, however, the
United States failed to stay on course. This nation's tax policy soon
became preoccupied with efforts to address large and persistent
federal deficits. This meant an ongoing search for additional revenues, a search made considerably more difficult by commitments
of key politicians not to raise taxes.

Even after the 1986 act, the U.S. individual income tax base
remained much narrower than the income tax bases of most of our
trading partners—principally because of generous exclusions for

fringe benefits, pension and life insurance savings, and housing expenses, particularly mortgage interest—so, in principle, further expansion of the income tax base remained possible, but the bipartisan coalition that moved the 1986 legislation had collapsed. Despite oft-repeated rhetoric in favor of having the market, not the government, direct people's resources, Republicans had no taste for removing tax breaks to further expand the income tax base. Instead, Republican leaders made tax cuts for investments, particularly a capital-gains tax cut, their first priority. Simultaneously, Democratic leaders concluded that the income tax rate reductions of the 1980s had been unduly generous to high-income families, and they viewed higher income tax rates as an essential component of tax-increase legislation to finance deficit reduction. Higher top rates, of course, were anathema to Republicans. The acrimonious and messy divorce from bipartisan tax policy caused by these divergent views turned into "gridlock."

The search for new revenues acceptable to both Republicans and Democrats required turning away from the income tax to other sources, but neither party thought the country ready for a new broad tax on consumption, such as a retail sales tax or a European-style value-added tax. Narrower targets thus came into view. The goal was to tax things that we wanted to consume less, slightly sinful things like alcohol and tobacco, and things we should use less of, like energy and fuels.

Why Can't We Tax
Alcohol and Tobacco?

There is no longer any real debate that smoking and drinking impose costs to society, including health and accident costs, that justify imposing alcohol and tobacco excise taxes in an effort to curtail consumption of these products. The Yale Health Plan, for example, informed its membership that cigarette smoking is responsible for more than one-fifth of all mortality from heart disease, doubles the incidence of coronary artery disease, and increases mortality by about 70 percent. A recent economic study claims that increased alcohol taxes would be the most effective policy to reduce deaths from drunk driving.[2] Both the federal and state governments have long imposed alcohol and tobacco taxes, but over time inflation has diminished the force of the federal levies.

Federal taxes on tobacco and alcoholic beverages are levied on a per-unit basis (per number of cigarettes or ounces of distilled spirits, beer, or wine) rather than as a percentage of price. As a result, the tax rate on these items declines over time due to inflation. In other words, excise taxes on alcohol and tobacco have declined as a percentage of expenditures on alcohol and tobacco as the general level of prices has increased. This is precisely the opposite effect from that inflation has had on the income tax.

Nevertheless, there have been very few explicit increases in federal tax rates on alcohol or tobacco during the past forty years. Congress raised the federal excise tax on tobacco from 7 cents to 8 cents per pack in 1951. That rate remained unchanged for more than thirty years until 1982 when Congress raised the tax to 16 cents per pack. Notwithstanding the 1982 tax rate increase, in 1989 the federal cigarette tax was about 11 percent of the average per-pack price, compared with 17 percent in 1975 and more than 30 percent in 1960, a decline from more than 30 cents per pack in 1950 to about half that in 1989 in inflation-adjusted dollars.[3] As a result of this erosion and a decline in cigarette smoking from its peak in 1982, tobacco tax revenue declined from 0.55 percent of gross national product in 1950 to less than 0.1 percent in 1989.

Everyone present at the 1990 budget summit knew that a cigarette tax increase was inevitable, but there was surprising difficulty in moving forward. Both Republicans and Democrats had key legislators from tobacco-producing states up for reelection that year, and the leadership of both parties had promised them that they would not be the first to advance a tobacco tax increase. This produced the suggestion that a member of the staff clothe himself in a white sheet, light as many cigarettes as he could possibly handle, and float into the room billowing clouds of smoke. Republicans and Democrats could then look up simultaneously and say in unison, "Aha! What about increasing tobacco taxes?"

Ultimately, the 1990 Budget Act did phase in an increase in

tobacco taxes from 16 cents to 24 cents per pack, effective in 1993. Even after this increase, however, federal tobacco taxes continue to be quite low in comparison both to historical levels in this country and to foreign rates.[4]

Simply indexing cigarette taxes for inflation would produce more than an additional $1 billion a year and would halt inflation from eroding the real effective tax rate on cigarette consumption. Tax revenues would also automatically rise with cigarette price increases if the current excise tax per pack were recalibrated as a percentage of the manufacturer's price. Doubling the tobacco tax to 48 cents a pack would yield an extra $4 billion a year.

President Clinton in 1993 did not propose any further increase in tobacco taxes as part of his deficit-reduction plan. He had decided to reserve this source of revenue to help finance increases in federal health insurance coverage, and in 1994, in connection with his health insurance proposals, he proposed an increase in the federal excise tax on cigarettes to 99 cents per pack. That change would have increased federal revenues by about $10 billion a year, but failed to pass Congress when Clinton's health proposals tanked. In 1995, President Clinton embarked on an extensive regulatory program intended to reduce teenage smoking, a program aimed at sellers and advertisers that is almost certain to be less effective than the dollar-a-pack tax on cigarettes that would have resulted from his 1994 proposal.

The failure of Congress to enact substantial tobacco tax increases over the past forty years is a tribute to the power of regional politics. Powerful tobacco-state representatives and senators have blocked or minimized such legislation. They are particularly effective whenever the margin for passage of important legislation is narrow, as it was, for example, in 1993. That year a handful of votes determined whether or not massive budget legislation would be enacted. Losing votes of Democrats from tobacco-producing states would have killed President Clinton's deficit-reduction package.

The difficulty of enacting increased or even indexed tobacco taxes pales in comparison to the political barriers to legislating sensible reforms in the taxation of alcohol. As I have said, the federal tax rate on cigarettes declined by about 50 percent in real terms during the period 1950 to 1990. During the same forty-year period, federal tax rates on beer and wine declined by about 75 percent in real terms, and the real tax rate on distilled spirits declined by nearly 70 percent. Measured in 1989 dollars, the tax on beer declined from about 75 cents a six-pack to less than 20 cents between 1950 and 1989, the tax on table wine declined from about 14 cents a bottle to 3 cents, and the distilled-spirits tax fell from about $7 a bottle to about $2.

Distilled spirits are currently taxed at $13.50 per gallon, or about 21 cents per ounce of alcohol. Beer is currently taxed at a rate of $18 per barrel, which is about 10 cents per ounce of alcohol, and table wine is taxed at $1.07 per gallon, a tax of about 8 cents per ounce of alcohol.

The old saw that a shot of liquor, a can of beer, and a glass of wine all have the same alcoholic content implies that a fair and neutral tax designed to curb the consumption of alcoholic beverages should be levied at an equivalent amount based on alcoholic content. Such a reasonable and sensible change in tax policy, however, is not at all likely as a political matter, even though, like cigarettes, the current taxes on alcohol are low, by our own historical standards and also in comparison to alcohol taxes in Europe or Japan, whether measured as a percentage of output or as a percentage of price.

Why is such a sensible policy change politically impossible? A few facts reveal why spirits are more heavily taxed than beer and wine. Much of this nation's consumption of distilled spirits involves drinks of scotch, vodka, gin, rum, or tequila, all of which are imported. Higher prices due to excise taxes, therefore, disadvantage producers abroad, not those located in the United States. The bourbon producers of Kentucky and Tennessee, along with the handful of other domestic producers of distilled spirits, simply do not have enough political clout to compete with domestic producers of beer and wine. The largest domestic producer of beer, however, the Busch brewery, which produces America's best-selling Budweiser and a variety of other brands, is located in St. Louis, Missouri, the hometown of Richard Gephardt, who until 1994 served as majority leader of the House of Representatives and is now minority leader. Moreover, beer taxes hit Joe Six-Pack right in the belly. A tax of 25 cents per alcohol ounce would raise the tax on a six-pack of beer from about 33 cents to 81 cents. Over this, politicians shed barrels of tears.

The winos and yuppies who drink wine also are safe, even though they have nowhere near the political appeal of a beer-guzzling sports fan. A tax of 25 cents per alcohol ounce on table wine would raise the tax per bottle of wine from about 21 cents to 70 cents. But more than forty of our states produce some wine, and all would like to produce and sell as much as California or France. This creates insurmountable political difficulties in obtaining a majority vote in the Senate for a substantial increase in the tax on table wine.

Indexing alcohol taxes for inflation would raise $1 billion to $2 billion a year and a uniform tax of about 25 cents per ounce of alcohol would raise an additional $4.5 billion per year. But such sensible tax reforms face daunting political hurdles.

An Energy Tax Crashes and Burns

The most important substantive decision taken in the budget legislation of 1990 and 1993 was, by far, Congress's refusal to enact either a tax on energy consumption generally or a large increase in the federal gasoline tax. In both the budget summit of 1990 and the deficit-reduction legislation of 1993, Congress seemed quite close to enacting a broad-based excise tax on energy consumption. In fact, such a tax passed the House of Representatives in 1993 but ultimately was not enacted because the Senate refused to go along.

In addition to providing a significant new source of revenue, an energy tax could encourage conservation, reduce our country's dependence on foreign sources of oil, and reduce pollution by making energy consumption more expensive. If such a tax were to reduce the demand for oil imports, lower world oil prices might result, and part of the burden of the tax might be shifted to foreign suppliers. Reducing this country's reliance on foreign sources of oil would decrease our exposure to volatile changes in energy prices and interruptions in oil supplies. Since an energy tax would raise energy prices, it would help to conserve energy resources and, at the same time, reduce emissions of carbon dioxide, thereby helping to decrease pollution. A potential outcome of such increased conservation would be a rise in innovation and productivity in energy consumption. Underpriced commodities tend to be abused. The net gain for the economy would probably be substantial. An energy tax should have no adverse impact on the nation's rate of savings.

Because energy consumption represents a greater percentage of consumption and income for low-income families than for middle- or upper-income families, such a tax requires some mechanism to offset its regressive burden on low-income families. A tax credit against electrical costs or a refundable income tax credit could solve this problem, however, and these ideas were part of the energy tax proposals considered in the 1990 budget negotiations.

A broad-based energy tax would have the additional advantage of raising substantial amounts of revenue, about one-fourth the revenue of an identical-rate broad-based consumption tax, such as a value-added or retail sales tax. This means that a 10 percent energy tax, for example, would raise approximately half the revenue of a 5 percent retail sales or value-added tax. A tax of 5 percent of the price of energy consumption (or an equivalent tax of about 35 cents per million BTUs) would raise about $20 billion of revenue a year, nearly $100 billion over a five-year period. The narrower base and higher rates of an energy tax would create a natural ceiling on its potential revenue-raising capacity in sharp contrast to a tax on consumption generally.

Depending upon the form it took, an energy tax would have different effects on families depending upon the region of the country in which they live. Taxing home heating oil, for example, would have a large impact on families in the Northeast, while gasoline taxes tend to impose the greatest burden on people who live in the western part of the United States. A tax based on the carbon content of energy sources, which has from time to time been proposed on environmental grounds, would adversely affect producers of high-carbon coal, particularly in West Virginia. To smooth these kinds of regional differences, President Clinton in 1993 proposed an energy tax based on heat (BTU) content, similar to that which was considered along with an ad valorem energy tax (a tax as percentage of price of energy products) in the 1990 budget negotiations.

People who participated in the budget summit negotiations of 1990 blamed the failure of a broad-based energy tax primarily on the spike in energy prices that occurred that year when Iraq invaded Kuwait. Oil prices doubled from $14 a barrel in July 1990 to $28 in September. This external price shock made it difficult, if not impossible, for politicians to tell their constituents that they were going to add another 5 percent or so to the price of energy products. Regional factors also played a role, particularly in creating exceptions for home heating oil use. When all was said and done, the 1990 legislation resulted in a nickel-a-gallon increase in the gasoline tax. Gasoline taxes, however, have historically been used to finance spending for highway construction, and it was difficult to get even half of the 1990 nickel increase targeted for deficit reduction, rather than additional highway spending.

As it turned out, the Iraqi invasion had nothing to do with Congress's failure to pass an energy tax. In 1993, when Congress returned to this issue at the urging of President Clinton, domestic energy and gasoline prices were again low, oil having fallen back to about $14 a barrel. After much debate and considerable arm twisting, a broad-based energy tax based on BTU content was included in the House version of the 1993 act, but it foundered in the Senate.

Some of the difficult political sledding of this proposed energy tax in the Senate was due to the fact that, unlike the 1990 proposal, the House's 1993 energy tax did not exempt energy used in manufacturing. As a result, many domestic businesses, where energy is a substantial component of price, such as steel and chemicals, argued that the tax would disadvantage domestic producers in comparison to foreign producers who would not have to pay it. Although these complaints were overblown, since energy prices tend to be higher abroad than they would have been here even with the tax, the failure to exempt manufacturing galvanized business opposition to the energy tax.

What ultimately killed the energy tax in 1993, however, was the opposition of key Democratic senators from oil-producing states, most notably David Boren of Oklahoma and John Breaux of Louisiana, both of whom served on the Senate Finance Committee. Their votes were crucial to move the Clinton tax bill from the Finance Committee to the Senate floor and ultimately also proved necessary for Senate passage of the 1993 deficit-reduction legislation. These senators simply said "No" to any broad-based tax on energy.

When the dust settled, the 1993 act imposed a lesser tax increase on energy consumption than had the 1990 legislation, a 4.3-cents-per-gallon increase in the gasoline tax as compared to 1990's nickel, bringing the total federal tax to 18.3 cents per gallon of gasoline and 24.3 cents per gallon of diesel fuel. For a brief while, the entire additional 4.3 cents per gallon went to deficit reduction for a total of 6.8 cents, but beginning in October 1995, 2.5 cents of that was diverted back into trust funds for highway construction.

In spring 1996 Senate Republicans, led by Bob Dole, attempted to repeal, at least for that election year, the 4.3-cents-per-gallon gas tax increase enacted in 1993. Thus began the 1996 Republican attack on the Clinton tax increases. President Clinton tried to respond by selling oil from the United States Strategic Petroleum Reserve in an effort to lower gas prices at the pump, but also said he would sign a gas tax repeal if Congress passed it. The American Petroleum Institute pointed out that, in inflation-adjusted dollars, a gallon of regular unleaded gasoline cost an average of only $1.14 a gallon in 1995, compared to $1.60 for a gallon in 1960 and $2.20 in 1980 (in 1995 dollars).[5] No one was listening. The savvy radio talk show host Don Imus suggested that the gas tax repeal would simply transfer money to the oil companies, remarking: "The money is now at least going to reduce the deficit. So what's this about? Politics, that's what. Beltway jive."[6] Ultimately Bob Dole abandoned his effort to repeal the gas tax increase in favor of a much more expensive 15 percent reduction in income tax rates.

Good policy, in contrast to politics, would move in the opposite direction. In 1996 the Congressional Budget Office concluded that, even with the spike in gasoline prices that spring, an increase in the gasoline tax of 50 cents per gallon would not raise the price of gasoline above its previous U.S. highs in real terms, or above price levels common in Europe and elsewhere in the world. In 1994, for example, taxes, on average, accounted for less than 30 percent of the price of premium gasoline in the United States, compared to 65–75 percent in Europe and nearly 50 percent in Japan and Canada.[7] Each additional penny of gasoline tax raises about $1 billion of revenue so that a 50-cent tax increase would raise about $50 billion a year, which could be used to reduce either income taxes or the deficit.[8] If such a gas tax increase were phased in, say at 10 cents a gallon a year, people would have time to adjust to the higher prices at the pump. To the extent that people chose to drive less in response to the higher prices that would result from such a tax, both pollution and road congestion would be lowered.

But not to worry. Congress isn't going to do this. Our recent experience with gasoline and energy tax proposals, as well as with increases in alcohol and tobacco taxes, illustrates the trap of confusing sensible tax policy proposals with legislation that can actually be enacted. Pressures for favored or punitive treatment of one sort or another are inevitable in the political process. Reminiscent of the higher taxes on imported distilled spirits, a tax on gas-guzzling automobiles was enacted in a manner to hit foreign luxury cars, not automobiles produced domestically. If an energy tax could have been imposed on oil imports, rather than both imported and domestically produced oil, its political prospects would have improved. But a tax limited to imported oil would raise serious problems with our trading partners, who would likely retaliate on American exports, and runs counter to this nation's efforts to reduce barriers to international trade in both the North American Free Trade Agreement and the recent GATT negotiations. Canadian oil imports, for example, which now account for about 15 percent of all U.S. oil imports, are explicitly exempted from such an import fee under the United States–Canada Free Trade Agreement.

Even if an energy tax could have been enacted, Congress's process of considering it showed that it would have been riddled with exceptions and special rates. Under the current diesel fuel tax, home heating oil, for example, is currently taxed at about half the rate applicable to identical diesel fuels used for other purposes, and certain agricultural uses are exempt altogether. This requires different-colored dyes to distinguish among identical fuels which are subject to different tax rates depending on their use. Needless to say, the IRS has discovered a whole lot of cheating going on; low-rate colors are far more popular than high-rate colors.

Conclusion

The failure of proposals for energy taxes and Congress's ability to enact only minor increases in federal taxes on gasoline, alcohol, and tobacco demonstrate the political difficulties of enacting sensible and relatively noncontroversial tax changes. Expanded and new exceptions to these taxes for small wineries and for specified uses of fuel offer further proof that common sense and logic are poor predictors of congressional decisions. In thinking about proposals for substantial changes in this nation's system of taxation, one must not forget that before an idea can become law, it must move through both houses of Congress and be signed by the president. That process guarantees imperfections and ensures special advantages for certain people and companies that others do not have the political clout to obtain.

The experience with these excise taxes, along with the 1990 enactment and subsequent repeal of a handful of excise taxes on certain "luxury" items, such as yachts, also demonstrates the difficulties of finding stable new sources of revenues for the federal government. The small increase in gasoline taxes and defeat of the energy tax mean that a retail sales tax or some other form of broad-based tax on consumption remains the only practical possibility for a major new revenue source for the federal government.

11

Read My Hips

The emphasis in the 1996 presidential campaign on tax policy issues in addition to tax cuts marks an important shift in the nation's political conversation about taxes. Not since Ronald Reagan's 1986 effort have we seen leading politicians pressing for major tax reforms. Presidents Bush and Clinton both presided over major tax legislation, but during their presidential campaigns both of them had advanced proposals quite different from those ultimately enacted on their watch, and both ultimately said they regretted the tax legislation they signed.

The general anti-tax attitude of the American people has served for nearly two decades as a caution to politicians of both parties, but Congress's 1988 effort to extend Medicare coverage to cover the costs of prescription drugs and catastrophic illnesses, paid for by the elderly, completely immobilized Washington's political leadership on issues of tax policy. This legislation produced a major political debacle not soon forgotten by presidential aspirants or the tax-writing committees of Congress.

Remember the Alamo

In 1988, Congress enacted the Medicare Catastrophic Coverage Act to expand substantially the drug and catastrophic health benefits provided to the elderly under Medicare. To avoid having these new Medicare benefits significantly increase federal deficits, Congress insisted that the elderly pay for them, principally through an additional tax calculated as a percentage of each elderly person's income tax liability. Because this was a progressive tax, many elderly people would have come out ahead, paying relatively little for the additional health coverage, but others—a very vocal minority, as it turned out—would have had to pay far more taxes than the value of the benefits they would get. The additional tax was as high as $1,000 a year for some people.

Many elderly people already received private insurance coverage for drugs and catastrophic medical expenses from their former employers or had bought private insurance coverage to pay for gaps in Medicare coverage. They saw only pain and no gain from this legislation. In addition, the calculations required to determine the additional tax due were so complex that they made an elderly person's health insurance claims seem like a walk in the park.

The Medicare Catastrophic Coverage Act first became a political catastrophe, then a nullity. On Thursday morning, August 17, 1989, an angry group of elderly constituents trapped Dan Rostenkowski, the Ways and Means Committee chairman, in his car in his hometown of Chicago, and wouldn't let him out. Many shouted "Liar," "Coward," "Recall," and "Impeach." One petite elderly woman, Leona Kozien, threw herself and her sign reading "Seniors for Repeal of the Catastrophic Act" on the hood of Rostenkowski's car. The 6-foot-4-inch Rostenkowski managed to escape on foot, and his driver later picked him up at a nearby gas station. Ms. Kozien admitted that she was nervous but insisted that Rostenkowski was more frightened than she was.[1] It was an incident from which Rostenkowski never quite recovered, and one that all of his congressional colleagues feared might happen to them.

In 1989 Congress repealed the Medicare Catastrophic Coverage Act of 1988. From then on, whenever Congress considered increasing payments required of Medicare beneficiaries or cutting their benefits in an effort to reduce deficits, someone piped up "Remember Catastrophic." It sounded like "Remember the Alamo"— a warning, to be sure, but far from a victory cry. Any proposal that then happened to be on the table was either promptly shelved or so whittled down as to be unrecognizable. Likewise, any suggestion that government spending increases or new government programs be accompanied by specific tax legislation to fund the additional spending raised the specter of the catastrophic Medicare retreat. The failure of "Catastrophic" was a political lesson learned too well.

Read My Hips

The year after the Medicare Catastrophic Coverage Act was repealed, President Bush and Congress negotiated the Budget Act of 1990. Many conservative Republican politicians and quite a few political pundits regard this deficit-reducing exercise as the reason Bush failed to win reelection in 1992.

In 1985 Congress enacted the Gramm-Rudman Act in an effort to limit federal deficits. It provided that if certain federal deficit targets were not met, automatic spending caps—known as sequestration—would come into effect and automatically impose across-the-board cuts in federal spending. Early in 1990 it became clear that the Gramm-Rudman legislation would require enormous spending cuts if new budget legislation was not enacted. Robert Reischauer, the director of the Congressional Budget Office, told Congress in July 1990 that the automatic sequestration under Gramm-Rudman would require a cut in defense spending by 42 percent and a reduction of non-defense discretionary spending by 64 percent.[2] Liberals would have applauded the first, and conservatives the second, but no one wanted both.

With this hammer of tens of billions of dollars in Gramm-Rudman sequestration hanging over their heads, key policymakers in the Bush administration and leaders in the Congress concluded it was essential to enact new budget legislation that made substantial progress in reducing projected deficits. Otherwise, they feared, the financial markets would predict renewed inflation and interest rates would soar.

In May 1990 the Bush administration and the Republican and Democratic leaders in Congress began "budget summit" negotiations with a goal to reduce projected deficits by $50 billion the next year and by $500 billion dollars over a five-year period. These goals were about twice as large as any previous deficit-reducing legislation during the 1980s. Before this saga ended in October of that year, there would be more twists and turns than on a Virginia mountain backroad. The Republican Party splintered, and the presidency of George Bush suffered wounds from which it never recovered. Even history was confounded by this legislation; its economic effects have never been known with any certainty. The combination of a war in Iraq and recession at home wreaked havoc upon the budget negotiators' deficit prognostications.

Discussions between the Bush administration and the Democratic congressional leadership were going nowhere fast until the morning of June 26. That day, after a breakfast meeting with congressional leaders, George Bush issued a statement announcing that a budget package must include not only domestic and defense spending cuts and reforms in budget rules and procedures, but also "tax revenue increases." The White House was completely unprepared for the political explosion this statement unleashed.

On the day George Bush accepted the Republican nomination for the presidency he had promised never to raise taxes. He told the Republican Convention in New Orleans: "Congress will push me to raise taxes, and I'll say no, and they'll push and I'll say no, and they'll push again, and I'll say to them: Read my lips, no new taxes." After that he made it clear on many occasions that this pledge applied to all taxes, not just income taxes. The *Economist* magazine described this as "about the most explicit election pledge in history."[3] But that same magazine, along with many of Bush's closest advisers, did not believe that abandoning the pledge would cost Bush politically. This was because polls had routinely showed, by margins of about 3 to 1, that the American people had long believed that Bush would break his no-tax pledge. Confirming their suspicion, however, cost Bush dearly with the American public generally, who decided to punish him for breaking his word even if it came as no surprise, and particularly within the Republican Party, especially among those who had always regarded him as a pretender to the throne of Reagan.

During the period following Bush's June 26 statement, Republicans and Democrats involved in the budget negotiations played a seemingly endless game of fence sitting, with neither willing to make a real first move. The Democratic leadership, particularly the Senate majority leader, George Mitchell, sensed Bush's political blood in the water and allowed his self-inflicted wound to fester. Having witnessed the shock and dismay that Bush's June tax statement had caused within the Republican Party, the administration was not about to make public a first offer of a budget proposal that included significant tax increases. In mid-July, a majority of House Republicans endorsed a no-taxes resolution, sponsored by Dick Armey of Texas, and sent a letter to President Bush opposing any increase in tax rates.

Newt Gingrich, who was then the House minority whip, did a bit of flip-flopping of his own, first expressing outrage at Bush's June 26 statement, then indicating in July that he, too, could "sponsor and support" some tax increases. In August, Gingrich sponsored new tax cuts and subsequently adamantly opposed any increased taxes. Gingrich ultimately torpedoed the agreement between the Bush administration and the congressional leadership. The *Washington Post* remarked: "Mr. Outside–turned–Mr. Inside has gone outside again."[4]

The president himself contributed to his political undoing, as well as to the public's cynicism and dismay, by waffling endlessly over this issue. In one news conference, shortly after the June 26 statement, Bush, unbelievably, compared himself to Abraham Lincoln, remarking, "Like Abraham Lincoln said, 'I'll think anew.' " Later that year, while jogging with his son George in a St. Petersburg baseball park, he told reporters to "read my hips," and he then proceeded to run away. Throughout this process, newspaper head-lines led off with words like "waffle," "retreat," "flip-flop," "blink," and "zigzag." Bush's public approval rating dropped by 20 points, 19 points in the month of September 1990 alone.[5]

The president's waffling, along with the Democrats' ability to portray Bush's obsession with cutting capital-gains tax rates as a do-mestic policy concerned only with helping the rich, ultimately did Bush in. It is, of course, impossible to know whether a more firm and forthright Bush performance would have alleviated either the Republicans' discontent or the public's cynicism over his breaking the "no new taxes" pledge, but Bush's floundering certainly did not help his political cause. Nor did it give the Democratic budget ne-gotiators any sense that they were negotiating with a president who had either the strength or the vision to maintain any core of poli-cies from which he would not vary.

The budget summit negotiations had much motion but no movement until September 7, 1990, when the negotiations shifted to Andrews Air Force Base outside of Washington. The negotiations at Andrews lasted only eleven days, but it seemed like at least a year. The twenty-five members of the House and Senate, with two aides each and other congressional staff, along with representatives of the Bush administration, spent a total of more than $60,000 for food and drink during the Andrews budget meetings.[6] About 125 people were served three large meals each day and enjoyed an un-limited stock of coffee, soft drinks, chips, pastries, ice cream sun-daes, and M&Ms. No one seemed to notice that the absence of any budget restraint on the negotiating process might itself be em-blematic of Washington's larger budgetary difficulties.

One Monday evening sitting in a room, waiting for another in an endless series of meetings to begin, I was watching a Washing-ton Redskins football game, drinking beer, when it occurred to me that this negotiation was like being in a minimum-security prison. The surroundings were pleasant enough and my companions did not seem particularly dangerous, but you simply could not leave.

President Bush had assigned three negotiators to act on his be-half: John H. Sununu, his chief of staff; Richard Darman, director of the Office of Management and Budget; and Treasury secretary Nicholas F. Brady. Mr. Sununu actually made many people angry on both sides, an odd technique in such negotiations. It was like being in a shower with the heat increasing gradually until it dawned on you how scalding it had become. You couldn't miss the heat, however, when former Senate majority leader and then Appropriations Committee chairman Robert Byrd of West Virginia, a courtly man who still regarded the Senate as a gentlemen's club, publicly scolded John Sununu for his arrogant behavior. Sununu had driven Senator Byrd over the edge by sitting with his feet propped up on the budget negotiators' conference table, chatting away with his colleagues, obviously having tuned out Senator Byrd and many others. Senator Byrd announced in his lengthy lecture that in his forty years in the Senate he had never been treated so rudely by a representative of the president of the United States. In private moments, even Sununu's ally Bob Dole referred to the administration's triumvirate as "Nick, Dick, and Prick."

Once the summit negotiators stopped posturing and started dealing, numerous proposals were exchanged between Republicans and Democrats. Although this intense eleven days of negotiations at Andrews never produced a final agreement, it did form the basis for the bipartisan agreement that ultimately emerged in October.

As we saw again in 1995, a budget agreement that both the president and the opposition party in Congress could accept was often stalled by political gamesmanship—repeated efforts by Republicans and Democrats to garner political advantage—and by deep differences in attitudes toward government and tax policy. Having reluctantly accepted that tax increases would be a necessary and substantial component of this deficit-reduction legislation, Republican negotiators wanted to fashion tax increases in a manner that would not inhibit economic growth. They were determined, therefore, to avoid any increases in individual or corporate income taxes, to resist particularly any increases in income tax rates, and to impose any additional new tax burdens on consumption. They wanted, as much as possible, to target consumption of items, such as alcohol, tobacco, and energy, which Americans should consume less.

The Democrats, on the other hand, had concluded that the tax changes of the Reagan era had unduly shifted the tax burden away from wealthy members of society onto the middle class. (As I have indicated, much of the increased middle-class tax burden in the 1980s was due to increased Social Security taxes.) This meant that Democrats wanted to concentrate tax increases on upper-income families. If this demanded an increase in income tax rates, that was just fine. In addition to spurring proposals by Democrats for increases in the top income tax rate and fortifying resistance to any capital-gains tax cut, this concern for middle-income tax burdens also engendered resistance to increased alcohol, tobacco, and gasoline or other energy taxes.

Thus, the Republicans regarded the most important element of the budget tax proposals that they stimulate, or at least not inhibit, economic growth. Democrats, on the other hand, cared most that the tax increases appear to be fair and be imposed primarily on upper-income families. These abiding differences echo in today's political debates over tax policy. As a result of this division, the tax issues were the ones on which the 1990 budget negotiations foundered. There was no straightforward way to bridge this philosophical and political gap. If there had been, the negotiations would have proceeded much faster to a conclusion and would have enjoyed much broader support. The leaders of the different political parties had no common vision of fair tax changes conducive to economic growth, and they were preoccupied with positioning for political advantage.

Nevertheless, the prospect of a Gramm-Rudman sequester was more than either side was willing to face, and on October 1, 1990, the White House and leaders of Congress announced agreement on a budget deal that was expected to reduce the deficit by $40 billion in the first year and $500 billion by 1995. The agreement was estimated to reduce projected defense and domestic discretionary spending by a total of $182 billion, to cut projected spending on Medicare and other benefits by $119 billion, to increase taxes by

$134 billion, and to save $65 million in interest payments on the public debt over the next five-year period.

Republican and Democratic leaders had committed to produce favorable votes for the budget agreement by more than one-half of each party's membership in both the House and Senate and thereby to pass the legislation in both houses of Congress on a bipartisan basis. The president had agreed not to veto it. The House Republicans, led by Newt Gingrich, however, refused to go along and, despite intense lobbying by President Bush, voted 105–71 against the agreement. Liberal Democrats were also unhappy with the deal, and Democrats voted against the bill by a 148–108 margin. The budget agreement had collapsed, and President Bush, Tom Foley (the Democratic Speaker of the House), and Robert Michel (the House Republican leader) had all suffered severe political wounds. None would recover.

In the month that followed the fatal October 5 House vote, the Democrats, who were in the majority of both the House and Senate, fashioned a new budget bill. The House Republicans had absolutely no clout. In fact, one day Bill Archer, the ranking Republican of the Ways and Means Committee who in 1995 became its chairman, asked Nick Calio, the White House's lobbyist, to convey a point to Dan Rostenkowski, then the Ways and Means Committee chairman. Archer told Calio, "You have a better relationship with Rosty than I do." It's not surprising that the Republican House majority elected in 1995 showed little taste for listening to, much less heeding, the views of Democrats.

The only leverage the Republicans had was in the Senate Finance Committee, where they had nine of the twenty votes, and a presidential veto threat, but nobody took the latter too seriously. This scenario did produce a bit of high drama. Early in October, following the House defeat of the budget agreement, much of the federal government was shut down for a few days. In his late show of October 9, 1990, Jay Leno remarked, "Because of Congress's failure to resolve the budget crisis, they had to close down a lot of public parks and monuments. Don't you think the country would be a lot better off if we reopened Yosemite and the Statue of Liberty and closed down Congress instead?" He could have said the same thing again when the government shut down at the end of 1995, but he didn't.

The budget summit agreement negotiated in September between the White House and congressional leaders did not contain any significant increases in income taxes. Instead, two-thirds of the revenues were to come from increased excise taxes and another 20 percent from increases in payroll taxes. The agreement, therefore, had substantially fulfilled the administration's desire to avoid income tax increases and to concentrate any necessary tax increases on consumption excise taxes.

In the Budget Act as finally enacted by the Congress in late October 1990, the overall contribution of tax increases to the total deficit reduction was expanded and the excise tax component was reduced from a total of $90 billion to less than $70 billion. Excise taxes contributed only about half of the total tax increases. Social Security and Medicare payroll tax increases had been expanded to account for 30 percent of the total, and individual income tax increases made up the rest. As finally enacted, there were about $40 billion of total income tax increases. The increased taxes were offset by roughly $18 billion of increases in the earned-income tax credit.

Thus, the short-term effect of the House Republicans' revolt was to end up with a Budget Act in 1990 much less to their policy liking. By repudiating the president, they also increased his vulnerability to primary challenges in 1992 by Pat Buchanan. In the longer term, however, Newt Gingrich's move paid dividends, at least for him. It solidified his image as a tax cutter and improved his standing within the Republican Party. Both George Bush's forced retirement by the 1992 election and Newt Gingrich's elevation to Speaker of the House through the 1994 elections owe much to the 1990 Budget Act.

In his last flop on this taxing matter, George Bush in March 1992 repudiated the 1990 budget agreement, saying, "If I had to do it over I wouldn't do what I did then." Characteristically, he didn't say much about policy but emphasized instead the "political grief it had caused him."[7] Continuing his lack of sure-footedness on this issue, however, Bush, in response to a question whether the decision was really a mistake, waffled one last time. "Well I don't know," he said, inspiring the *New York Times* to label him "President Needle" and the *Washington Post* to write an editorial headlined "Flip, Flop, . . . Flip?"[8]

House Republicans, at least, had achieved clarity. Tax increases were absolutely to be avoided; tax reductions would be praised, promoted, and pushed. Beginning in 1990, and especially in 1991 and 1992, Newt Gingrich and his allies in the House and Senate urged President Bush to reduce taxes to stimulate the economy, which then was in recession. Bush simply trotted out his well-worn proposals to reduce capital-gains taxes.

In 1994, Republican candidates for the House of Representatives signed a "Contract with America," which promised substantial tax reductions and a balanced budget within the next decade. In 1996 tax cuts became a centerpiece of the Republican campaigns for the presidency and the Congress. There would be no more flip-flopping about taxes, at least in this wing of the party. In 1993 and 1994 President Clinton allowed Republicans to recapture the tax-reduction issue politically, and they are not about to let it go.

Bill Clinton Disguises Himself as Robin Hood

Ironically, the Budget Act of 1990, which probably felled the Bush presidency, became the blueprint for President Clinton's initial budget proposals in 1993. The Clinton administration, which had come into office promising a tax cut for the middle class, promptly shifted ground and made deficit reduction its key domestic priority for 1993. Two key veterans of the 1990 budget summit had been appointed to central Clinton administration economic positions: Leon Panetta, the House Budget Committee chairman, was appointed President Clinton's director of the Office of Management and Budget, and Lloyd Bentsen, the Senate Finance Committee chairman, was named Treasury secretary. Based in substantial part on the advice of these two people, Bill Clinton concluded that a major effort at deficit reduction was essential to the long-term health of the American economy.

It had become clear that the deficit was not simply going to wither away. In 1992, the federal government had a deficit of about $290 billion, or nearly 5.5 percent of gross domestic product (GDP)—a very high figure but still below the record 6.3 percent reached in 1983. The last year the federal budget had no deficit was in 1969.

The cumulative federal debt held by the public in 1992, including foreigners, was about $3 trillion, soon to be $4 trillion.[9] Interest on the federal debt paid to the public that year was about $290 billion, more than 20 percent of total federal spending and about 5 percent of GDP. The share of federal spending to pay interest on the federal debt has been rising for some time and is now at an all-time high, either as a percentage of total federal outlays or as a percentage of GDP. To combat these trends, the Clinton administration in 1993 proposed new taxes, some reduction in the growth of federal spending, particularly for defense, and extension of the 1990 act's budget procedures and rules. After a protracted battle, and with no Republican votes, Congress ultimately acquiesced.

During his campaign, Bill Clinton had routinely attacked what he called "Reagan-Bush" tax reductions for "the rich." His deficit-reduction tax proposals fulfilled his campaign promise of higher income tax rates on upper-income individuals. The top federal income tax rate under Clinton's 1993 Tax Act exceeds 40 percent—an increase of about 10 percentage points. Democrats became committed to the belief that increasing the top income tax rates will not inhibit economic growth.

Somewhat surprisingly, President Clinton's proposals contained only a faint echo of a long history of redistributional tax politics in the United States—beginning with Wilson, continuing with Roosevelt, and up to the present—which traditionally has insisted on increases in taxes on corporations. Clinton sought to increase the corporate tax rate from 34 percent to 36 percent, but he proposed to offset this change with new tax breaks, including restora-

tion of a tax credit for equipment purchases that had been repealed in 1996. The Clinton administration defended this proposal by citing the controversial contention of some economists
that purchases of equipment play an especially important role in
stimulating economic growth.[10] Congress settled for an increase in
the corporate rate to 35 percent and dropped the tax credit proposal.

Ironically, President Clinton's legislation expanded the differential between the top capital-gains and ordinary income rates
by leaving the capital-gains rate at 28 percent while increasing the
top rate on ordinary income above 40 percent. Clinton also proposed a targeted capital-gains tax cut, valuable mostly to owners of
certain small and medium-sized businesses, and this idea was accepted by Congress with some modifications. Like the paradox of
the Republican longtime anti-communist Nixon opening the door
to China, capital-gains tax cuts were apparently far easier for Congress to swallow when proposed by a Democrat president.

Tax relief for middle-income taxpayers, promised in Clinton's
campaign, was neither recommended nor enacted. Instead, the
president proposed income tax increases for Social Security recipients with more than $32,000 of income and a broad-based en-
ergy tax. Congress accepted the increased income taxes on Social
Security, but, as Chapter 10 describes, rejected the energy tax in
favor of a 4.3-cents-per-gallon increase in the federal gas tax.

The energy tax was only one case where the Clinton administration proposed to use the tax system to direct investment or consumption or even to substitute for direct regulation. Other
instances included provisions that deny income tax deductions for
lobbying expenses and deny deductions for executive compensation in excess of $1 million if not sufficiently linked to the perfor-
mance of the executive's company. In early 1996 the Clinton
administration was considering special tax breaks to reward good
corporate citizens, but they had not yet decided how to measure
corporate citizenship.

Bill Clinton's effort to focus tax increases predominantly on
high-income families—cloaking tax increases in Robin Hood
garb—was not entirely successful. Polls following the 1993 act

found the vast majority of the American people believed that the 1993 legislation had increased their taxes. In the midterm elections in November 1994, Republicans captured a majority of the House of Representatives for the first time in forty years running on their Contract with America that, along with other things, promised a variety of tax reductions to the American people. As one of its first acts, the new Republican majority amended the House rules to require a supermajority vote—60 percent—to raise income tax rates, a move challenged as unconstitutional by a number of Democratic members of the House.

President Clinton's State of the Union address to Congress in 1993 marked the end—for a brief two years—of divided government in the United States. The Democrats' outpouring of applause on that occasion demonstrated their enthusiasm for controlling both ends of Pennsylvania Avenue. An era of bipartisan compromise over matters of tax and budget policy had temporarily ended. Liberated from any responsibility for governing, congressional Republicans were freed to behave purely as the opposition, a role many found quite congenial. They certainly were not going to be duped into any bipartisan summit or voting for tax increases. Not one Republican voted for the Clinton Deficit Reduction Act of 1993, which barely passed the House and squeaked through the Senate by only one vote.

The legislative process, however, was not made as smooth as one might imagine by Democrats having to compromise only with themselves. Many deals had to be struck before Clinton could get his slim victory. Many skeptical Democrats, fearful of voting for tax increases, surely would have taken a walk had they been willing to hand their party's first president since Jimmy Carter a major political defeat in his first year in office, his honeymoon year. Instead they gave the Republicans an issue, one that, along with President Clinton's 1994 failed health-reform proposals, Republicans used to recapture both House and Senate majorities in the 1994 midterm elections, the first time the Republicans had enjoyed a House majority in forty years. Once again, tax increases in the name of deficit reduction had carried a steep political price.

In Great Britain, 1993 also marked the end of a tax policy era.

For the first time since Edward's abdication of the throne in 1936, the monarch agreed to pay taxes. On this side of the Atlantic, President Clinton's political mistake may have been in spreading the pain of increased taxes far more broadly.

In October 1995, President Clinton did a great imitation of George Bush when he told the Business Council, a group of officers of large U.S. corporations, "Probably there are people in this room still mad at me because you think I raised your taxes too much. It might surprise you to know that I think I raised them too much, too." He blamed Democrats in Congress for making him do it. He repeated this to a Houston fundraiser, and this time the press picked it up. At a press conference a few days later "George Clinton" clarified: "If we said anything which implies that I think we didn't do what we should have done . . . I shouldn't have said that." He went on: "My mother once said I shouldn't give a talk after 7 o'clock if I'm tired, and she sure was right." By this time, headlines read "Two Whoppers," "Clinton's Tax See-Saw," and, in the *Kansas City Star,* "Clinton's Tiny Crocodile Tears Reveal His Transparent Dishonesty." Unlike Bush, Clinton had had enough trouble with his body parts that he never told the press to "read my hips."

In 1995 and 1996 both President Clinton and the Republican majority in the Congress proposed tax cuts, not increases, as part of their proposals intended to balance the federal budget within the next seven to ten years. Bob Dole in 1996 said he could balance the budget while also handing out large tax cuts. The era of tax increases in the name of deficit reduction seems to have ended, at least for a while.

Conclusion

In the "good old days," tax legislation proceeded along a straightforward path: The president proposed legislation; the House Ways and Means Committee held hearings and fashioned a bill, which then passed the House and was sent to the Senate. The Senate Finance Committee held public hearings on the House bill, then drafted its own bill, which was amended on the floor of the Senate. The House and Senate bills were reconciled in a Conference Committee and approved by both chambers. The bill was then forwarded to the president for his signature, which was invariably forthcoming.

This process no longer necessarily holds. In the past fifteen years, tax legislation has sometimes taken this route, for example, in 1981 and 1986 at the behest of President Reagan and in 1993 at the urging of President Clinton. But we have also seen tax legislation initiated by the Senate in 1982, by a bipartisan blue ribbon commission in 1983, and by a bipartisan "summit" among representatives of the White House and congressional leaders in 1990.

Regardless of the path that tax legislation follows, however, leadership always is a critical component. The extraordinary efforts of Ronald Reagan in 1981 and 1986 and of Bill Clinton in 1993 demonstrate that strong leadership both sets the agenda for change and vastly improves the likelihood of Congress enacting coherent legislation. Presidential leadership alone, however, is never enough. Strong leaders must also reside in the Congress: Wilbur Mills in the 1960s and early 1970s, Bob Packwood in 1986, and Dan Rostenkowski and Bob Dole throughout the 1980s offer important examples of crucial congressional leadership.

The challenge of providing genuine political leadership on tax matters has become more difficult in recent times. The decline of the tax-writing committees' power, the proliferation of relevant actors, particularly congressional staff, and the general loss of party discipline have made the flow of information to policymakers and power over decisions more disorderly and diffuse. The increased partisanship that has accompanied the enhanced political salience of tax issues also thwarts prospects for bipartisan tax legislation. Often political advantages from making the other fellow into a villain far outweigh the potential political benefits from forging sound tax legislation.

Television also creates new difficulties for writing tax legislation. The glare of C-SPAN's klieg lights sometimes serves as a threat that foolishness or avarice on behalf of one company or some narrow group of constituents might show up on the evening news, but far more often television transforms public hearings into occasions for political posturing, rather than for information gathering, learning, and serious debate. Television makes it especially threatening for a member of Congress in a public hearing to admit a lack of expertise or to ask a witness for help even in arcane areas of tax law. Every politician now fears that an obscure C-SPAN moment will become the centerpiece of an opponent's vicious thirty-second attack commercial. It is far better politics never to show weakness, never to let one's guard down. As a result, writing coherent tax legislation has become an even more difficult task.

Most important, the public's tendency to focus on proposed tax changes with reference only to the potential impact on their pocketbooks confounds politicians. Today's public perspective on tax policy seems both to begin and to end with the question "How much is this going to cost or benefit me?" In these circumstances, the ability of politicians to muster public support for any tax reform is seriously limited.

12

Just the Facts,
Ma'am

It is astonishing how confident
people both outside and inside the Congress can be in predicting
the consequences of tax law changes, when those consequences are
impossible to know, given the current state of knowledge. You
name the person who will predict the effects of a particular proposal, and I can almost always tell you what they will say. It was not
surprising when Jack Kemp told television reporters "his opinion"
that the rate of economic growth would double if the vague tax reform recommendations of his Tax Reform Commission were enacted, that the size of U.S. GDP would grow from $6 trillion to $12
trillion in ten years. Such estimates should be taken for what they
are: expressions of a religious belief, not a consensus of predictions
of the economics profession. In the political process, economic predictions routinely serve to justify, and sometimes mask, ideological

battles. Clear and noncontroversial answers to crucial questions simply do not exist. Theoretical controversies, limitations of data, and incomplete and inadequate public and politicians' understandings of the limitations of information all conspire to complicate and confound the legislative process. Predicting and assessing the effects of tax changes always calls for knowing the unknown: the effects of the change on people's behavior and the ways in which those effects are reflected in private markets for goods and services, for capital and labor. Commonly, the short-term effects will differ from those in the long run.

It is not necessary or practical here to review all of the important factual disputes that envelop the tax legislative process. One important example is who bears the burden of the corporate income tax. We know that the corporate tax burden causes some combination of lower wages, increased prices, and reduced returns to suppliers of capital. What we don't know is how much of each, a question that has long produced varying and controversial answers from economists. Even the key congressional staffs often take different views. Sometimes the staff of the Joint Committee on Taxation allocates corporate income taxes to owners of capital; at other times it claims that who bears the economic burden of the tax is so uncertain that it can make no allocation. The Congressional Budget Office has used three variations of who bears the corporate tax burden in recent years, sometimes treating the tax as borne by owners of capital, sometimes treating the tax as borne by labor, and sometimes half by labor and half by capital.[1] Who in fact bears the burden of corporate income taxes depends on the details of corporate tax law, in particular on the rules for the recovery of capital expenditures, but the economic analysis usually ignores these details. Needless to say, who pays the corporate tax is a very important question in assessing the fairness and economic effects of a tax system and of proposed tax changes.

Often there is an economic consensus. It just flips from time to time. Prior to the early 1980s, for example, the economics profession generally agreed that labor supply was not very sensitive to changes in taxation. An influential study by the economist Jerry Hausman in 1981 reversed this consensus, but other empirical studies subsequent to the 1986 Tax Reform Act have raised serious doubts about the methodology and results of the Hausman study.[2]

Another key question involves the effect of taxation on savings and investment. Indeed, estimates of the economic effects of replacing the income tax with a consumption tax often depend critically on the assumed responsiveness of savings to changes in the rate of return. Economists admit that this is "one of the more contentious issues in public finance."[3] The public finance economist Don Fullerton asks why opinions vary so widely regarding the "much-studied" effects of taxes on savings and investment. He wonders, "Are the reasons political rather than economic?," but he then retreats to academic safety, concluding that "more research is needed."[4]

I have previously noted one other example of mistaken certainty. When the highest tax rate on individuals was lowered from 70 percent to 50 percent in 1981 at the behest of Ronald Reagan, many people claimed that lowering tax rates would put an end to the tax shelter phenomenon. Never has a prediction about taxpayer behavior proved more wrong. The number of dollars thrown at tax shelters tripled or perhaps even quadrupled between 1981 and 1983.[5]

When major tax changes are being considered, predictions about their likely consequences are routinely advanced by politicians and professional economists in the government, business, and the academy. Sometimes the differences in predictions are obvious. All its political proponents and many economists, for example, claim that replacing the income tax with a flat-rate consumption tax will lower interest rates. To the contrary, Martin Feldstein, a Harvard economist, who was chairman of Ronald Reagan's Council of Economic Advisors, has suggested that interest rates would rise. Perhaps the wisest course is to confess uncertainty and admit it depends on how the Federal Reserve responds.

Talking about the likely effects of a 1996 tax cut proposal by the presidential aspirant Bob Dole, Herbert Stein, the chairman of the President's Council of Economic Advisors under Richard Nixon and Gerald Ford, candidly remarked:

To show him that's not only good politics but also good economics, his advisers trot out a bunch of economists, some of them Nobel Prize winners. They say that if we cut taxes, growth will speed up, we won't lose as much revenue as you might think, and everyone will be happy.

But there's another bunch of economists who say that cutting taxes will increase the deficit so much that the growth rate will slow down and everyone will be worse off. Probably some of them won Nobel Prizes, too. And there are other economists who say: Nobody knows, it could go either way, it all depends on the nature of the tax cut, among other things.[6]

One of the "other things" that makes the effects of tax changes on the economy so hard to predict is that the macroeconomic consequences usually do not turn on the tax changes alone. For example, tax cuts accompanied by equal spending cuts to produce a neutral effect on federal deficits will tend to have quite different effects on the economy than deficit-increasing tax cuts without offsetting spending cuts. Moreover, the overall economic effects of a tax change often depend on decisions of the Federal Reserve. For example, the potential economic stimulus of a tax cut can be dampened if the Fed fears inflation and moves to increase interest rates.

Only rarely is the true uncertainty of economic predictions stated so straightforwardly. In addition to Herbert Stein, a notable exception is the eminent British public finance economist A. B. Atkinson, who in a 1995 book on a flat-tax proposal confessed: "Policy-makers may be taking a serious gamble if they base plans for tax and benefit reform on predictions of increased labour supply (and tax revenue)."[7] A Nobel laureate in economics, Wassily Leontief, stated the difficulty more generally in his Presidential Address to the American Economics Association: "In no other field of empirical enquiry has so massive and sophisticated a statistical machinery been used with such indifferent results."[8] Senator Paul Douglas of Oklahoma, an economist himself, put it more colorfully when he remarked, "If you laid all the economists in the world end to end, they wouldn't reach a conclusion."

But economic uncertainty about the likely consequences of tax policy changes creates political opportunities. The economic debates make it relatively easy for politicians or other policy advocates to find economic support for their proposals. Former staff members from congressional tax staffs and the Treasury Department now man tax policy departments at accounting and consulting firms. These firms routinely churn out economic predictions that are used to lobby Congress for specific tax changes beneficial to their clients. Charles McLure, who served as head of the Treasury's tax economists in the Reagan administration, says that the "current state of the art in public finance . . . may lead to a feeling that virtually any policy can be supported by a selected reading of the existing public finance literature, especially since there is so much uncertainty regarding the values of several key parameters."[9]

Nevertheless, the public has great difficulty resisting the claims of presidential aspirants and other politicians that they have discovered a tax proposal that provides a tax cut for everyone that would so stimulate economic growth as to reduce or eliminate budget deficits. The temptation to believe that hard choices can be avoided remains too great.

A David Letterman–style top ten list may supply some sense of the difficulties. Here are ten questions no public finance economist likes admitting not having answers for:

1. At what tax rate do people work less?
2. What is the effect of income taxes on total savings?
3. To what extent does an increase in domestic savings translate into an increase in domestic investment, rather than investments abroad?
4. What is the effect of the Social Security system on overall savings?
5. How much do Individual Retirement Account (IRA) provisions increase total savings?
6. To what extent do corporate taxes determine business locations?
7. Why do corporations pay dividends?

8. Who ultimately pays the corporate income tax—workers, shareholders, customers, or all owners of capital?
9. How completely do foreign exchange rate adjustments compensate for tax law differentials among countries?
10. What is the effect of the overall level of taxes on economic growth?

Many additional fundamental questions of this sort have been hotly disputed in the economics literature, questions that potentially could have a very significant impact on the struggle to enact sensible tax policies.

The genuine uncertainty about these issues stands in sharp contrast, however, to the confidence of political actors about the future consequences of their actions. No politician can admit uncertainty about the consequences of his economic proposals. Like those who hold different, but firm, views of what God demands, tax ideologues know exactly what is right and what is wrong, which economists' findings should be embraced as truth, which should be tossed aside. Controversial factual propositions hardly slow the claims of true believers in the wisdom of competing tax policies. Daniel Patrick Moynihan, the Democratic senator from New York, cogently explained the danger: "It is quite possible to live with uncertainty; with the possibility, even the likelihood that one is wrong. But beware of certainty when none exists." He concluded: "Ideological certainty easily degenerates into an insistence on ignorance."[10]

Conflict over Values

A great politician, the economist T. S. Adams, who served as the Treasury's top tax adviser during the youth of the income tax from President Wilson's administration through President Coolidge's, knew tax lawmaking, even then, to be a "hard game" in which people tried to shift tax burdens to others. He observed in 1928 that anyone "who trusts wholly to economics, reason and justice, will in the end retire beaten and disillusioned." Dr. Adams viewed "class politics" as "the issue of taxation."[11]

Louis Eisenstein, an eminent tax lawyer, described the contest over tax policy as a battle among ideologies, describing an ideology as a system "of ideas and beliefs suitably equipped with the necessary vocabulary . . . presented as bodies of objective truth which only the prejudiced or benighted can fail to approve."[12] He added, "The ideologists of taxation are constantly attributing their own preferences to some higher disinterested wisdom."[13] Let us look at the ideologies. Eisenstein identified "three primary ideologies" of taxation: First, the "ideology of ability," which "declares that taxes should be apportioned in accordance with the ability to pay them and that ability to pay is properly measured by income or wealth."[14] This ideology was emphasized by George Mitchell in his unyielding campaign against George Bush's proposals to cut capital-gains taxes, by Bill Clinton in his 1992 presidential campaign and his 1993 proposals to increase income taxes on the rich, and in Democrats' attacks in 1995 and 1996 on Republican proposals for flat-rate or single-rate tax reforms.

This ideology of ability, Eisenstein claims, is opposed by the "ideology of barriers and deterrents," which insists that progressive taxes "dangerously diminish the desire to work; . . . fatally discourage the incentive to invest; . . . and irreparably impair the sources of new capital." The ideology of barriers and deterrents seeks the immediate removal of progressive taxes on income and wealth to avoid "impending disaster" and eventual "decline and decay, since neither capital nor ambition will be available." This, of course, is the ideology now urging the nation to move to a flat tax, particularly one that excludes either savings or investment income.

Finally, Eisenstein points to the "ideology of equity," which is "closely associated with the eloquent theme of equality among equals," the notion "that those who are similarly situated should be similarly treated and those who are differently situated should be differently treated." Eisenstein identified three categories of supporters of each of these ideologies: those who would directly benefit from the ideology by virtue of either pecuniary or political rewards; those who are paid to believe; and those who simply believe based on their own judgments.[15]

It is telling that none of Louis Eisenstein's ideologists demands a simple, or even comprehensible, tax system. Generally, as we have seen, wealthier citizens are better able to turn tax ambiguities and complicated rules to their advantage in minimizing the taxes. Ambiguity and uncertainty also have a tendency to reward the most aggressive adversaries in a self-assessment system of reporting income tax liability such as ours where only a small percentage of returns filed each year are audited by the Internal Revenue Service. Of course, no one would ever design a tax system to benefit its strongest adversaries and to penalize those most diligent in trying to comply with its requirements, but simple tax rules nevertheless are often lacking strong advocates. We need an ideology of simplicity.

The adherents of each of these ideologies of taxation tend to ignore the inevitability of political compromise, the fact that the nation's tax laws always are a response to competing ideologies, competing interests, and competing groups. Conflict among the purposes of fairness, economic efficiency, and simplicity is inevitable. To ignore or reject the certainty that such conflict both demands and is reflected in inevitable political compromises is to be a foolish utopian, one who denies the existence of ever-present economic, social, legal, and political complexities. The one genuine certainty is that political compromises inevitably will change over time as the public changes the identity of the politicians who represent them. As the power of different ideologists varies, the particular political compromise shifts, and the tax law changes.

Paint-by-Numbers Lawmaking

The tax law also changes in response to short-term economic circumstances, political fads, vivid stories, and recently from misguided numerical constraints. Since 1986 virtually all tax legislation has been a revenue-raising part of "Omnibus Budget Acts," which have had the principal mission of deficit containment. In making these laws, Congress has subordinated the traditional tax policy-making goals of improving tax equity, simplifying the tax law, promoting economic efficiency, and stimulating economic growth to the overriding goal of ensuring specific annual revenue increases from tax changes during the "budget window" (usually five years). At its worst, this exercise has involved extraordinary games to time the revenue effects of particular legislation, typically accelerating revenue gains into the budget window and postponing revenue losses until after that five-year period expires.

In 1986, tax reform legislation was facilitated by the tax-writing committees' decisions to attempt to make that legislation revenue neutral—neither to increase nor decrease revenues, at least in the short term—and not to change in any significant respect the distribution of the income tax burden among people with different levels of income. By agreeing to these constraints, the House and Senate tax-writing committees decided that the 1986 legislation would serve only two purposes: first, to bring greater tax neutrality to economic decision-making and, second, to improve the "horizontal equity" of the tax law—in other words, to impose more nearly similar income taxes on people who are similarly situated. As Chapter 8 describes, these revenue and distributional constraints played quite a constructive political role in allowing the 1986 legislation to go forward, but it was crucial that these constraints were imposed internally by agreement among the tax policymakers themselves.

In the decade since 1986, that success has lulled congressional decision-makers into illusions of precision. Congress today wants tax policymaking to turn on simple numerical answers, reminiscent of the supercomputer Deep Thought, which in the science fiction classic *The Hitchhiker's Guide to the Galaxy* revealed that the answer to the "Great Question of Life, the Universe and Everything" was "42."[16] Disputes over policy are transformed into disputes over whose computers—the administration's or the CBO's—to use.

Armed with their staff's mathematical answers to both revenue and distributional questions, tax policymakers frequently have avoided the difficulties of exercising judgment to strike an appropriate balance among ambiguous and often conflicting tax policy goals. In doing so, they have constrained themselves to write law that conforms to misleading or wrongheaded mathematical straitjackets.

Virtually all of the tax legislation enacted during the decade following 1986 has been in response to specific budgetary requirements established by Congress either in budget legislation or in Joint Budget Resolutions. Under the Gramm-Rudman Budget Act of 1985 and its 1987 amendments, estimates of the annual revenue effects of budget legislation could trigger across-the-board spending cuts. The budget rules of the 1990 and 1993 acts allowed no revenue-losing measure to be enacted unless the revenue losses were offset by equivalent revenue gains or reductions in certain categories of federal spending. In virtually every year since 1986 the House and Senate Joint Budget Resolutions have required the tax-writing committees of the House and Senate to produce legislation that meets specific revenue targets. In such circumstances, estimates of the annual revenue effects of legislation have become critically important to the tax lawmaking process.

In the 1993 Budget Act, for example, personal income tax rate increases were made retroactive to the beginning of that year, with deferred payments allowed for three years solely to satisfy five-year revenue targets.[17] New and large penalties on marriage were also enacted for high-income taxpayers for the sole purpose of conforming to a specific combination of revenue and distributional targets, while not violating President Clinton's desire not to raise the top income tax rate above 40 percent.[18]

There is no need here to detail the arcana of the various budget requirements. My point is that by virtue of these limitations on the tax legislative process, Congress has mistakenly elevated the importance of estimates of the annual cash-flow revenue effects of tax legislation for each year of a five- or ten-year budget period. Potentially serious spending and tax consequences attach to these numbers, and, as a result, politicians are often primarily concerned about whether the tax or budget legislation under consideration produces revenue estimates that "come out right." The primacy of estimates of revenue effects has, of course, diminished the capacity of the traditional concerns of tax policy—fairness, economic growth and efficiency, and simplicity—to influence the contours of tax legislation.

These budget constraints have also turned many key legislators into revenue-estimate tricksters in an effort to achieve legislative outcomes they desire. For example, in both 1990 and 1991, Phil Gramm and Newt Gingrich introduced IRA legislation which would have lost massive amounts of revenue after the relevant five-year budget window had expired, but would have produced large short-term revenue gains by accelerating cash receipts into the budget period. Both Republican and Democratic legislators have advanced new expanded IRA savings accounts where huge revenue losses are "backloaded." A variation on this theme was contained in legislation proposed by House Republicans in 1995 to increase dramatically business deductions for depreciation of equipment, but to do so in a way that shifted big revenue losses to years after the five-year budget window.

Probably the most venerable technique for taking advantage of revenue-estimating rules, which depend on the annual amount of cash received by the government, is the "speedup," simply moving revenues that would otherwise be collected in a later year to an earlier year. For example, in 1969, the last year that the federal budget was in surplus, the budget surplus was made possible in part by changing the rules for the deposit of withheld income and payroll taxes, so that revenues that otherwise would have been collected in 1970 were moved up into 1969.[19] In 1991, Congress enacted extraordinarily complex requirements for payments of estimated taxes by individuals solely to accelerate revenues into that year to "pay for" temporary extensions of unemployment compensation benefits. In 1994, Congress financed a portion of the tariff reductions from the GATT Uruguay trade agreements by speeding up deposits of certain excise taxes from a due date in October to September 29, solely in order to move the revenues into an earlier fiscal year.[20] The most egregious use of budget scorekeeping rules is to finance permanent revenue reductions with temporary revenue increases, for example, by selling government-owned assets to "pay for" permanent tax changes. In many of these cases, revenue losses from the tax reductions will continue to decrease federal receipts long after the proceeds from the asset sales or tax payment speedups have been spent.

Legislators, of course, need to know the general size and direction of the revenue effects of proposals they are considering, but congressional budget rules that require uncertain and frequently meaningless revenue estimates to serve as a straitjacket on policy outcomes make no sense. Such a process inhibits thoughtful tax policymaking and undermines public respect for both the laws that are adopted and the lawmakers that enact them. The refusal of key congressional players to stop promoting legislation that has been constructed to produce favorable five-year cash-flow revenue results when longer-term revenue consequences are known to be quite adverse is indefensible. Congress, however, has so far been unwilling to enact budget rules or procedures that make legislators accountable for the readily foreseeable long-term consequences of their decisions.

While there is much to be said in favor of a balanced budget amendment to the Constitution, one of its unfortunate consequences would be to heighten even further the critical role of revenue estimates in the tax legislative process. A requirement that Congress enact a budget that is estimated to be in balance for the next year or the next two years, which is what the proposed balanced budget amendments call for, could elevate to Olympian heights the gamesmanship of legislators in shifting money from one year to another.

Overall budget limitations such as those contained in the Gramm-Rudman Act and the 1990 and 1993 Budget Acts have played an important role in constraining the growth of federal deficits. While they have not worked as well as their authors or their strongest proponents would have us believe, the cumulative federal debt would certainly now be much higher had these rules not been in place. Conceding this positive effect, however, does not require denying the adverse consequences that these rules have had on the substance of tax legislation during the past decade.

Don't Underestimate
the Colorful Anecdote

In addition to fashioning tax laws to match controversial and con-tested mathematical constructs, Congress has long been exces-sively vulnerable to memorable anecdotes. It used to be said that opponents of tax increases hide behind carefully selected widows, but now those who would tell a good story to influence tax policy are far more creative than that.

In 1978, the House Ways and Means Committee was consid-ering repeal of a provision that had been enacted two years earlier, which had eliminated the forgiveness of capital-gains tax on assets held until the owner's death. Rather than imposing a deathtime capital-gains tax, Congress in 1976 had changed the law to require that a decedent's cost basis in an asset carry over to his heirs, thereby collecting the capital-gains tax when the heir ultimately sells the asset.

During the 1978 hearings, which provoked many outcries con-cerning the complexities of the new requirements, a pig farmer ap-peared before the committee and vividly recounted the difficulties that the new law posed for him in determining the cost basis of each of the pigs that he had inherited from his father. Shortly thereafter, Erwin N. Griswold, former dean of the Harvard Law School and solicitor general of the United States, told the committee of the heartaches the new rule would cause his heirs in determining their tax liability when they sold his extensive stamp collection, which he had acquired over many years.

The pig farmer's story, coupled with Griswold's testimony, doomed the provision. Whenever anyone would argue in favor of retention, or even amendment, rather than repeal of the 1976 statute, a member of the committee would pepper him with ques-tions about the pig farmer's problems. I always tell my students: in a court of law, first argue the law, then the facts, then public pol-icy, but in Congress, create memorable anecdotes. Numerous tax rules have been enacted to respond to some story or other.

The stories that have wreaked the most havoc with the tax law involved tales about high-income individuals or profitable corporations that used tax-incentive provisions or loopholes to escape income tax. Mrs. Dodge, of the automobile family, narrowly avoided a beating at the hands of Congress because in 1966 she had earned $1 million of tax-exempt interest from state and local bonds and had paid no tax. To respond to her situation and those of a handful of others, Congress in 1969 adopted a so-called minimum tax. New stories about other high-income people paying little or no tax inspired significant amendments to this provision in 1976 and again in 1982. Likewise, the expressions of outrage generated by the announcement in 1985 that the laborers on General Electric's assembly line had paid more taxes than this highly profitable company led to a corporate minimum-tax provision as a major innovation of the 1986 Tax Reform Act.

Corporations and individuals are subject to these alternative minimum taxes only if the computation of the minimum tax produces a greater tax than that due under the regular income tax computation. Both of these minimum taxes are imposed at lower rates than the regular corporate or individual income taxes and apply to a broader measure of taxable income, including certain tax credits, exclusions, and deductions that reduce regular income taxes.

Congress enacted these minimum taxes for one specific objective: to limit the ability of individuals or corporations that have substantial economic income to avoid all tax liability. Here, then, we have two congressional policies at loggerheads. The exclusions, deductions, and credits that reduce these people's and companies' taxes were all enacted to provide incentives for particular conduct or investments, but, at the same time, Congress determined these provisions to be counterproductive when taxpayers use them to avoid all or virtually all of their income tax liability. Congress enacted a minimum tax because of an overriding concern for the loss of public regard for the income tax when high-income individuals or profitable corporations are able to pay little or no tax because of these tax advantages.

Many commentators have long regarded the enactment of

minimum taxes as a sign that Congress has failed: it should repeal either the incentives or the minimum taxes. A more realistic assessment, however, accepts Congress's multiple interests and goals and admits that the minimum tax simply reflects congressional trade-offs among competing objectives. Although originally enacted in response to stories about only a handful of high-income people or profitable companies who paid little or no tax, the minimum taxes today affect hundreds of thousands of individuals and corporations. This is an important, indeed classic, example of how complex tax provisions can grow from the combination of a few colorful anecdotes. It is also a perfect illustration of Congress's habit of compromise.

Conclusion

Many politicians and their supporters have come to regard tax policy positions as a litmus test of loyalty, often to a particular philosophy of government, sometimes to a specific constituency. They routinely insist on the truth of controversial factual claims about the economic consequences of their proposals. Often they are far more concerned with short-term political advantage than long-term policy goals.

In 1995 many leaders of the new Republican majority in Congress proposed fundamental new directions for federal tax policy. House Majority Leader Dick Armey and several presidential candidates proposed substituting for the current income tax a so-called flat tax; presidential hopeful Richard Lugar urged a national sales tax; Ways and Means Committee Chairman Bill Archer embraced some form of tax on consumption; Senate Budget Committee Chairman Pete Domenici called for a progressive consumption tax. In 1996 calls for a new tax system were also heard from Bob Dole and Jack Kemp, but they largely avoided specifics.

At the same time, the Republican majority in Congress was pushing income tax reductions that would return to the public somewhere between $150 billion and $350 billion depending upon the level of anticipated spending savings over the next seven years.

The prospect of enacting such a substantial tax cut presented a genuine opportunity for the Congress to marry short-term tax relief and long-term policy goals, but, even though the same key players were involved, this tax-reduction effort was totally disconnected from the more fundamental tax reform and restructuring movement. Why should any such tax reductions not be targeted to simplifying the existing income tax, to reducing the massive costs of tax compliance currently imposed on taxpayers, and to improving the economic efficiency and growth-enhancing potential of the income tax? Why instead did Congress make the centerpiece of this legislation a $500-per-child income tax credit, which advances none of these important tax policy goals? Simple. A per-child tax credit had become a major political priority of an important "pro-family" Republican constituency and had been endorsed by pollsters' focus groups. Whatever the merits of an additional per-child tax credit, it cannot be claimed to satisfy any of the criteria motivating these same politicians' long-term tax reform proposals. The long-term policy goals were silenced in the jockeying for the political advantage of immediate tax cuts. This is not unusual.

PART III

THE FALL?

13

Taxing What You Spend
Instead of What You Make

In 1921, when the income tax was only eight years old and a fraction of its current size, Chester Jordan, a public accountant from Portland, Maine, told the Senate Finance Committee that he could reduce the size of his accounting firm from eight to three members if Congress only would substitute a tax on "spendings" for the income tax.[1] That idea was strongly seconded by Ogden Mills, then a congressman from New York, who later was to serve as Herbert Hoover's secretary of the Treasury.[2] After Congress refused to go along with his suggestion, the demand for Chester Jordan's services grew, he changed his name to Price Waterhouse, and the rest is history. (I made that last part up, of course, but it should have happened that way.)

Chester Jordan's proposal for taxing consumption rather than income was not a new idea, even in the 1920s. John Stuart Mill had been a fan of taxing consumption, and Alexander Hamilton had only praise for consumption taxes. Hamilton claimed that with consumption taxes people could choose how much to pay; as he put it, "the rich may be extravagant, the poor may be frugal."

In 1942 Franklin Roosevelt's Treasury secretary, Henry Morgenthou, advanced a progressive-rate tax on spendings to finance the Second World War, but once again Congress rejected a consumption tax.[3] Instead, the Revenue Act of 1942 began the conversion of the income tax, which had applied only to high-income people, into a tax on the masses. Had this episode turned out differently, the income tax might have remained narrowly targeted to high-income people, and a consumption tax might have become the federal government's mainstay revenue raiser instead of the income tax.

In the early 1970s, President Richard Nixon came close to proposing taxing consumption by substituting a value-added tax for corporate income and payroll taxes.[4] Several years later, in 1979, Ways and Means chairman Al Ulman did recommend a 10 percent value-added tax. Some people claim this was why he failed to win reelection in 1980.

When Ronald Reagan and Republicans and Democrats in the Congress retained and strengthened the income tax in 1986 rather than replacing it with a consumption tax, many observers thought that signaled the demise of the political movement to replace the income tax with a consumption tax. The Democrats' successful political efforts in the 1990 and 1992 campaigns to portray the tax changes of the 1980s as excessively favorable to the rich, coupled with accumulating evidence that most of the gains in real incomes during the period since 1973 have been garnered by high-income families, also made any serious effort to repeal the income tax seem far-fetched. President Clinton's success in 1993 in raising income tax rates for high-income people appeared further to reaffirm the continuing central role of the progressive-rate income tax in assuring fairness in this nation's distribution of tax burdens.

But the Republicans' sweep of the congressional elections of 1994 dramatically changed the political landscape. Proposals for substituting a consumption tax for the income tax vaulted back into the forefront of the nation's political dialogue. Republican Senate Budget Committee chairman Pete Domenici of New Mexico and Democratic senator Sam Nunn of Georgia introduced legislation to replace the individual income tax and a portion of the Social Security payroll tax with a progressive-rate tax on consumption and to substitute a valued-added tax for the corporate income tax. The new Ways and Means Committee chairman Bill Archer of Texas and Republican presidential candidate Senator Richard Lugar of Indiana said that they too wanted to replace the income tax with a consumption tax. Lugar proposed a retail sales tax to be collected by the states, which he claimed would put the IRS out of business. In 1995, Dick Armey of Texas, the new Republican majority leader, and Republican presidential candidate Steve Forbes urged replacing the corporate and individual income taxes and the federal estate tax with a flat-rate tax on consumption, which they simply called a flat tax. Pat Buchanan looked to revenues from new tariffs to reduce or replace the income tax. In early 1996, a Republican commission appointed by Senate Majority Leader Bob Dole and Speaker of the House Newt Gingrich and headed by Jack Kemp, former tax-cutting congressman, advanced a vague proposal to replace the income tax with a single-rate consumption tax. Bob Dole, as the Republican presidential nominee, also urged a major tax restructuring to give us a "fairer, flatter, and simpler" system. Radical revision of the nation's tax system had become an issue in the 1996 campaign for president and congressional consideration of proposals to replace the income tax with some form of consumption tax inevitable.

The 1996 election results may slow this movement a bit, but will not bring it to a halt. Now that these politicians, among others, have given voice to public discontent with the existing income tax and have offered serious policy alternatives, sustaining the status quo has become politically unattractive. This genie will not return easily to its bottle.

The Many Faces of Consumption Taxes

As Chapter 1 describes, for this nation's first century, taxes on consumption in the form of excise taxes on specific commodities and tariffs on imported goods were virtually the only taxes imposed by the federal government. As the recent batch of legislative proposals vividly shows, there are many modern ways to tax consumption. The key common features of consumption taxes, regardless of how they are structured, are that the tax base is equal to retail sales, and that the tax generally does not impose a burden on savings or investments. If a person spends less than her current income, the difference is savings, which is exempt from consumption taxation. If a person spends more than her current income, she either draws down prior savings or borrows to finance the spending; either way, a consumption tax should be imposed on such spending.

Young people and the elderly often spend more than their current incomes while people in middle age tend to save part of their current incomes for retirement, their children's education, or the down payment on a house. Thus, in comparison with a tax on income, a consumption tax imposes relatively greater burdens on the young and the old. An income tax typically imposes its greatest burdens in the higher-earning years of middle age. For very wealthy people, however, age may make little difference; their income will almost always be greater than their consumption in any particular year.

Under an income tax, the pre-tax return on savings is reduced by the tax rate, except for specially favored or exempt savings, like amounts in an IRA. In other words, an income tax of 20 percent generally reduces a 10 percent pre-tax return on savings to 8 percent after tax. In contrast, the distinguishing characteristic of a consumption tax is that the pre-tax and after-tax rates of return on savings are generally identical; savers typically get the full 10 percent pre-tax return. This result can be achieved with consumption tax alternatives either by allowing a deduction or exclusion of savings from the tax base or by exempting investment income from tax.

The most common types of consumption taxes are retail sales taxes and "credit-method" value-added taxes. Retail sales taxes are commonly imposed by state and local governments in the United States. As most Americans know all too well, retail sales taxes on goods and services are collected from consumers by retail businesses who pay the tax to the government. Often retail sales taxes exempt such things as food or clothing, requiring the checkout cashier to decide whether a chocolate Easter bunny is food or a toy and whether a Halloween costume qualifies as exempt clothing. The *Wall Street Journal* reported that, because cities and counties also commonly impose sales taxes, in 1990 there were approximately 50,000 separate sales tax jurisdictions in the United States. It is common for large multi-state corporations to file more than 200 different state and local sales tax forms monthly.

The most common form of consumption taxes elsewhere in the world is a tax on value added (sales minus purchases). Value-added taxes (VATs) are now imposed by twenty of the other twenty-two OECD countries at rates that range from a low of 6.1 percent in Switzerland to a high of 20 percent in Sweden and Denmark. The difference between the value of a business's sales and its purchases is its value added. The cumulative value added by manufacturers, wholesalers, and other intermediaries through the retail sale of a good or service necessarily equals the total value of the retail sale so that a retail sales tax and a VAT at the same rate are economically equivalent unless they have different exemptions. A retail sales tax taxes only on the occasion of sales to consumers directly, while a VAT taxes in stages based on the excess of a business's sales over its purchases, thereby collecting a portion of the tax at each level of production.

Most other nations' value-added taxes are "credit-invoice" VATs, which determine the tax by applying the tax rate to the sales price of the good or service provided by a business and allowing the business an offsetting tax credit for value-added taxes included in the prices they pay to other businesses for their purchases of goods or services. Like retail sales taxes, this kind of VAT is often separately stated as a part of the good's or service's purchase price. The ultimate consumers—non–business purchasers—do not get any credits with respect to their purchases. Typically, nations that impose value-added taxes exempt exports and tax imports so that the tax is imposed by the country where the goods and services are actually consumed.

Both value-added and retail sales taxes are usually imposed on less than a full consumption base. In addition to common exemptions for food, clothing, and housing, which are intended to relieve the regressive impact of such consumption taxes on lower-income families, many services are often excluded from the tax base. Common examples include medical and hospital care, services provided by state and local governments, public transportation, financial services provided by banks and savings institutions, foreign travel, and often legal and accounting services.

The widespread experience of European and other nations with these taxes makes it clear that a credit-method VAT would be workable in the United States. The IRS estimated in 1984, the last time it seriously considered a VAT, that such a tax would apply to about 20 million businesses. The IRS claimed it would take eighteen months after enactment to put a VAT into effect because of the new administrative techniques required to collect such a tax. If such a delay actually occurred, almost an entire congressional term would pass before any revenues from the new tax would be collected. This would cause a long wait for the politicians, who would take the political heat from adopting this new federal tax. The pain of this new tax could not instantly be alleviated by new government spending. This is an unappealing prospect for any politician, which increases the likelihood that any new value-added tax could be enacted only if its revenues are used to replace existing taxes even more despised by the populace.

Curiously, few of the current consumption tax proposals follow either the common value-added or retail sales tax forms. However, before considering the more exotic variations of consumption taxes, which is the next chapter's task, I shall address briefly the key claims of consumption tax proponents: first, that a consumption tax would be more fair than an income tax; second, that it would be simpler; and third, that it would stimulate greater savings and therefore increase the nation's economic output.

Is a Consumption Tax Fair?

Consumption taxes are used in the states and throughout the industrial world as a part of tax systems that typically also contain progressive-rate income taxes. Clearly consumption taxes have a role to play as a part of a modern tax system. Consumption taxes, for example, impose a tax burden on purchases by people with illegal sources of income who evade income taxes and on retirees, who may have only nontaxable sources of income. Indeed, comparison of this nation's tax system and those of our trading partners reveals that the greatest disparity is their greater reliance on taxes on consumption.

Of the twenty-five member countries of the Organization for Economic Cooperation and Development (OECD), only the United States and Australia have no VAT, although Australia does have a wholesale sales tax.[5] In the United States, consumption taxes account for only about 17 percent of total federal, state, and local revenues—compared to an average of 30 percent for OECD member countries—and the U.S. federal government's share of that is quite small.[6] Less than 5 percent of federal revenues come from excise taxes on specific kinds of consumption, and the federal government has no broad-based tax on consumption. As a percentage of gross domestic product, consumption taxes range between 5 and 8 percent in Canada and European countries; in the United States, they amount to less than 2.5 percent of GDP. Only Japan is substantially lower, collecting less than 1.5 percent of its GDP in such taxes.

The current proposals in the United States, however, unlike the practice elsewhere, would completely replace both the corporate and individual income taxes, and sometimes the estate tax as well, with some form of consumption tax. This would elevate consumption taxes to a unique function. No modern industrialized nation relies on consumption taxes to the exclusion of income taxes as a way of raising revenues. When confronted with this fact, Bill Archer, the Ways and Means Committee chairman, responded,

"Bermuda does." But our society and economy are a long way from that small island nation, which relies almost exclusively on tourism to keep its economy afloat. What's fair taxation in Bermuda may not be fair for the United States. In our case, the question becomes whether taxing only amounts consumed and not amounts saved would be regarded as fair by the American people.

In response to this question, proponents of replacing the income tax with a consumption tax often invoke the venerable philosophers Thomas Hobbes and John Stuart Mill (and sometimes the sociologist and economist Thorstein Veblen), who urged that people should be taxed on what they "use." As Mill put it, people should be taxed on what they remove from the "common societal pool" for their own consumption. This philosophical political stance leads, of course, inexorably to the conclusion that it is the use of resources (consumption) and not their possession (wealth or savings) that should be taxed. This tautological claim reminds me of the Mother Goose rhyme "Little Bo Peep," which after it informs us that the poor dear has "lost her sheep" insists also in telling us that "she doesn't know where to find them."

This position treats as a "common good" a family's power to consume out of private wealth holdings and ignores the ability to pay taxes that unspent wealth represents. It is difficult, however, for people who have no wealth to regard other people's private wealth holdings as being in a "common pool." They sure don't have any access to this particular pool.

For people without wealth, the common good, if there is any, must obtain from the benefit that their family will realize as a result of the increased savings of the wealth holders. The "common" benefit from this "common pool" of savings, therefore, must lie in an assumption that increased wages will occur because of the additional private savings of others. This philosophical argument thus collapses into a claim about the economic growth that its proponents expect from taxing consumption instead of income. Some people believe such growth will occur and will increase everyone's income; others deride it as "trickle-down" economics.

A second claim by consumption tax advocates is that consumption taxes are fairer than income taxes because consumption is a better measure than income of people's ability to pay taxes over their lifetimes. Over a lifetime, an individual's total consumption will equal what that person has earned, plus any gifts and bequests that they have received, plus earnings on their savings, minus any gifts or bequests they make. Classifying people and measuring tax burdens with respect to their annual income has some obvious distorting characteristics, such as classifying students and elderly people as poorer than they may be, and also makes early consumers seem poorer than early earners. Consumption tax proponents complain that taxing income overemphasizes annual variations in savings.

Economists' view of savings as a temporary postponement of consumption has led many to argue in favor of using consumption or lifetime income as an index of people's relative well-being.[7] A lifetime view has also been defended as a better approach in advancing equality of opportunity over equality of income. However, high lifetime income may not reflect a high current ability to pay taxes since capital markets often do not permit people to borrow against their future earnings. Short-term precautionary savings, which is an important component of total savings, typically serves to smooth people's consumption over several years, rather than over a lifetime.

One philosopher, Norman Daniels, argues that a lifetime perspective in public policy is fair because *"consistent* differential treatment by age will equalize over time."* He argues that the young and the old may be treated differently at any moment in time but *over time* people will be treated both ways.[8] The validity of this claim, however, depends on consistent treatment of various age groups over a long period of time, something that no Congress can assure and that prior congressional behavior has proved false.

Our system of government, with new elections of the House of Representatives and one-third of the Senate every two years and of presidents every four years, does not give one Congress the power to prevent different legislation by a subsequent Congress. It is impossible, therefore, for any legislative body to make a viable binding political commitment to fair taxation over any person's lifetime. Indeed, as we have seen, each new Congress is tempted to change the tax law, and all at least threaten substantial change. The fact that no current Congress can effectively constrain policies of future Congresses encourages self-interested people lobbying legislators to try always to maximize their *present* interests. This alone might well make it of special concern to legislators and their constituents to know who wins and who loses in terms of their present status.

In addition, a generation that experiences its peak income-producing years during wartime, when higher taxes are required to pay for the nation's defense, may appropriately pay more in lifetime taxes than a generation whose peak earnings occur during peacetime, when taxes historically have been lower. An income tax, not a consumption tax, tends to produce this result, and this may help explain Congress's choice during the Second World War to extend the income tax to the masses, rather than accept the Roosevelt administration's recommendation to enact a progressive consumption tax.

Ultimately, a lifetime view is not likely to hold much sway with legislators. As one economist on the staff of the Joint Committee on Taxation has put it, politicians do not regard an individual who is making $200,000 in a current year as having the same current ability to pay taxes as an elderly individual currently earning $35,000 even if their lifetime incomes are identical.[9]

Most opponents of consumption taxation emphasize that since lower-income people consume a greater portion of their income than higher-income people, consumption taxes are more advantageous to higher-income people than income taxes. A consumption tax ignores a person's ability to pay taxes that results from savings. There can be little debate that if the federal income tax were to be replaced with a flat-rate consumption tax, the tax burden on low- and middle-income individuals would increase relative to that of upper-income individuals.

There are several ways—such as by exemptions for food, clothing, and medical expenses, by new income or payroll tax credits, or by exceptions for a specified amount of wages—to reduce or even eliminate the regressivity of consumption taxes at the bottom end of the wealth or income distribution. But it is difficult without quite high top rates to achieve substantially progressive taxation at the upper levels of income or wealth by taxing only consumption and not taxing either income or wealth.

Herbert Stein, chairman of the Council of Economic Advisors for both Nixon and Ford, put well the ultimate test of the fairness of a consumption tax:

> The question is whether a person who has an income of, say, $200,000 and spends on consumption $40,000 should be taxed like a person who has an income of $40,000 and spends $40,000 on consumption or like a person who has an income of $200,000 and spends $200,000 on consumption.[10]

Would a Consumption Tax Be Simple?

One of the major advantages claimed on behalf of consumption taxes is that they would be much simpler than the current individual and corporate income taxes. The nature of this advantage, however, depends on the type of consumption tax that is levied. Retail sales or value-added taxes that are imposed at a single rate without significant exemptions are, of course, simpler to administer and comply with than multiple-rate taxes with important exemptions. South Carolina, for example, imposes a lower sales tax rate on purchases by persons over age eighty-five. Such exemptions increase compliance costs.

There are data that suggest that the costs of administration and compliance of retail sales taxes may be only about one-quarter to one-half as great as those for the income tax, but since such comparisons are between state sales taxes with rates in the range of 4 to 8 percent and the federal income tax with rates up to 40 percent, it does not seem wise to place too much stock in such estimates.[11] No one has any experience in trying to enforce a retail sales tax at a rate of 20 percent or more, which would be the range of rates necessary to replace both the individual and corporate income taxes. If enactment of a federal retail sales tax were to become the occasion, as it should, for coordinating and making uniform the various sales tax rules of the states, a combined federal-state rate as high as 30 to 35 percent might occur in some states. Such high tax rates would increase dramatically incentives for tax-avoidance maneuvers and outright evasion. Of the five countries that have ever imposed retail sales taxes at rates in excess of 10 percent, two shifted to value-added taxes to facilitate collection. One expert has concluded that 10 percent is the maximum feasible rate for a retail sales tax, and the countries of the former Soviet Union and Eastern Europe are all marching toward value-added taxes.[12]

The advantage of a value-added tax is that it is collected from all companies, rather than just retailers, thereby spreading the costs of compliance over more businesses. One reason for the widespread international use of the credit-method form of value-added tax is that multistage collection of the tax makes it harder to evade. In order to claim tax credits for purchases from other firms, an invoice showing that the selling firm paid tax on the sale is required, and this eases enforcement, at least for sales among businesses. The Congressional Budget Office, using heroically favorable assumptions, has estimated that the administrative and compliance costs of a credit-method VAT could be as low as one-tenth the size of those costs under the current corporate and individual income taxes.[13]

The main advantage of both retail sales taxes and value-added taxes is that the tasks of compliance and collection are on businesses rather than families. This means that most American families would never have to deal directly with the enforcement of the tax, even though they might pay the tax through higher prices. No tax returns—not even a postcard—would be required from individuals, except for self-employed individuals who would have to file business tax returns under a value-added tax. As the next chapter will show, however, the consumption tax proposals apparently enjoying the greatest support in the United States do not enjoy this advantage because they require collection from individuals of at least some portion of the consumption tax.

Would a Consumption Tax
Increase Savings?

Many proponents of taxing consumption rather than income claim that exempting savings from tax will stimulate additional savings and, in turn, enhance economic growth. Indeed, government policies designed to increase our national savings and business investment are particularly timely now. Over the past decade and a half U.S. rates of savings and investment have been low compared both to our own historical experience and to the savings rates of our international competitors. The 4 percent net rate of national savings in the United States is currently below the savings rates of virtually all OECD countries, and our average 3.6 percent net savings rate in the decade of the 1980s compares quite unfavorably with the 10.2 percent rate of West Germany and the 17.8 percent rate of Japan during that same decade, as well as to our own prior levels of 7–10 percent.[14]

Likewise, the U.S. investment rate has long been lower than that of other countries, although by borrowing more than $1 trillion from foreigners between 1982 and 1994 we have been able to invest more than we could finance from domestic saving. During the past three decades, for example, the Japanese net private investment rate has averaged two and a half times greater than that of the United States, while that of Germany has been two-thirds greater.[15] Moreover, a far greater proportion of this nation's private investment goes into housing relative to the corporate sector, when compared to our international competitors. Indeed, in recent years, the United States has had the lowest corporate investment per dollar of housing investment and the lowest ratio of corporate to non-corporate investment when compared to the United Kingdom, Australia, Germany, and Japan.[16]

But, as Chapter 12 has shown, predictions about the likely effects of tax changes often vary widely, and the economic evidence about the effect of a choice between consumption and income taxation on national rates of savings and investment remains controversial. Although, under a consumption tax, each dollar a person saves will allow her to consume more at a future point in time than would be true under an income tax, some people may decide to save less because, under a consumption tax, the elimination of a tax on savings would permit a small level of current savings to grow to a specific desired amount to be spent at some future time. To put the point more precisely, an income tax encourages "target savers," who want to have a certain amount accumulated at a certain time, say for their children's education, to save more, while a consumption tax encourages additional savings by people whose amount of savings increases with greater rates of return. Both kinds of people no doubt exist, but despite the application of great amounts of data and time, massive computer power, and considerable talent, economists simply do not agree on the likely amount of additional savings that would occur if the federal government were financed solely through consumption taxes rather than income taxes. Indeed, as I shall discuss in Chapter 15, there is considerable economic evidence that both the Social Security and Medicare systems have had a substantial adverse impact on aggregate domestic private savings in this country even though both are financed by flat-rate taxes on wages.[17]

Most economists, however, have concluded that a consumption tax will result in greater national savings than an income tax so long as such a shift does not increase federal deficits. For example, Alan Auerbach, University of California professor and former chief economist for Congress's Joint Committee on Taxation, has estimated that a deficit-neutral replacement of the corporate and individual income taxes by a retail sales or value-added tax would increase long-run national savings by about 2 percent and would increase per capita output anywhere from 1 percent to 8 percent. Auerbach also concludes, however, that much of this benefit would be lost if, in the shift to a consumption tax, rules were adopted to preserve in some fashion ongoing deductions for the cost of assets purchased under the income tax. Given past congressional responses to tax transitions, some protection for these deductions seems likely.[18] The range of estimates by other economists also varies substantially. For example, Michael Boskin, chairman of George Bush's Council of Economic Advisors, estimates that moving to a consumption tax from the current system would increase economic output in the long run by 5 percent to 10 percent per year but his estimates of the benefits are many times greater than those of Brookings economist William Gale and Congressional Budget Office economists William Randolph and Diane Lim Rogers.[19]

Shifting from the current income tax to a consumption tax would treat all savings alike and therefore remove incentives for savings in forms that now enjoy tax-favored treatment. The income tax now favors retirement savings through employer-sponsored pension plans, retirement annuities, life insurance, and owner-occupied housing. The economic consequences of removing the relative tax advantages of these long-term forms of saving have not been studied in detail, but raise serious social and economic issues.

The globalization of capital markets adds further uncertainty about the potential impact of additional savings on the nation's economic growth. Global mutual funds today allow even unsophisticated U.S. residents to invest their savings abroad rather than in the United States. Moreover, when an individual contributes to the capital of a U.S. multinational corporation, say by purchasing newly issued shares, these funds may be used to finance the company's investments abroad. On the other hand, reduction or elimination of U.S. taxes on capital income may serve to attract investments from foreigners.

The economic effects of the globalization of capital markets are not yet well understood, but at minimum, they have made it more difficult for this nation to increase domestic investments simply by increasing domestic savings, even if we could be confident that a shift in tax policy would have the desired effect on the nation's overall level of domestic savings.

Conclusion

A broad-based consumption tax would likely serve this nation well if it replaced a substantial part, but not all, of the existing income (or payroll) tax and if it were constructed in a manner that experience shows works well, namely as a retail sales tax or European-style value-added tax. Even these taxes are not problem-free, however. Compared to income taxes, consumption taxes favor capital-intensive over labor-intensive industries. One survey done by the Information Technology Association of America, for example, found that smaller but growing technology firms would be particularly disadvantaged by a shift to consumption taxes.[20] Several European nations have recently begun providing special incentives for labor-intensive industries because of fears and political forces that have suggested that their reliance on consumption taxation may have skewed the playing field too heavily in favor of capital-intensive businesses.

The nation's governors and mayors have long resisted the federal government entering into consumption taxation. They have two reasons for this. First, the states have long regarded sales taxes in any form as their exclusive domain. Second, governors and mayors are concerned that a federal move to a consumption tax would eliminate the current income tax advantage for state and local borrowing. When the press got wind that Richard Nixon was seriously contemplating a value-added tax proposal, governors and mayors told him and John Connally, his Treasury secretary, in no uncertain terms that they would regard such a proposal as an extremely unfriendly act and would vigorously oppose any federal VAT.[21] The uniform opposition of governors and mayors was an important—perhaps even decisive—factor in dissuading President Nixon from proposing a value-added tax as a partial substitute for Social Security and corporate income taxes in the early 1970s.

Of course, if state political leaders could be convinced that the federal government would abandon the income tax altogether and leave that source of revenue entirely to the states, perhaps a deal could be struck. A suspicious governor, however, might well accept nothing less than repeal of the Sixteenth Amendment as convincing evidence that Congress in fact had permanently ceded income taxation to the states, not a likely occurrence. Moreover, consumption tax advocates might well regard their victory as fleeting if state income tax increases were an early consequence of repeal of federal income taxes.

As an old English proverb put it: "Sickness comes in on horse-back, but goes out on foot."[22]

14

The Flat Tax, the "USA" Tax, and Other Uncommon Consumption Taxes

The American public has not yet embraced the idea of replacing the income tax with either a retail sales tax or a value-added tax, the common forms of taxes on consumption. Instead, the tax reform that, so far at least, seems best to have captured the public's imagination is a "flat tax," an uncommon form of consumption tax that the public may mistake for an income tax. Nevertheless, polls throughout 1995 and surprising support in early 1996 for the campaign of Steve Forbes, who made the "flat tax" the centerpiece of his effort to capture the presidency, have revealed something of a groundswell of popular support for replacing the existing income tax with a "flat tax." Support for the flat tax apparently cannot be judged by the level of support for any particular candidate; only 18 percent of the people who claimed to support a flat tax voted for Forbes in the Iowa primary.

It is hard to know, however, exactly what the public is trying to tell us.

This is not surprising. So far at least, the flat tax is an imaginary tax, thought up by two Stanford professors, Robert Hall and Alvin Robushka, in 1981 and embraced by a variety of politicians since, but so far not enacted by any government, state or federal, domestic or foreign. The public may not yet know what a flat tax is or how it would affect them, but people do seem to like the idea.

Clearly, the most appealing feature of the flat tax is the promise that the annual tax return will be diminished into a simple post-card that everyone might fill in easily and quickly. The IRS is supposed to shrink as well, some say disappear.

Combining such simplicity with low tax rates has almost irresistible appeal. And that is exactly what the flat tax is supposed to do. But will the public accept the trade-offs necessary to achieve such massive simplification and low rates of tax? The pure form of a flat tax would eliminate many tax deductions and exclusions now available under the income tax, including deductions for state and local taxes, for home mortgage interest, and for charitable deductions, as well as tax advantages for fringe benefits, such as employer-provided health insurance and retirement savings. That these beloved tax allowances would disappear under the flat tax may not be known by those who answer the pollsters' questions.

Support for the flat tax apparently also stems from the belief that this tax would treat everyone the same. This involves two hopes: first, that enactment of a flat tax would eliminate politicians' ability to use the tax system as an instrument of social and economic policy or as a vehicle to reward their campaign contributors or pet projects and, second, that avenues for tax avoidance will at last truly be closed. The extent that public support for a flat tax reflects a deep public commitment to a single flat rate of tax—to taxing Michael Jordan's millions at the same rate as John Jordan's thousands—is far from clear.

To be sure, much of the political momentum for the flat tax reflects public distaste for the current income tax monster. Let's slay the income tax dragon by making a radical change, the kind of radical change a flat tax seems to promise.

The ignominious collapse of President Clinton's 1994 health-reform proposals sounds a note of caution, however. No matter how much the citizenry despises and even fears the status quo, politicians are quite capable of constructing something they will like even less. Bill Clinton's health-reform ideas served him well in the 1992 presidential campaign, when he was able to paint with a broad brush, talking in great generalities about the need for fundamental change. Only when his broad principles for change took detailed shape did his reform program collapse. This translation into detailed statutory proposals is a step that flat-tax proponents have so far avoided.

The "USA" Tax

Another uncommon form of consumption tax has been advanced by Senators Pete Domenici and Sam Nunn. In addition to an 11 percent VAT on businesses, the senators propose taxing individuals at progressive rates on their total annual consumption—a so-called expenditure tax. Senators Nunn and Domenici have designed their progressive tax on consumption in an effort to avoid the substantial tax reduction for high-income families that would occur under the flat-rate consumption tax alternatives. Only India and Sri Lanka have ever adopted such an expenditure tax, and those taxes were repealed soon after they were enacted.

Under this personalized consumption tax, a family's annual expenditures on consumption would be computed by adding up all the receipts available for consumption and subtracting any amounts saved. Amounts received minus amounts saved equals consumption, to which progressive rates would then be applied. The only reason to collect a consumption tax from individuals rather than businesses is to allow personal exemptions or to impose progressive tax rates.

Senators Nunn and Domenici have modified the standard form of expenditure tax in an effort to make their proposal more appealing politically. They would exempt, for example, much consumption financed out of sales of people's existing assets and often would defer the tax on consumption from borrowed funds. These modifications require complex rules to track both borrowing-financed consumption and consumption from dispositions of preenactment assets.[1] In addition, even though their consumption tax exempts savings generally, the senators have nevertheless provided additional benefits for specific forms of savings, such as for bonds issued by state and local governments. Such an exemption retains the relative advantage that such assets enjoy under the current income tax. The senators call their tax an "Unlimited Savings Allowance" or "USA" tax. Maybe the "U" really stands for unusual.

Senators Nunn and Domenici also allow both businesses and individuals to offset their consumption tax liability with the Social Security payroll taxes they pay and have attempted to craft a consumption tax proposal that would not shift dramatically the total taxes paid by people at different levels of income, even though amounts saved would be exempt from tax. The tax rates of their proposal are higher than those of other consumption tax proposals because of both their Social Security tax credit and their effort to limit the distributional shift from their tax. Under the current income tax, a married couple with $25,000 of income is taxed at a rate of 15 percent, a 28 percent rate kicks in at about $40,000 of taxable income, and the top rate of nearly 40 percent is applicable only to income in excess of $250,000. In sharp contrast, under the Nunn-Domenici USA tax, a married couple with taxable consumption between $5,500 and $24,000 would pay tax at a rate of 27 percent and a top 40 percent rate would be applicable to all amounts over $24,000. With this rate schedule, the senators have not enjoyed a rush of co-sponsors.

Senators Nunn and Domenici introduced their "USA" tax in 1995 with 291 pages of statutory changes, thereby enabling tax experts to know precisely what the tax looks like and to tear it apart line by line. Steve Forbes and Congressman Dick Armey have provided no such target for their flat tax. Congressman Armey introduced only a five-page outline of a flat-tax statute. Steve Forbes preferred thirty-second commercials. This accords them great flexibility in responding to tough questions about how the tax would actually work. In taxes, the devil resides in the details.

Donning Dark Glasses and
a False Mustache

Neither the political proponents of the flat tax nor the parents of the "USA" tax have labeled their proposals consumption taxes. Instead, they have decided to disguise what they are doing and have constructed their proposals to look more like an income tax than a sales tax.

They also often insist on using an income tax label, referring to their proposals as consumed income taxes, savings-exempt income taxes, "USA" taxes, or simply flat taxes. As Professors Hall and Robushka of Stanford, the inventors of the Armey-Forbes flat tax, once confessed in a candid *New York Times* editorial, there are many "economically equivalent ways to impose consumption taxes." Despite their economic similarities, however, all methods are not *politically* equivalent. Politicians want to avoid a sales or value-added tax look as well as any separate statement to consumers of the amount of taxes included in the price of the goods and services they buy. Achieving close association with the income tax apparently is also desirable politically, notwithstanding the decline in the public's support for the income tax. Politicians must believe that both of these features—looking more like an income tax than a sales tax and invisibility to consumers—provide them political cover. They may think a good disguise and a clever label allows them to deny that any federal consumption tax is being suggested.

It is especially important politically not to let elderly consumers know that they are paying a new tax on their purchases of goods and services. The AARP wouldn't like that at all. The chairman of Congress's Joint Economic Committee, Senator Connie Mack of Florida, a state with a large politically active elderly population, recently voiced his opposition to a retail sales tax because of its burden on the elderly. At the same time, however, he said he supported a consumption tax in a different form—a so-called flat tax—which should indirectly impose economic burdens on purchases of goods and services by the elderly similar to those imposed directly by a retail sales tax at the same rate. The key difference is that the flat-tax form makes it much more difficult to know that it is consumption that is being taxed.

Both the flat tax and Senators Nunn and Domenici's business tax are variations on a form of value-added tax that resembles an income tax: a "subtraction-method value-added tax" or a "business transfer tax." This kind of VAT taxes the difference between the total receipts from a business's sales of goods or services and the total amount of the business's purchases of goods or services from other businesses. The difference between sales and purchases is the business's value added and the tax rate is applied to that amount. This subtraction-method VAT is used in New Hampshire and Michigan and seems to be enjoying great favor among consumption tax advocates.

At the same tax rate, a subtraction-method VAT and the common European-style credit-method VAT should produce identical results. Take, for example, a retailer who purchases a product from a manufacturer for $2,000 and sells it to consumers for $3,000. The "value added" by the retailer is $1,000. Under a 10 percent credit-method VAT, the retailer must pay tax of $100—$300 (10 percent of the sales price) less a $200 credit for the tax previously paid by the manufacturer. With a 10 percent subtraction-method value-added tax the retailer would subtract $2,000 of purchases from $3,000 of sales and pay 10 percent of the $1,000 difference, or $100—exactly the same amount. Unlike the more common credit-method VAT, a subtraction-method VAT has the political virtue of looking like a corporate income tax, and it does not show up as a separate charge to consumers.[2]

A subtraction-method VAT also has certain substantive advantages. It makes implementing exceptions, such as for food or clothing, and multiple tax rates more difficult. Economically, this is a major advantage. Over time, however, politicians will no doubt come to regard this virtue as a disadvantage and, despite the practical complexities, they will find a way to benefit their favorites.[3]

The flat-tax proposal of presidential candidate Steve Forbes and House Majority Leader Dick Armey essentially splits the collection of a single-rate subtraction-method value-added tax between businesses and individuals. Rather than denying businesses any deduction for wages, as is usual under a subtraction-method value-added tax, the flat tax allows businesses to deduct wages in addition to purchases from other businesses. This type of consumption tax is collected at each stage of production, as under a typical value-added tax, except for the tax on wages, which is paid by individual wage earners. In combination, the total of the business and individual tax bases equals total sales, putting aside any exemptions.

Rents, royalties, dividends, interest, and capital gains would not be taxed to individuals. None of the currently available income tax deductions or tax credits would be allowed to individuals under the Forbes-Armey flat-tax proposal, although other flat-tax variations would retain some deduction for home mortgage interest and certain charitable contributions. The refundable earned-income tax credit currently allowed to low-income workers under the income tax would be repealed. A tax rate of about 20–23 percent should apply to the individual-level wage tax, depending on the deductions allowed, if the tax is to be revenue neutral. Flat-tax proponents insist, however, that additional economic growth and future cuts in federal spending would soon allow the rate to be lowered to 17 percent without increasing federal deficits.

The principal advantage of this division of a value-added tax between businesses and individuals is that it permits the exemption of a certain amount of wages from tax and thereby eliminates for wage earners the regressivity of a standard flat-rate tax on consumption. The amount of the exemption or standard deduction will, of course, vary depending on both the flat-tax rate and the other exclusions, deductions, or tax credits allowed. Congressman Armey, for example, would allow a personal deduction of about $20,000 for a joint return and an additional deduction of $5,000 for each dependent and no other deductions. Thus, the individual-level tax would apply only to total wages in excess of $30,000 for a married couple with two children. These numbers are, of course, subject to change, but the goal is to exempt some substantial amount of wages from the tax base. This exemption eliminates the regressivity of a sales tax on the consumption of low-income wage earners, although many of these workers would have to give up substantial earned-income tax credits in exchange. Low-income people, such as retirees, whose income is from sources other than wages, would obtain no benefits from such an exemption, and if they learn that the tax is similar to a sales tax, they may press for some of the more usual sales or value-added tax exemptions for food and clothing. The flat tax would permit the imposition of progressive rates on wages, and some economists have suggested this variation, without explaining why wages but not investment income should be subjected to progressive tax rates.[4]

Under the flat tax, businesses, including corporations, partnerships, and self-employed individuals, would be taxed on gross business receipts from the sales of goods or services minus the costs of business purchases of goods or services, cash wages paid, and any contributions to retirement plans for employees.[5] Businesses would not be taxed on any financial receipts from interest, dividends, borrowings, or equity issues, nor would they be allowed any deduction for payments of interest, dividends, repayments of loans, or retirements of equity. Since an immediate deduction would be allowed when a business purchases goods or services, no depreciation or inventory accounting would be required. No deductions would be allowed for any business costs of providing fringe benefits to employees. Businesses, therefore, would get no deductions for the cost of health insurance, life insurance, or child care they provide their employees, to name only a few of the more important fringe benefits. The tax rate applicable to businesses would be identical to that for individuals, but no exemption would be provided for small businesses or for businesses with only a small amount of taxable net receipts.

To date, their income tax labels and disguise have deflected the public from realizing that the Forbes-Armey flat tax is a kind of value-added tax and that the "USA" tax is also a form of consumption tax. So far the critical details have remained buried with experts, notwithstanding the unambiguous admissions of the flat-tax inventors, Professors Hall and Robushka. They are clear: "We want to tax consumption."[6] But the income tax characterizations by politicians have been far more effective than either the analy-

ses of experts or the concessions of its creators. Polls say that public enthusiasm for a value-added or sales tax is far lower than for a
"flat tax." Go figure.

Politicians' claims that they are advancing an income tax, when
their proposal is in substance a consumption tax, confound efforts
to evaluate the flat tax. Should the political spin be taken seriously
and these proposals scrutinized as if they were income taxes? Or
should the political rhetoric be put aside in favor of substance, and
the flat tax compared to alternative methods of taxing consumption? One cannot ignore the income tax garb, when this seems certain to shape the public's perceptions both before and after
enactment, or ignore the consumption tax underneath, when this
will determine the tax's economic burdens and financial consequences.

Let us return to two central questions addressed in the prior
chapter about retail sales and value-added taxes: Would the flat tax
or USA tax be fair? Would they be simple?

Are These Consumption Taxes Fair?

Unlike the standard forms of sales or value-added tax, which are
collected entirely from businesses, both the Nunn-Domenici USA
tax and the flat tax impose individual-level taxes in an effort to
achieve greater fairness in the distribution of the tax burden. The
USA tax accomplishes this by applying a progressive-rate schedule
to an individual's total annual consumption in an attempt to
achieve an overall distribution of taxes similar to that under the individual income tax while, at the same time, shifting taxes away
from savers to consumers.

In contrast, the flat tax is not concerned about keeping the
overall distribution of taxes generally unchanged. It will operate
much like other flat-rate consumption taxes in shifting taxes from
high-income individuals to people with less income. By providing
an exemption for a specified amount of wages, however, the flat tax
would eliminate the adverse impact of more common forms of consumption taxes on low-wage workers, and would do so without dis-

torting people's choices of what to consume, as would special exemptions for items such as food and clothing. In my view, either of these taxes improves upon a European-style value-added tax or a retail sales tax in terms of their fairness although any ultimate judgment about their fairness should take into account the arguments discussed in the prior chapter for taxing consumption rather than income.

In addition to the choice between taxing consumption and taxing income, these two proposals also raise questions about the fairness of a single tax rate compared to a progressive-rate schedule. Although a progressive tax rate schedule has been a feature of the U.S. income tax for more than eighty years and a progressive-rate federal estate tax has been in place for seven decades, flat-rate taxes are quite common in this nation's tax system. As the prior chapter indicates, most state sales taxes are levied at a flat rate, although the tax rates differ from state to state, and many states exempt certain goods and services, such as food or clothing. Both the federal wage tax that funds Social Security and the wage tax that finances Medicare hospital insurance for the elderly are flat-rate taxes. The corporate income tax is basically a flat-rate tax. Until 1993, the alternative minimum income tax on individuals was a flat-rate tax, although it now has two rates, 26 and 28 percent; the second rate was undoubtedly added to satisfy someone's desire for an extra tax bite out of the pockets of upper-income individuals.

In some respects, the flat tax would unquestionably be fairer than the income tax. As both Vivien Kellems and Angela Boyter told the Congress, a flat-rate tax would eliminate the penalty on marriage. So long as the exemption level for married couples is twice that for single people, any flat-rate tax will treat married couples and single people the same.[7] A clean solution to the marriage penalty; no small accomplishment.

Multiple tax rates generally serve one of two purposes: they enable the legislature to favor certain types of investments or consumption, or they implement a political consensus that fairness requires progressive rates at least somewhere in the tax system. In Europe, value-added taxes have been imposed with multiple rates based on the kind of items purchased. Lower rates are imposed on such things as food, clothing, and medicine to eliminate some of the tax's regressivity and higher rates are placed on some luxuries in an effort to introduce some progressivity into the tax. Such multiple rates are also often used to favor or disfavor certain forms of consumption. This is why, for example, the European taxes on gasoline and alcohol are generally higher than the standard VAT rate.

In this country, the flat-rate taxes on wages used to finance Social Security and Medicare benefits were designed, and have been embraced by the American public, as programs of social insurance under which wage earners and their employers make contributions through a payroll tax equal to a fixed percentage of wages (or some portion thereof) and, in exchange, receive cash benefits and hospital insurance during retirement or upon the disability or death of a wage earner. Although the flat-rate Social Security payroll tax is regressive when viewed in isolation, the Social Security system is quite progressive when its benefits are taken into account. Thus, one cannot assess the fairness of these flat-rate wage taxes while ignoring the benefits they finance without getting an extremely distorted and misleading picture.

This is not true, of course, of all flat-rate taxes. For example, the retail sales taxes imposed by the states are used to finance the general expenditures of state government. Progressive-rate income taxes at the federal level have often been justified as necessary to offset the regressivity of these state sales taxes.

There is nothing new in imposing taxes at a flat rate. It happens all the time. But the existence of a flat rate alone does not tell you much. In order to evaluate such a tax, we have to know both the tax rate and what tax base is subject to the flat-tax rate. We also have to know how the flat-rate tax fits into the nation's system of taxes and expenditures. More than eighty years ago when this nation adopted the Sixteenth Amendment, achieving fairness in the distribution of the tax burden was the essential reason for taxing income and for taxing it at progressive rates. The truly radical feature of the Forbes-Armey and other flat-tax proposals is that they would completely eliminate the income tax as a source of federal revenues and replace it with a flat-rate tax on consumption. Will the American public view such a flat-rate consumption tax as fair?

Progressive income tax rates have long been defended as an essential element of taxation based on ability to pay. The argument is that an extra dollar means less the more of them you have; in other words, that an additional $1,000 is less valuable to a person earning $300,000 than to a person earning $30,000, so that it is fair to tax a greater percentage of the richer person's income. Even if true, this does not tell you that any particular progressive income tax schedule is fair. A top income tax rate as high as 91 percent, as we had in the 1950s and early 1960s, is not fair; it is way too high.

Progressive income tax rates have also been viewed as necessary to offset other more regressive taxes, such as payroll and excise taxes, state and local sales taxes, and some property taxes. This may be an important reason why the progressive income tax has done little to reduce the economic disparities in American society.[8]

But even if the case for progressive taxation is weaker than some supporters admit, critics of progressive taxation themselves argue from a highly questionable premise. They presume that a market economy rewards the strong and leaves behind only the lazy, the weak, or the undeserving. On this view, income and wealth are manifestations of merit, not of luck and good fortune.

But market distributions are not inherently fair.[9] Even when the market is functioning perfectly, both capital and labor income depend on the public's demand for the product or service being supplied. People in endeavors where demand proves strong will do well; people who work or risk their capital in places where demand is weak will do badly. Rewards to both are often outside an individual's control. The enormous public demand for Madonna to sing "Material Girl," for Vanna White to turn letters and clap, and for Michael Jordan to play basketball has made them all very wealthy people. If public tastes shifted and demand for their services decreased, their incomes would decline dramatically without any change in their abilities or work effort.

In addition, most income derives from the joint use of multiple resources provided by different people. It is usually impossible to know which person produces what share of the total output. Who gets what often depends on their relative bargaining power.

In fact, an important share of market returns to both capital and labor is due to government institutions. American democratic political institutions enable the private market to function. Laws and means to enforce them, police, and criminal and civil courts all affect the income that can be earned by private citizens. The economic condition of people in countries, such as those of Eastern Europe, with very different laws and government institutions proves that. Surely, some substantial portion of the nation's output, of income from both labor and capital, must be conceded to be a societal rather than an individual creation.

Finally, returns to capital and labor are dramatically affected by luck: being born, for example, into a family of wealth or education rather than a family of poverty or ignorance. Most of the wealth advantages of the very rich are attributable to inherited wealth and enormous one-shot gains. Both of these sources of great wealth often are morally arbitrary.

We must therefore question the typical starting point of people who attack the moral validity of progressive taxation, of those who implicitly or explicitly assume that the market rewards people who deserve it and denies rewards only to undeserving people. Even if the market economy functioned perfectly, the ethical justification for its distributions of income and wealth would be dubious.

When the market functions imperfectly, as it always does—when the economy is burdened by inflation or unemployment or both; where industry is organized to produce monopoly benefits, perhaps through legal barriers to entry; when political influence or patronage produces private advantages; where genuine equality of opportunity is absent—even modest ethical claims for the justice of a market distribution of income and wealth are weak. One need not believe that the rewards of personal dedication and integrity are nil, or that the lazy and inefficient do better than the industrious and efficient, to concede that little of what we own is truly attributable to individual merit alone. Perhaps this is why Gerald

Ford's Treasury secretary, William Simon—probably the most conservative Treasury secretary since Andrew Mellon—remarked, "There appears to be a widespread consensus that an element of progression is desirable in the tax structure."

The essence of the debate over progressive taxation is captured in this anecdote offered by Dan T. Smith, a former assistant secretary of the Treasury in charge of tax policy and a professor of finance at Harvard. Mr. Smith had visited a one-room Montana schoolhouse and asked three children what would be a fair tax on a family with an income of $5,000 if a family with an income of $2,000 paid a tax of $200:

> The first child said, "500 dollars," thereby showing a predisposition for proportional burdens and perhaps a desire to make use of a newly acquired familiarity with percentages. A second child immediately disagreed, with the comment that the payment should be more than 500 dollars because "each dollar isn't so important" to the family with the larger income. A third child agreed, but with the reservation that the additional tax over 500 dollars shouldn't be "too much more or they won't work so hard."[10]

Progressivity in taxation will not lead the United States inexorably to become—as some believe—a "provincialized backwoods, with a decaying obsolete technology, where all privacy and individuality will be abolished and a person might be beheaded for demonstrating a modicum of intellectual or entrepreneurial independence."[11] The case against progressive income taxes ultimately must turn on the adverse impact of such taxes on economic production and output, their adverse effect on economic growth.

Even a radical restructuring of the nation's tax system does not require us to abandon a commitment to fairness in the distribution of the tax burden. As the *New York Times* columnist William Safire, who called the flat-tax proposal "draconian," put it: "Most of us accept as 'fair' this principle: the poor should pay nothing, the middlers something, the rich the highest percentage."[12] Tax restructuring does not require a redistribution of taxes from upper-income families to those who are worse off.

The 1986 Tax Reform Act demonstrated that a desired level of progressivity can be achieved with very few different tax rates. Even a flat-rate tax contains within it at least two rates: zero and the flat rate. The tax-simplification potential of the flat tax depends far more on its definition of the tax base than on its single flat rate. The key question is whether the flat tax sacrifices too much fairness in its laudable effort to achieve much needed simplification.

Steve Forbes's opponents for the 1996 Republican presidential nomination have been almost as critical about the fairness of the flat tax as the Democrats, such as Democratic House Leader Richard Gephardt, who lambasted it as an unwarranted sop to the rich. Steve Merrill, governor of New Hampshire and chairman of Bob Dole's campaign committee, told the *David Brinkley Show* that any tax change like the flat tax that reduced taxes on the wealthy required the loss to be made up from somebody else. He claimed that either the deficit would rise or the ordinary people of New Hampshire were going to be hit with a tax increase. Pat Buchanan said the flat tax looked like something thought up by the boys at a yacht club. Lamar Alexander called it a "nutty" idea. Phil Gramm complained that it was not fair to tax individuals on their wages but not on their interest, dividends, and other investment income or capital gains. He put forth his own single-rate tax that would be imposed on individuals' receipts of these items as well as wages. Dick Armey wrote letters at least to Alexander and Gramm urging that they curb their "overheated rhetoric" on the flat tax.

Would These Consumption Taxes Be Simple?

As the prior chapter has shown, the common forms of consumption taxes—retail sales taxes and European-style value-added taxes—would greatly simplify the tax lives of many Americans by eliminating all tax returns and payments except from businesses. Neither the USA tax nor the flat tax goes this far. Both retain some individual-level tax in addition to the tax on businesses. The USA tax contains a progressive tax on individuals' consumption; the flat tax has a tax on individuals' wages.

It is not at all clear how the USA tax stacks up against the income tax in terms of complexity. As compared with the current income tax, the USA tax would, over the long term at least, eliminate the need to keep records of the costs of particular investment assets, which would be deducted when purchased, and would eliminate a variety of tax-planning gambits since all reinvestments of the proceeds from sales of assets would not be taxed. But, because of complex transition rules and rules that sometimes defer the tax on consumption out of borrowed funds, the USA tax requires much additional new recordkeeping. At least one prominent tax lawyer, Martin Ginsburg, regards its complexities and tax-planning opportunities as sufficiently troublesome to render the tax virtually unworkable.[13]

On the other hand, the claim that the flat tax would simplify the tax system for a large number of Americans is both straightforward and true. Enormous simplification would, of course, be achieved by taxing individuals on only their wages, instead of taxing all sources of income. Further simplification occurs by not allowing tax deductions or credits for items like state and local taxes, medical expenses, unusually large uninsured theft or casualty losses, child-care expenses, etc. Indeed, if Congress had the will, a great deal of simplification could be achieved simply by eliminating such adjustments under the current income tax.

The claim that most people could file their tax returns on a postcard under the flat tax is true. We now collect more than $400 billion a year by a 15 percent flat-rate Social Security tax on wages without requiring individuals to file any piece of paper, postcard or otherwise. Indeed, most people could file their current income taxes on a postcard if they have only wage income or wages, interest, and dividends and do not itemize their deductions or claim the earned-income tax credit.

When the Treasury Department in 1984 advanced the tax reform ideas that formed the basis for the Tax Reform Act of 1986, it suggested freeing a large number of people from any obligation to file a tax return. The IRS would just send them a bill or a check for their refund. Although the creaky computers at the IRS might screw it up, tax-return filing requirements could be eliminated for a very large number of people even under the current tax law. Bob Dole proposed eliminating tax-filing requirements for 40 million people, a realistic suggestion. Return-free tax collection could be made even more widely available if Congress would eliminate exclusions, deductions, and tax credits in exchange for lower tax rates.

Postcard tax returns for wage earners would be coupled under the flat tax with an exemption from tax of individuals' receipts of non-wage sources of income. People living off investment income, such as interest, dividends, rents, royalties, or capital gains, or Social Security would not have to file even a postcard.

Under the flat tax, as under more typical value-added or sales taxes, most of the complexity resides at the business level. As the previous chapter indicates, many businesses are quite small, and for them complying with consumption taxes is not a picnic. Indeed, Jane Six-Pack, the heroine of Chapter 5, would be required to file a business return under the flat tax. Let's see what her tax returns would look like under the flat tax.

The issues that caused the Six-Packs to pull out their hair under the current system may not get a whole lot easier under the flat tax: (1) Jane's work clothing, (2) Jane's home office expenses, (3) their child-care expenses, (4) Joe's use of the company truck to commute to and from work, (5) their income from renting a room in their house, (6) their home mortgage interest deduction, (7) their payroll tax obligations for babysitters and other household helpers, and (8) the dependency exemption for Joe's mother.

First, because the flat tax would allow a substantial deduction for dependents, the Six-Packs must determine whether Joe's mother qualifies. On the other hand, the flat tax would eliminate the credit for the Six-Packs' child-care expenditures. No child-care deductions would be allowed, and employers' child-care reimbursements would receive no tax advantages. This is simpler than current law, but harsher. Third, Jane and Joe's difficulties in knowing their tax responsibilities for their household helpers would remain unchanged under the flat tax. Such Social Security obligations would not be affected by this change.

Fourth, as Chapter 5 told, the current income tax allows Jane to deduct the costs of her work clothing. How would the flat tax treat Jane's work clothing? Probably the same. In filling out her business return as a self-employed physical therapist, Jane would face many questions similar to those she now must answer under the income tax, and there is no reason for the rules for deducting work clothing to be different. Likewise, Jane's home office expenditures raise flat-tax questions identical to those under the income tax, and they will prove no easier to answer. Many in Congress think the current rules are too harsh, but more lenient rules produced much litigation. The difficulties do not change one iota by moving to a flat tax.

Renting a room in one's home would probably be a separate business under the flat tax and also require the filing of a business tax return. Thus, in addition to Joe's postcard return for his wages and Jane's business return for her physical therapy work, the Six-Packs might have to file a business return for the rental income from their tenant. Perhaps the two businesses can be combined in one return, but that won't make the task any simpler. Again, issues similar to those under the income tax must be resolved. (Congress could, of course, simplify matters by exempting some amount of rental income from renting rooms of one's house under either the flat tax or the income tax, but so far it hasn't.)

Rather than taxing fringe benefits to employees, the flat tax denies employers deductions for fringe benefits. Joe's employer must learn whether Joe's personal use of the truck is a disallowed fringe benefit. Resolving this question may well draw heavily on the income tax precedents.

Finally, the complexities the Six-Packs faced in determining the amount of interest deduction allowable under the income tax will either disappear completely or remain unchanged, depending on whether Congress allows any deduction for home mortgage interest. As this review of the Six-Packs' tax situation under the flat tax illustrates, many questions that have plagued the income tax may continue to drive some taxpayers mad under the flat tax. There are at least 20 million families like the Six-Packs who will find themselves in flat-tax boats that look frighteningly like the income tax boats they thought had just sunk.

Sheltering personal consumption from tax through business deductions would continue to be one of America's favorite indoor sports under the flat tax. The income tax has long struggled with how to treat business meals, travel and entertainment, skyboxes, club dues, conventions, business meetings at resorts, and the like. The annual congregation of corporate jets at the Kentucky Derby and the Super Bowl is no accident. Taxpayers have long been creative in finding ways to mix personal pleasure with deductible business meetings. The current income tax rules are unduly complex, reflecting years of accumulated political compromises, but in this regard at least the tax collector's task may not become easier under a flat tax.

Much of the complexity under the current income tax for big businesses is due to depreciation and inventory accounting and to rules allowing tax credits for income taxes paid to foreign governments. All of these problems would disappear under the flat tax, which would produce major simplification for large businesses. But the flat-tax treatment of international income may create enormous opportunities for tax avoidance for large businesses in the absence of complicated anti-avoidance rules. Businesses would have huge incentives, for example, to move interest deductions offshore and interest income to the United States.

Fringe benefits would create new problems under the flat tax. First, since fringe benefits would not be taxable to individuals, but would not be deductible by employers, they would not be offset by the personal exemption. Many low- and middle-income employees will therefore prefer cash compensation to fringe benefits. More important, their exclusion under the income tax has induced many employers to provide such things as pensions and health insurance to their employees. Flat-tax advocates so far have told us nothing about what, if anything, will replace the current tax stimulus for employers to provide health insurance and retirement income for their employees.

There might well be opportunities for tax shelters under the flat tax. Since business purchases of assets would be deductible, a business might, for example, reduce or eliminate its tax liability by purchasing art for its walls or land for future development in years when it would otherwise owe taxes to the government. It could then sell the art or land in years where other deductions are sufficiently great that tax losses would otherwise occur. Senators Nunn and Domenici determined that special rules were necessary to stop such transactions under the USA tax.

The flat tax also contains incentives for businesses which would owe tax to merge with businesses that have excess deductions. The current income tax has a series of (excessively complex) rules to limit such acquisitions of tax losses. The flat tax may have none. How long can that last?

No tax returns would be required from trusts or their beneficiaries under the flat tax because no investment income would be taxed. That is a simplification.

None of the foregoing comments about the flat tax turn on whether it has one single rate or multiple rates. Contrary to popular belief, multiple tax rates are not now a source of very much complexity in the federal income tax, and flat-rate taxes are not necessarily simple in design or compliance.

One major simplification that would be achieved by a flat rate is eliminating the need to worry about the attribution of income, deductions, and losses among family members. But changes in the taxation of children and trusts in 1986 minimized this problem under the current income tax. Moreover, the large exemption— or zero bracket—under the flat tax may still enable people to save taxes by shifting income or deductions among family members.

A single flat-tax rate also in principle allows great flexibility in choosing whether to collect taxes from businesses or individuals. When business and individual rates are the same, collection from the business at the business rate can either serve as a withholding tax or as a final tax.

Even a single-rate tax, however, typically has multiple rates. Many entities will be tax exempt, thereby enjoying a zero rate. These include not only the various levels of government, but also a large variety of nonprofit organizations, including charities, such as the Red Cross, schools and universities, churches, arts and health organizations, and a host of private foundations. In addition, businesses that have no income in the current year will enjoy a zero marginal tax rate. Businesses that operate abroad also typically will face different and multiple foreign tax rates. These kinds of variations in tax rates are inevitable, even in a flat-rate system, and, as under the current income tax, they will create many opportunities for reducing taxes by shifting income and deductions among different entities.

Flat-tax rates also do not eliminate the advantages of postponing taxes. Thus, moving taxable receipts and deductions both among business entities and from year to year—the two most important tax-planning games under the current income tax—should remain an important area of tax planning under the flat tax. Tax lawyers and accountants need not fear for their livelihoods.

Much of the simplification that would be achieved under the flat tax could also be accomplished under the income tax if Congress were willing to make trade-offs in favor of simplification similar to those the flat-tax proposal makes. Perhaps such a serious political commitment to simplification is possible, if at all, only in the context of a radical restructuring of our tax system of the sort that the flat tax contemplates. But there is no inherent reason for flat-tax politics to be so dramatically different. Moving to the flat tax may elevate simplification to the dominant goal of tax reform. But, if the past is prologue, caution is warranted; simplification has not been the hallmark of tax lawmaking.

Will a Flat Tax Keep Government Small and Increase Americans' Freedom?

Congressman Armey's flat-tax proposal is the centerpiece of a bill entitled the "Freedom and Fairness Restoration Act." Congressman Armey and other flat-tax advocates not only are convinced that the flat tax would make the nation's tax system simpler and fairer, they also view the flat tax as the lynchpin in reducing "the power and reach of the Federal establishment." Steve Forbes, Dick Armey, and the *Wall Street Journal* have all claimed that Congress will not raise tax rates under a flat tax because "everybody would have the same rate and you cannot raise it without everybody knowing and complaining." This faith that enacting a flat-rate consumption tax will hamstring the voracious appetite of the Congress for revenues seems naive. In 1990 Democrats proposed a "millionaires' surtax"—a higher tax rate on income over $1 million. This prompted Phil Gramm to say "millionaires today, thousandaires tomorrow," and in 1993 Democrats in Congress did enact a special surtax for incomes over $250,000. The claim that moving to a flat-rate tax will guarantee the people of this nation lasting freedom from high tax rates, from narrowly targeted taxes, from special tax advantages, or from unfair tax differentials is a pipe dream. It denies all historical experience.

Indeed, the most dramatic source of tax growth in the United States over the past forty years has been in the Social Security payroll tax—a flat-rate tax on wages. The Social Security tax rate was originally set at 1 percent of wages, and was expected to grow to 5 percent. Today, the tax rate exceeds 15 percent and an additional tax of nearly 3 percent of wages is imposed to pay for hospital insurance under Medicare. Social Security's share of federal revenues has grown from 10 percent of total budget receipts in 1954 to nearly 40 percent in 1994. At the state level, tax revenues supplied by flat-rate retail sales taxes have been the most important source of state revenues for half a century, and they have also grown at a brisk pace. These two examples alone should give pause to those who claim that a flat tax will necessarily constrain the growth of government.

There simply is no reason to believe that by enacting the flat tax Congress will forswear its long-standing practice of legislating selected tax increases directed at particular kinds of expenditures, specific forms of income, or specific classes of people. One need not consult a psychic hotline to envision a future congressional session enacting a special "surtax" of 20 percent or so on the interest, dividends, wages, rents, royalties, and capital gains of taxpayers whose total income exceeds $100,000 or $200,000. Such visions, realistic visions, could go on and on. Nothing short of a constitutional amendment that would bar such a tax can guarantee that future Congresses will behave as Steve Forbes and Richard Armey want them to.

How Do You Get There from Here?

It would be a straightforward exercise to replace the progressive income tax rates with a flat rate and larger exemptions. That alone would achieve some advantages of the flat tax, such as elimination of the marriage penalty, but the rate structure change is only a small part of the move to the flat tax. The two key changes wrought by the flat tax, as we have seen, are taxing consumption rather than income and eliminating a host of tax deductions, exclusions, and credits. Much of the concern about the flat tax relates to the elimination of the special tax provisions of the current income tax. Homeowners, for example, are worried about the effects on the value of their homes from elimination of the deductions for home mortgage interest and property taxes; charities wonder how a tax system with no deduction for charitable gifts will affect their funding; state and local governments are concerned about losing the current tax advantage for state and local borrowing and the federal tax deduction for state and local income and property taxes.

The question whether special tax advantages of this sort should be retained or eliminated is not unique to the flat tax or other consumption tax alternatives. This issue would be central to any proposal for radical restructuring of the current income tax, even if the reform were to continue to tax income rather than replace the income tax with a consumption tax. Politicians in this country have long viewed the tax law as something of a playground, a way to change people's behavior, to redirect the nation's resources, to reward friends and punish enemies. Far too often, they treat the tax law as chicken soup—a generic cure-all for every economic and social ill the nation happens to be facing.

Since 1974, the federal government's budget has explicitly recognized the existence of so-called tax expenditures—provisions of the income tax law that are considered alternatives to government spending. Tax expenditures for federal budgetary purposes are defined as revenue losses due to departures from the "normal structure" of the individual and corporate income taxes[14]—a highly controversial and contested notion since we have never had an income tax with a "normal structure." But the "tax expenditure" list is the federal government's effort to classify and measure the spending equivalents of many special tax breaks, and it includes estimates of the costs of numerous tax exclusions, deductions, deferrals, or credits intended to encourage particular economic activities or to benefit particular categories of taxpayers.

In 1993, the federal "tax expenditure budget" identified 120 separate tax expenditures and estimated that their total revenue cost was just over $400 billion.[15] Many of these provisions date from the inception of the income tax. As much as 95 percent of their total estimated revenue costs is due to provisions enacted at least twenty-five years ago. To take only a few examples: Congress has long provided income tax advantages for buying state and local government bonds rather than corporate or federal government bonds, for homeownership, for charitable giving, for drilling for oil and gas, for exploring for and developing minerals, and for harvesting timber. Income tax provisions encourage employers to pay and employees to accept a wide variety of fringe benefits in lieu of cash, including such things as life and health insurance coverage, compensation deferred until retirement, subsidized meals on the employer's premises, mass transit passes, and parking places.

Many of these tax expenditures serve useful social functions, and they probably could not be replaced by direct expenditures in the current political and fiscal climate, even if one could design a better-targeted, fairer, and less costly direct-spending alternative. As congressional failures to respond to the tax shelter phenomenon clearly demonstrate, it is extremely difficult for Congress to muster the necessary votes to eliminate even those tax-expenditure provisions that have outlived their usefulness. The beneficiaries of these provisions have come to regard them as vested rights and strongly, and often effectively, oppose efforts at restriction or repeal.

Moreover, modern-day "conservatives," who want to get government off our backs and make it smaller, draw a great (and frequently false) distinction between the government subsidizing an activity such as oil drilling by writing checks to oil companies and giving the same companies a tax write-off for identical behavior. Tax reductions for drilling for oil presumably reduce the size of government, while direct subsidies or government loans would make it larger. Tax breaks keep all the money in private hands, even though the government is calling the shots. This way of directing resources is appealing to politicians who claim to want to keep government small.

When the tax system is used to direct private spending, long-term social and economic consequences follow. Consider these two important examples: Income tax preferences for owner-occupied housing have directed much of this nation's productive investment capital into housing. As a result, the share of our investment in housing is disproportionately high relative to other nations with which we compete in the global economy. Of course, the key provisions for preferring owner-occupied housing entered the income tax at the beginning, early in the twentieth century.

Similarly, this nation's health-care-financing system is predominantly employment based because employer-provided health insurance is exempt from both income and Social Security taxes. Because of these tax advantages, which date from the 1940s, employers today find that about 65 cents of additional health coverage is worth a dollar of cash wages for most of their employees. The flat tax would eliminate the current income tax advantage for all fringe benefits and, in doing so, would equate the tax treatment of employer-provided health insurance and cash wages. Such a change might well be wise as a matter of both health policy and tax policy. The existing system of employer-provided health insurance is a historical accident—one that probably no one would choose now if we were beginning fresh. During World War II, employers and unions circumvented federal wage ceilings by offering medical fringe benefits. The popularity and generosity of employer-provided health insurance boomed after the war, because Congress sheltered them without limit from income and Social Security taxes. Given a clean slate, no one would choose to build such an employer-based system of health insurance. But we are not starting from scratch. Today employer-provided health insurance is by far the largest source of private health insurance in this country; more than 150 million Americans get their health insurance that way. Congress cannot simply terminate the existing tax advantage for such health insurance and put nothing else in its place without risking a disastrous rise in the number of uninsured Americans. The notion that this kind of change can be made simply as a natural consequence of replacing the income tax with a consumption tax or something called a flat tax is not simply naive; it courts political and social disaster.

Homeowners are worried that potential buyers will pay less for houses if they will not be able to deduct interest on their home mortgages or their local property taxes. One estimate—no doubt the highest since it was performed for the real estate industry—suggests a decline in the value of owner-occupied homes by $1.5 trillion, due to the elimination of deductions for home mortgage interest and property taxes. Another independent analysis suggests an average decline in housing values of 40 percent and significant defaults on mortgages.[16] Proponents of the flat tax claim that a decline in interest rates and in tax burdens overall will compensate homeowners for any loss in the value of their houses. But who can be sure? A truly sharp decline in housing prices might stimulate foreclosures and might even shock the savings and loan industry and secondary mortgage markets. The federal government's risks in mortgages backed by the Veterans Administration or FHA could also increase. Only by making such a change gradually over time by phasing out these deductions rather than repealing them instantaneously can policymakers be confident that any negative effects on housing values will be moderate. The USA tax and some versions of the flat tax would simply retain the deduction for home mortgage interest, but this, of course, necessitates higher tax rates to raise the same revenue. It also encourages borrowing when one key purpose of the proposed change is to encourage savings.

The repeal of deductions for state and local property and income taxes by the flat tax, along with the fact that bonds issued by those governments would no longer enjoy tax advantages, raise serious questions about the flat-tax effects on the finances of state and local governments. States that now "piggyback" on the federal income tax will either have to accept the flat tax themselves or enact a new income tax statute when the federal income tax is thrown overboard. At a Senate Finance Committee hearing, Congressman Armey's Republican colleague Senator Alphonse D'Amato of New York expressed great concern about the potential impact on state finances. Mr. Armey clearly wants the high-tax state of New York to become more like his own low-tax state of Texas. But he gave Senator D'Amato no clue where in New York to look for oil.

The flat tax would treat charitable contributions identically to taxable personal consumption. The USA tax would allow a deduction for charitable gifts, but this would provide no advantage to such gifts over personal savings, which also would be deductible. What will such changes do to fundraising by charities? Will the federal government provide charities with another form of financial help?

The flat tax would also eliminate tax incentives for employers to offer their employees pensions. I don't know about you, but I can say with absolute certainty that if my pension savings, which are my only real savings, had been available to me without any tax penalty during my twenties and thirties, I would have driven faster cars, taken more expensive vacations, drunk better beers and scotch, and perhaps even worn fancy clothes. Today, I would have far less in my retirement savings than I do. Small amounts of savings compound to substantial sums when left to grow for thirty or forty years. Much psychological and economic evidence suggests that, without special tax incentives for retirement savings and corresponding tax penalties for pre-retirement withdrawals, many people in their twenties, thirties, and even forties would put much less money into this form of long-term savings.

One of the flat-tax creators, Alvin Robushka, stated that a flat tax would eliminate many pension plans.[17] The American Academy of Actuaries reported that replacement of the income tax with any form of consumption tax could have a major adverse impact on the private pension system, which now contains more than $2.3 trillion in savings for workers' retirements. Robert E. Heitzman, Jr., the author of the report, stated that "one unintended casualty could be the nation's private pension system." He continued, "If all forms of savings were given tax-favored treatment, employer-sponsored pensions could be jeopardized. Losing this major source of private savings would ultimately work counter to the goal of increasing the nation's savings rate."[18]

Shifting to a less universal example of the potential dislocations from these kinds of major tax reforms, consider the effect on divorce settlements. Divorcés who are paying alimony are allowed to deduct these amounts under the current income tax and such payments are taxed to the recipient. Child support is not now deductible by the payer or taxed to the recipient. Under the flat tax neither alimony nor child support would be deductible or taxed to the recipient. Under the Nunn-Domenici USA tax, both alimony and child support would be deductible by the payer and taxable to the recipient. What will people who entered into divorce agreements under current rules do? Will they have to renegotiate their divorce settlements? No one will like that!

The Nunn-Domenici USA tax attempts to provide relief to people who paid income taxes on their salaries, purchased investment assets with after-tax dollars, and now want to spend their savings, on the ground that it would be unfair to impose a second tax on their consumption financed from these after-tax receipts. Transitional relief for such transactions, however, would require complicated rules and higher tax rates and also may change significantly the distribution of the consumption taxes by exempting from tax the consumption of people who have such assets. Nevertheless, claims for "transitional relief" will be widespread, and, as the 1986 tax reform vividly demonstrated, when Congress chooses who will get such relief, it is often not a pretty sight. Access, political affiliations, and political contributions have often been more important than the merits of the claim. Congress has often been willing to pay important constituents a few million, sometimes even a few hundred million, to buy off their opposition to major changes in policy.

In this chapter I have attempted to assess realistically the flat tax's strengths and weaknesses. First, its proponents clearly overstate its advantages. Congressman Armey plays Pollyanna when he claims that the underground economy will virtually disappear with a flat tax.[19] Nor is the IRS going to wither away. Tax lawyers and accountants will continue to have plenty to do. The flat tax, for example, provides incentives for tax planners in some instances to transform interest which would not be deductible into items that are deductible, such as rents, royalties, or increased prices for purchases. Tax lawyers are experts at converting loans into leases, interest into rent. Multinational corporations would have incentives to locate interest deductions abroad and interest income in the United States where it would not be taxed. And the 20 million owners of small businesses will be sorely disappointed when they learn that the flat tax, at best, will lower their costs of tax compliance by only a small fraction of what its advocates claim.

Second, the transition to a flat tax will be neither as smooth nor as abrupt as Congressman Armey's five-page flat-tax statute implies. It is a safe bet that when Congress enacts a flat tax the five pages will have multiplied a hundredfold.

Third, and perhaps most important, the shift in the distribution of the tax burden under the flat tax is worrisome. It is far from clear that trading a progressive-rate income tax for a flat-rate consumption tax will improve the lives of hardworking folks who go to work every day and try to do the right thing. Many small businesses with incomes below $100,000 almost certainly will face a tax increase. As many conservative Republicans have already recognized, the elimination of all taxes on capital gains, interest, dividends, and other investment income of individuals is not likely to sit well with the American people.

Fourth, one has to ask whether a belief in American exceptionalism requires the United States to adopt a form of consumption taxes untried elsewhere in the world instead of moving toward a standard form of value-added tax or retail sales tax. In part, of course, people's answer to that question will turn on their views of the extent to which personalizing the consumption tax, as both the flat tax and the USA tax do, satisfies their concerns about the fairness of a retail sales or value-added tax.

There are collateral consequences of choosing a unique form of consumption tax that require analysis and discussion. For example, one major difference between the flat tax and the consumption taxes prevalent throughout the world is the flat-tax treatment of imports and exports. Typically, sales or value-added taxes impose tax only on consumption that occurs within the country. Goods produced in the country but exported for consumption elsewhere are not taxed, while imports are subject to the value-added or sales tax.

In contrast, under the flat tax, this system is not available; instead imports would not be taxed but exports would. Thus, for example, if Ford sells cars manufactured in the United States to be used in the United States, their full retail sales value would be included in the flat-tax base. Likewise, if Ford or any other U.S. automobile manufacturer sells automobiles made in the United States to a foreign dealer for use abroad, the manufacturer's sales price would be subject to the U.S. flat tax. But a U.S. dealer of cars made in Japan, Germany, or another foreign country would be taxed only on the excess of the dealer's total receipts from its sales over the costs of the cars from the foreign manufacturer. As a result, the costs of manufacturing cars abroad would not be included in the U.S. flat-tax base; only the foreign car dealer's markup would be subject to U.S. taxation.

Economists, including the inventors of the flat tax, claim that we should be indifferent to this distinction because currency exchange rates—the value of the dollar relative to other currencies—will adjust to compensate for these tax differences. But U.S. automobile manufacturers and other U.S. companies that compete with products from abroad will not readily accept the economists' assurances that exchange rates will adjust so perfectly. Domestic businesses undoubtedly will resist rules that impose a U.S. tax on the full retail price of products manufactured in the United States but tax only the dealer markup of products manufactured abroad. They will view such a tax as fundamentally unfair to American businesses and perhaps as seriously disadvantaging U.S. manufacturers competitively. This will be an important, perhaps even decisive, issue. U.S. businesses vehemently opposed President Clinton's 1993 proposed energy tax because of its potential disadvantages to domestic versus foreign products.

But, despite all the questions raised here, the proponents of the flat tax are on to something very important. They have tapped into a wellspring of public dissatisfaction with the current income tax and into people's longing for radical surgery, surgery not only on the income tax we now hate, but also surgery on the political process that keeps making it worse, making it more complicated and less fair, congressional session after session. The American public seems to regard the 1986 tax reform as a promise failed and is desperately seeking a tax system that can't be put asunder by the special interests, a tax that cannot be avoided by hiring expensive tax advisers. This accounts for the public appeal of the flat tax's promise to treat everyone the same.

Flat-tax advocates are right that a broad tax base with low rates causes fewer and less significant economic distortions than a high-rate tax with numerous exclusions, deductions, and credits. Reducing or even eliminating many tax deductions, credits, and exclusions—the expansion of the tax base which lies at the heart of the flat tax—points the right direction. Broadening the tax base would permit Congress to raise the same revenues with lower tax rates, and with lower tax rates simple rules are more easily justified and defended. Distinctions among people that are important at higher rates are far less significant at low rates, regardless of which tax base—income, wages, or consumption—we are talking about. As we have seen, many of the priorities for broadening the tax base are the same under a flat-rate consumption tax as under the income tax.

The essential point is this: If Congress has the political will to make such major changes in the tax base and to maintain them over time, much simplification can be achieved and tax rates can be lowered substantially. Whether the tax is imposed at one flat rate or a few different rates is of relatively little consequence in terms of the costs of compliance or economic efficiency, although it may be important in determining how the tax is distributed among the populace.

The essential political vision of flat-tax advocates is important. Our creaky old income tax has built up lots of barnacles over a long period of time. Tax incentives and benefits enacted decades ago have acquired a life of their own. Prying them off the current Internal Revenue Code is no easy task. In principle, Congress could commit itself to serious simplification of the income tax without the kind of massive change in the tax system that the flat tax implies, but it may well be that no such simplification is politically possible absent a massive shift in the nation's tax structure.

The fear, of course, is that a massive reform of the sort the flat tax implies will introduce as many new problems as it eliminates. Some of the problems from change, which I discussed here, highlight the fundamental wisdom of the trite adage "An old tax is a good tax." That the flat tax has never been tried anywhere in the world makes such a move even more frightening. Our experiences with tax legislation make us properly fearful that the promise of simplification will be lost through a series of political compromises. To be sure, the income tax might well be a lot simpler than it is now; likewise, the flat tax will be a lot more complex than its proponents proclaim.

Comparisons between a real income tax forged through decades of accumulated political compromises with any ideal tax—flat or otherwise—imagined in the solitude of the ivory tower or floated on the political hustings inevitably favor the latter. But such comparisons should be avoided; they ignore all our experience with the tax legislative process.

15

Back to
the Future

All the proposals for radical re-
structuring of the nation's tax system—those to reconstruct the income tax and those to cast it out in favor of a consumption
tax—attempt to answer the same question: How should the American government in the twenty-first century raise the revenues necessary to finance the public expenditures the people demand in
a manner that is fair, is reasonably simple, and encourages economic growth? As the foregoing chapters have demonstrated,
achieving these three goals at once is no easy task. We need to encourage savings and investment and promote economic growth
without making the distribution of the nation's taxes unfair. A
simple tax system will prove elusive for many in our complex modern society. Uncertainty about the economic and social conse-

quences of tax changes is omnipresent. Creating a public consensus for change is difficult, mustering a political majority well nigh impossible.

The American people are mad at the income tax—and have good reasons for being angry—but that does not mean that they have rejected the idea of taxing income or have accepted the proposition that the federal government should tax only consumption rather than income. Many politicians' taste for untried forms of consumption taxes masquerading as income taxes supports this view. The American people are angry at the way income is taxed, angry about how the income tax now works, angry at the way tax policy is made, angry at the way the tax law gets written, and angry at how the tax law is administered. They want a simple tax law and would probably prefer a tax system more friendly to savings, but only if that does not produce a major redistribution of taxes away from wealthier taxpayers to those with lower incomes and less wealth. They also want their tax dollars to be well spent. Government waste feeds anti-tax frenzy.

The status quo is neither stable nor satisfactory. Change we must and change we will. This chapter tells what to change. Here I propose moving forward by returning to the original purpose and scope of the income tax. However, let me begin by examining ways to encourage additional savings in the income tax.

Encouraging Savings in the Income Tax

A major impetus for shifting from the income tax to a consumption tax is to increase our national rate of savings. That can be done with tax policy changes far less radical than replacing the income tax with a consumption tax.

The current income tax now encourages personal savings in three major ways. First, there are tax incentives for retirement savings through employer-sponsored pension plans and purchases of retirement annuities. Second, the tax law exempts from taxation investment earnings in connection with life insurance contracts. Third, the income tax encourages homeownership.

These three forms of long-term savings constitute the bulk of most families' wealth. Owner-occupied housing alone accounts for a quarter or more of the net wealth of most households and up to 70 percent for many. Life insurance and pension savings account for another 20 percent or more of household wealth. This means that, on average, about one-half of total personal wealth is in the form of assets that already enjoy protection from the income tax. For many middle-income families, these assets along with the promise of future Social Security benefits make up virtually all of their personal savings.[1]

Within the existing income tax, there are additional ways to increase private savings. Since 1986, Congress has changed pension rules to limit the amounts that qualify for favorable income tax treatment and has also made employer pension plans more costly and complicated. Many of these changes were made solely to increase government revenues in the short run. Simplifying the pension rules and easing some of the limitations could help increase this important form of savings. In 1996 Congress took some steps in this direction for employers with fewer than 100 employees in connection with legislation raising the minimum wage. Making it much simpler for all businesses to establish and maintain pension plans should be a priority.

Additional savings might also be encouraged by expanding opportunities for individuals to save through tax-advantaged individual retirement accounts (IRAs). The Budget Act passed by the House and Senate in 1995 but vetoed by President Clinton, for example, would have increased the number of people eligible for such tax-favored savings accounts and also would have enlarged the potential uses for such accounts by allowing savings for education, medical expenses, and the purchase of a home, in addition to retirement. To the extent that such options encourage people to withdraw money earlier from preexisting IRA savings accounts, they could have an adverse effect on savings, but the more liberal withdrawal rules may encourage additional savings by people who are reluctant to tie their money up until retirement. Another option would be to allow special tax breaks for savings for up to a specified amount of education expenses in education savings accounts that could be used for a variety of job-training expenses as well as for children's education.

Economic research about the effectiveness of IRAs in expanding private savings has been inconclusive. Some economists believe that most taxpayers have simply shifted savings from taxable savings accounts to non-taxable IRA accounts; other analysts believe IRAs have had a significant positive effect in increasing private savings. In either event, IRA tax incentives could be better designed to produce greater increases in savings for the revenue dollars they cost. People might, for example, be allowed a tax break only for savings that exceed some percentage of their income, rather than for the first dollars of savings up to a ceiling, currently $2,000. Such a revision clearly would enhance the potential positive effects of IRAs on private savings.

Although the current tax law encourages homeownership, it also encourages borrowing by homeowners. In the early 1990s, the Japanese government, among others, recommended to the United States that it should make U.S. tax policy more favorable to savings by limiting Americans' ability to deduct the interest costs of borrowing for current consumption. Economists are in uncommon universal agreement that limiting or eliminating such interest deductions will reduce current consumption and increase savings by encouraging people to borrow less so that their savings increase. The 1986 Tax Reform Act attempted to move in this direction by eliminating the income tax deduction for credit card purchases, for department store credit purchases, and for automobile loans, but much of the potential benefit of this change was lost by subsequent amendments, which allow homeowners to deduct interest on "home equity" loans even if the proceeds are used to finance a vacation or buy a car.

Banks and other financial institutions have been aggressive and very successful in encouraging home equity loans and lines of credit to get around the limitations on interest deductibility. Some credit cards are now structured as home equity lines of credit. As a result, the 1986 act failed to curb borrowing, but now allows tax advantages for borrowing only to homeowners and increases the prospects that someone will lose his home, rather than just his car, when the economy takes a sharp downturn.

Eliminating interest deductibility on home equity loans used to finance consumption would encourage savings without the shock of a complete repeal of the deduction for home mortgage interest. An overall cap on home mortgage interest deductions as a percentage of income could further serve to limit income tax incentives for borrowing. Alternatively, Congress might convert the home mortgage interest deduction to a tax credit of, say, 10 or 15 percent of the interest paid as a way to decrease the tax savings from borrowing. Any of these changes should increase private savings while avoiding the political outcry and curbing the adverse effect on home values that could accompany outright repeal of the home mortgage deduction.

Additional income tax changes are also available to improve the composition of our national savings and investments. Our income tax law, for example, currently overtaxes corporate income, in sharp contrast to its favored treatment of housing investments. By taxing corporate income first under the corporate income tax and then again by the individual income tax when distributed as dividends, the current tax system discourages equity investments in corporations and encourages companies to finance their investments through borrowing. Corporations have repurchased their own shares and increased their borrowings, sometimes through leveraged buyouts, to reduce this double tax burden. Such differential taxation has affected greatly the financial structure of corporations and the allocation of investment capital in the United States. The disparity between the income taxation of housing and corporate investments helps explain why the United States has an extremely high proportion of national investments in housing relative to corporate investments compared to other industrial nations. Building a house creates jobs only while the house is being built; corporate investments create jobs that may last many years. Congress should redress this disparity by eliminating the double tax on corporate income.

The income tax can be made friendlier to savings and more

neutral about the allocation of investment capital without dramatically shifting taxes from richer to poorer citizens. These kinds of changes also would protect the long-term nature of most savings now given a tax break under the current income tax. In so doing, it would ensure that tax reform would not destabilize the private pension system.

The Missing Savings Link: Social Security

Nothing in the American tax system provides a starker political contrast with the income tax than the Social Security and Medicare payroll taxes. If railing against the income tax and the IRS is a no-lose political act, attacking Medicare or Social Security is no-win. The resistance of the American public to income tax increases throughout the 1980s and 1990s was matched by their easy acceptance of payroll tax increases during the same period to finance Social Security and Medicare. But the American public's willingness to pay additional taxes to ensure the future financial stability of these programs may be nearing an end. By putting the compliance burden on employers and avoiding any requirement for individual employees to file payroll tax returns, the Social Security and Medicare taxes have avoided the complexities and compliance difficulties that now haunt the income tax. But many of the other reasons for the decline in public support for the income tax are now present in the Social Security and Medicare systems.

First, the rise in the tax bite of the Social Security and Medicare payroll taxes now means that a large number of working Americans pay more payroll taxes than income taxes. The earned-income tax credit was enacted and expanded to offset this increased burden for low- and moderate-income workers, but since that credit is claimed by filing an income tax return and directly offsets income taxes, its link to payroll taxes is not apparent to workers. The willingness to pay these taxes is diminishing each year as more and more young people have come to believe they will never receive the promised retirement benefits. Recent polls show that more members of Generation X believe in the existence of UFOs than in the likelihood of collecting Social Security benefits. In contrast to the automatic income tax increases due to bracket creep, the increased payroll taxes were explicitly enacted by Congress, but the total size of the Social Security and Medicare tax take is beginning to cause political rumblings. This is why Jack Kemp, among others, suggested that employees' payroll taxes should be deductible under the income tax.

Second, the Social Security system contains marriage penalties analogous to those of the income tax. The Social Security benefit structure disadvantages married couples when both spouses have worked. An estimated 370,000 men and women over age sixty-five are now living together without marrying. Hilde Waring, age seventy-four, a widow who lives in the Bronx with widower Marvin Goldman, says, "Some years ago I might have gotten married, but certain things have changed my mind, mainly Social Security and taxes."[2] Recent increases in the income tax on Social Security benefits have exacerbated this problem. Two single people living together can each earn $25,000 per year, a total of $50,000, before their Social Security benefits are taxed, but if they marry, Social Security benefits are taxed whenever their joint earnings total $32,000. In the future, as a greater proportion of the population eligible for Social Security benefits includes men and women who have both worked and therefore are separately eligible to receive benefits, the number of retirees who would face substantial losses of Social Security income from marrying will increase dramatically. Such marriage penalties may produce some of the same disdain for the Social Security system that we have experienced under the income tax.

Third, strong and accumulating economic evidence suggests that this country's feeble rate of private savings may, in substantial part, be due to the increased retirement income protection and retirement medical-care insurance provided through Social Security and Medicare.[3] The security these programs provide our elderly citizens is extremely valuable, but by providing a safety net against unexpected medical expenses and a guaranteed inflation-adjusted monthly income for as long as one lives, the Social Security and

Medicare programs have significantly decreased people's need to save for retirement. The great benefits of these programs may have come at a significant cost in reduced national savings. Giving up the benefits that Social Security and Medicare provide would make no sense, but we must begin looking seriously for ways to reduce their costs.

Despite these problems, Social Security has not yet made it to the forefront of the tax reform agenda. In his quest for the presidency, Steve Forbes urged major structural changes in Social Security, but got the typical political response. He was told by politicians of all stripes to leave Social Security alone. There are three reasons why politicians are reluctant to advance changes in Social Security. First, as I have indicated, Social Security has long been regarded as the dangerous third rail of American politics. Because of the perceived political risks of talking about major changes of any sort, if politicians can postpone addressing its problems, they will.

Second, Social Security currently is producing cash surpluses. The United States government now collects more in Social Security payroll taxes than it pays in benefits. However, in another couple of decades at the latest, the current tax rate will not be adequate to fund current benefits. Without any changes, actuaries currently estimate that the Social Security and Medicare trust funds will run an annual cash deficit of nearly $600 billion by the year 2020, a deficit of $1.7 trillion a year by 2030. These projections may well be overly optimistic. If they are close, combined Social Security and Medicare payroll tax rates would have to exceed 25 percent to fund current benefits. Without other structural changes in Medicare and Social Security, the payroll tax rate will have to be raised to an unacceptably high level, benefits will have to be cut, or federal borrowing will explode. A combination of incremental changes made now would go a long way toward addressing the Social Security problem. Such changes could include extending the retirement age, eliminating the current overstatement of the consumer price index used to measure cost-of-living benefit increases, and perhaps other small benefit reductions or tax increases. Solving Medicare's long-term financial shortcomings is considerably more difficult.

But most of today's politicians regard these as problems for some future generation, even though relatively small steps taken now might produce large positive long-term benefits.

Third, since both Medicare hospital insurance and Social Security benefits are financed by taxes on wages—taxes that themselves impose no direct burden on savings—the adverse impact of these programs on national savings is generally not seen as a tax reform problem. But these taxes do decrease the amount of after-tax income available to younger workers, who might otherwise save at least some of it, and the benefits go to retired older citizens, who are more likely to spend the money. More important, Medicare transfers can only be used for health insurance, and the Social Security benefits structure is designed so that low-income workers, who need the money to spend during retirement, receive benefits equal to a higher proportion of their pre-retirement wages than do higher-income workers. The dramatic decline in the rate of U.S. savings has coincided with a substantial increase in total consumption by the elderly, due in substantial part to the intergenerational distribution of income from young to elderly people through Social Security and Medicare.[4]

Of the tax reform proposals recently advanced, few have made any effort to integrate Social Security payroll tax issues into the tax reform debate, and even these proposals avoid addressing any structural issues of Social Security itself. For example, the Kemp Commission recommended that employees be allowed to deduct their share of Social Security payroll taxes from either a reformed income tax or a personal consumption tax. The Nunn-Domenici USA tax would allow tax credits for Social Security payroll taxes to offset the consumption tax obligations of both businesses and individuals. Each of these changes would maintain the existing funding, benefits structure, and trust fund accounting of Social Security. Neither would have any real effect on the long-term financial viability of Social Security or Medicare or on their impact on the total level of private savings. But they would decrease the tax bite from Social Security and, by so doing, might make further payroll tax increases politically palatable.

The effect of Social Security and Medicare on the level of national savings depends on how the government finances, spends, and accounts for these programs. A number of more drastic proposals have been advanced designed to minimize the adverse effects of the Social Security system on the nation's level and rate of savings. A full discussion of these ideas would require a second book, but a brief look at two of the policy options illuminates the crucial issues. The first idea would convert all or part of the Social Security system into a private retirement savings system; the second would simply change the federal budget's accounting for both Social Security and Medicare.

A number of people have suggested that the Social Security system should be converted into a private pension system where each person's retirement benefits are linked directly to investment returns on their pension contributions.[5] Such a system has enjoyed success in Chile, has been adopted by Argentina and Peru, and is being considered in other countries facing long-term financial difficulties with their Social Security systems.[6] It would be very difficult, however, for the United States to change from the existing Social Security system to a fully privatized system and also protect the expectations of current retirees and employees.

Complete privatization of Social Security would require substantial additional financing to fund Social Security obligations to current retirees and people who will soon reach retirement. Although the cash coming into the Social Security Trust Fund currently exceeds benefit payments and, as a result, federal budgets claim the Social Security Trust Fund is running large surpluses, supposedly to fund future benefits, in reality the Social Security system now has unfunded liabilities that far exceed its assets. Using business accrual accounting procedures rather than cash flows as a measure of its condition demonstrates that the present value of the net unfunded liabilities of the Social Security system is more than $11 trillion.[7] A major new source of funds, either in additional taxes or in federal borrowing, would be necessary to fund those liabilities if existing Social Security taxes were channeled into individuals' private pension contributions.

Complete privatization of the current Social Security system would also eliminate much, if not all, of its redistributional force.

Under an actuarially based private retirement savings system, low-wage workers would no longer receive a higher return on their contributions than high-wage workers, as they now do under the current Social Security benefit structure. Crediting mandatory contributions, even in the form of payroll taxes, to each individual's retirement account would eliminate the complex benefit formula that now serves both to accomplish and to mask redistributions from higher- to lower-income workers.

In contrast, privatizing only a part of Social Security could retain much of this redistribution and still serve both to increase private savings and to reduce the long-term fiscal pressure facing Social Security. Partial privatization of Social Security was proposed in 1995 by Senators Bob Kerrey, a Democrat from Nebraska, and Alan Simpson, a Republican from Wyoming. Senators Kerrey and Simpson would allow workers to reduce their Social Security payroll taxes by 2 percent and transfer that money into a personal retirement savings plan. Their Social Security benefits would be correspondingly reduced. Individual workers would generally bear the investment risks associated with these private investments, although the government could guarantee some minimal return. On average, this wealth should grow at a much faster rate than "Social Security wealth," which depends on the growth of wages and returns on U.S. Treasury bonds. Risky investments, however, would no doubt make some people do worse.

The potential for the expanded retirement security that such a program might provide is shown by the fact that in the past seventy years the rate of return on the Standard and Poors portfolio of common stocks has averaged more than 10 percent annually, compared to a 5 percent return on government bonds. Wage compensation, which constitutes the Social Security tax base, has grown even more slowly, an average of less than 3 percent during the period 1960–1994. At an 8 percent compound return, someone who put $15 a week into such a fund would accumulate more than $250,000 after thirty-five years of working and more than $500,000 after forty-five years.

Such a partial privatization of Social Security could retain the benefits to low- and middle-income workers of the current Social

Security system, while transforming a substantial amount of "government spending" into "private wealth." Private retirement savings accounts under such a system ultimately would become an important source of wealth for all workers. People themselves, rather than Congress, would have control over this accumulation of funds. In contrast, simply investing a share of Social Security payroll taxes in common stocks without privatizing these funds would keep the assets and their control with a government agency and would also maintain the status of this form of retirement savings as government spending rather than private wealth.

One variation on this idea would limit this partial privatization of Social Security to people under age fifty at the time of enactment in order to protect the expectations about benefits of people nearing retirement age. Senators Kerrey and Simpson proposed coupling their partial privatization proposal with a gradual increase in the Social Security retirement age from sixty-seven to seventy and with certain other changes to constrain future Social Security deficits.

Opponents of even a partial privatization of Social Security are concerned, however, that privatization would unduly increase private risks and eviscerate Social Security's ability to redistribute retirement income to low- and moderate-income workers. They rightly point to Social Security's success in keeping the elderly out of poverty. In 1994 more than half the people over age sixty-five would have had incomes below the poverty level without their Social Security benefits. This view has led to proposals to keep the current Social Security tax and benefits structure in place, but to invest 40 to 50 percent of Social Security taxes in the stock market in an effort to obtain greater returns. Advocates of this change are confident that a requirement that Social Security funds be invested in a broad market index fund, such as the Wilshire 6000, will limit market disruptions and inhibit government favoritism for particular industries or firms. The intent here is to move from a pay-as-you-go Social Security system to a partially funded one, whose returns are linked to capital market growth rather than wage growth. This would have the advantage of allowing more wage earners to benefit from increased returns to invested capital. All sides now seem willing to adapt Social Security to the risks associated with stock market fluctuations.

Ultimately, the political question is which of these kinds of changes creates a more stable source of retirement income. Much more work remains to be done, but I am inclined to believe that shifting some part of Social Security payments into mandatory private accounts along with additional matching private contributions, while keeping a significant amount of retirement income within the Social Security system, will bolster public confidence and political support for the system. Such a system permits each worker to obtain significant retirement benefits based on their own earnings and investment experiences, although it does entail more private risk and somewhat greater administrative costs than the current system. Such a plan not only should increase the nation's savings but might also have a positive effect on work effort. But opponents of privatization aren't out of line when they point to the possible unraveling of Social Security that partial privatization might begin. Maintaining a substantial stake in Social Security benefits for everyone is the only way to guard against such an event.

At the opposite extreme from these kinds of major substantive changes in Social Security is a minimalist change, limited to the way the federal government accounts for Social Security and Medicare in the budget. Today, the federal government simply adds up the cash tax payments that it receives and the outflows of cash benefits it pays to "know" whether Social Security or Medicare is running a "surplus" or a "deficit." An alternative would be to account for Social Security and Medicare on an accrual basis, which would require the government to acknowledge and estimate the accrued unfunded liabilities of Medicare and Social Security in its annual and projected budgets. The financial statements of businesses currently take into account their future obligations to pay pensions and health benefits to their workers during retirement. The federal government should do the same. Changing from cash to accrual accounting for these programs would change nothing substantively, but would have enormous political ramifications over time. Ultimately these changes in the federal budget would show deficits in these programs so large that they would force policy changes attentive to long-term consequences.

A specific example from the 1995 budget debate demonstrates the importance of such budget scorekeeping rules. The 1995 Budget Act, as proposed by the Senate Finance and Budget Committees, would have raised the age of eligibility for Medicare health benefits from age sixty-five to age sixty-seven beginning in the year 2003. Under current cash-flow budget accounting rules, however, this amendment did not count as saving any money for the federal government because it did not change cash outlays during the 1996–2002 budget period, even though its enactment would have substantially reduced accrued liabilities under Medicare. Because this change did not save any cash in the 1996–2002 seven-year "budget window," Senator Kennedy was able to eliminate the provision on the Senate floor as "not germane" to the Budget Reconciliation Act. This proposed change in the age of benefit eligibility did not count as a deficit-reducing measure under the rules of the Senate, although no one doubts that it would have reduced Medicare spending significantly in 2003 and in all years thereafter.

If the federal deficit were determined by accruing both liabilities and assets of the Social Security and Medicare systems, reaching a "balanced budget" at a specific point in time would mean something very different than it does today. Congress would have to pay attention to the long-term impact of policy changes.

Senators Kerrey and Simpson have proposed a more modest change in federal budget accounting: using a thirty-year, rather than a five- or seven-year, budget period. This change, too, would serve to introduce greater concern with the long-term effects of policy into the legislative process. For example, it also would have counted substantial savings from the proposed change in the eligibility age for Medicare benefits.

In an era when budget scorekeeping drives policy outcomes, as it has for the past decade, a "simple" change in budget scorekeeping rules can have far-reaching policy implications. Combining a partial privatization of Social Security with this kind of change in federal budget accounting would almost certainly translate over time into a significant positive impact on the nation's rate of savings.

Making the Income Tax Simpler

The major impetus for replacing the income tax with some form of consumption tax is to inspire greater private savings and, by so doing, to increase economic growth and the nation's output. But much of the public's support for tax reform exists because of its promise of major simplification of the tax system. The wish for a postcard tax return, or none at all, may be the greatest stimulus to tax reform.

As Chapters 13 and 14 have indicated, most current tax reform proposals generally have three components: a shift from income to consumption taxation, a flattening of the tax rates, and the elimination of many of the tax breaks—the exclusions, deductions, and tax credits—of current law. As we have seen, whether moving to a consumption tax would achieve significant simplification depends on its form. By taking individuals out of the tax collection process completely, the standard forms of value-added or retail sales taxes dominate other alternatives on simplification grounds.

A single tax rate eliminates potential advantages from shifting income among family members and, if the business and individual rates are the same, also offers prospects for moving tax collection from individuals to businesses. The realistic potential to achieve great simplification by shifting tax burdens from individuals to businesses is limited, however, by the fact that people assess the fairness of a tax system by looking at how much individuals pay. The American public will not support a tax system that it does not believe to be fair.

Much simplification is also achieved in each of these tax reform proposals by eliminating many of the tax breaks of the existing income tax. Most of the tax reform proposals, for example, would eliminate special tax incentives for a large variety of specific business expenditures and activities and would eradicate deductions for state and local property and income taxes, deductions for mortgage interest and charitable contributions, credits for child care, the earned-income tax credit, the exclusion of interest on municipal bonds, and tax breaks for a host of fringe benefits, including those for health and life insurance and employer-sponsored pension funds. Purging the tax law of such provisions would substantially simplify tax administration and compliance and would produce significant additional revenues that could be used to reduce tax rates.

The rub, however, is that many of these special tax advantages were enacted by Congress to achieve important social or economic purposes, and hence are not easily eliminated. It is hard to believe that all these tax breaks would disappear in any tax revision, but the key point here is that, if they can be eliminated, the tax law would be much simpler, regardless of whether income or consumption is taxed or whether tax rates are flat or graduated. The Tax Reform Act of 1986 slaughtered few sacred cows and also retained a host of narrowly targeted benefits, such as for independent oil producers and ethanol manufacturers. Provisions such as these continue to enjoy substantial political support within Congress, and hardly a day passes without some politician suggesting a new tax cut for people and companies who behave in certain ways. Republican presidential candidate Lamar Alexander, for example, suggested a new tax credit for gifts to charities that help the poor. Both the Democrat Eleanor Holmes Norton and the Republican Jack Kemp favor special low federal tax rates for residents of the District of Columbia. Bill Clinton's labor secretary, Robert Reich, has floated the idea of new tax breaks for companies that are particularly good to their workers. Newt Gingrich in 1995 proposed a new tax credit for purchases of laptop computers, but after a few days' reflection withdrew the idea as "nutsy."

There are various ways to simplify the existing income tax short of eliminating all of the current income tax breaks. For example, as Bob Dole suggested in his presidential campaign, the IRS could eliminate altogether the requirement of filing a tax return for many of the 45 million to 50 million individuals and married couples who currently file the simplest tax forms, Forms 1040EZ and 1040A. There is no reason why the IRS cannot make all of the tax calculations for people who have only wage, dividend, and interest income and who take the standard deduction or who claim itemized deductions only for state and local taxes and home mortgage interest. For them, even a postcard return is superfluous. The IRS currently gets all the information necessary to complete these returns from employers, banks, states, governments, and other third parties on Forms W-2, 1099, and 1098. It simply needs to update some of its creaky old computers to do this job. The IRS had considered allowing a return-free system for such people in 1986 but abandoned the idea.

This could spare many millions of people the costs and agony of filing tax returns. Henry Bloch wouldn't like it, but the public might. Those people who do not trust the IRS to compute their taxes correctly could check the IRS's tax calculation themselves or with a tax-return preparer, presumably for less than the current fee for preparing a tax return and with less pain.

Second, the old standby of tax-simplification efforts, increasing the standard deduction, always eases tax compliance for large numbers of individuals. The number of people who claim the standard deduction could be further expanded by enacting floors or ceilings on itemized deductions to reduce the number of itemizers.

Other provisions could readily be simplified if they are retained. The interest deduction and child-care provisions scream for simplification, to name but two. The current rules allowing deductions for home equity loans could be eliminated and only interest up to a specified dollar limit might be deductible. This would permit elimination of complex and futile rules that now require individuals to trace the uses of borrowed funds. Single parents who work and working couples could be allowed a tax credit for a specified dollar amount of child-care expenses simply by showing that they paid it. This would eliminate two pages of complex, and widely ignored, statutory requirements.

Great simplification could be achieved by replacing the earned-income tax credit with a Social Security tax exemption for a certain amount of wages. Such a change would also permit easier and more timely delivery of benefits to recipients. It would require some mechanism to keep the costs of such a change reasonable by targeting this relief principally to low-wage workers.

Any serious effort to simplify the tax law should address the inordinate tax compliance costs of small businesses. The current income tax provides the same rules for your neighborhood hardware store as for large multinational corporations, even though the bulk of business income tax revenues come from the latter. Inventory accounting, foreign tax credits, and pension rules, to name but three, could be greatly simplified for small businesses without any significant revenue costs. In fact, Congress should consider enacting a greatly simplified income tax code applicable only to small businesses. The key to achieving income tax simplification is for Congress to make it a real priority.

The Simplification Missing Link: State and Local Taxes

Curiously, the tax-simplification movement has so far ignored completely state and local taxes, which, for many people, serve to complicate tax filing and to increase significantly their costs of tax compliance. Congress has never been willing, for example, to allow state income tax deductions only for those states whose income tax liability turns on federal income tax calculations. This would enable everyone to calculate their state tax liabilities as a percentage of their federal taxable income, while allowing each state to set its own income tax rate. No state income tax return would then require more than a postcard.

It is not at all clear what would happen to state taxes if the federal government were to replace the income tax with some form of consumption tax. Perhaps congressional proponents of such a change believe that state income taxes will simply wither away if the federal government abandons the income tax, but that does not seem likely. State revenue needs are increasing as the federal government is devolving greater responsibilities, such as for Medicaid and welfare, to the states. In addition, states have long had consumption taxation entirely to themselves, adopting retail sales taxes free from competition with the federal government. Virtually every state imposes such a tax. But there is a limit to the combined federal and state tax rates that can realistically be applied to consumption. If the federal government were to abandon income taxation altogether, many states would undoubtedly move to fill this vacuum. A federal postcard tax return under a flat tax would provide little benefit to the American people if state tax returns looked like the current federal tax forms.

When Congress gets down to the hard work of federal tax reform, it must pay careful attention to the likely responses by the states. Any large change in our federal tax system necessarily must involve the states as well as the federal government, but, so far, no one is saying so.

Back to the Future

No one should doubt that replacing the current corporate and individual income taxes with a flat-rate tax on consumption would shift substantial amounts of taxes from higher- to lower-income families. The flat tax, which taxes only wages and not investment income at the individual level, has little chance of enactment, because, once they understand it, the American people will not accept such a tax as fair. Indeed, the Sixteenth Amendment was added to the Constitution to redress such a situation. There is no reason to believe that complete substitution of any form of consumption tax for the income tax would be politically stable.

As I have mentioned, when Treasury Secretary Joe Barr revealed in January 1969 that 154 people with more than $200,000 of income paid no income taxes, he generated a groundswell of public outrage. Mrs. Dodge, who had $1 million of tax-exempt state and local bond interest, was subjected to special bashing. In 1986 the American public was again infuriated when it learned that the workers on General Electric's assembly line paid more taxes than the company. Such stories have enormous political force. These events involving only a few hundred taxpayers were directly responsible for adding the complex individual and corporate minimum taxes to the income tax.

In the not so distant past, in the elections of 1990 and 1992, great political hay was harvested by Democrats' complaints about undertaxation of the "rich." With taxes only on consumption, Warren Buffet or Bill Gates could well become the next era's Mrs. Dodge. The untaxed-Midas anecdotes that will surely flow from the elimination of the income tax, coupled with the wide disparities in taxes of people with similar levels of income but very different patterns of consumption, will inevitably create a backlash against a purely consumption-based tax system. Indeed, the fear of such backlashes is at least part of the reason why consumption tax proponents in the Congress have cloaked their proposals in income tax garb. But you cannot fool all the people for all time. Complete elimination of the income tax and substitution of consumption taxes is an unstable outcome, even in the unlikely event that such a plan could be enacted into law. Replacing the income tax with a consumption tax may well repeat Margaret Thatcher's disastrous error of replacing extremely unpopular property taxes with an even more unpopular "community charge."

More than a century ago, Adam Smith stated this basic principle of tax fairness: "The subjects of every state ought to contribute towards the support of government, as nearly as possible in proportion to their respective abilities." Ability to pay has been measured historically in a variety of ways, although the task has always been essentially the same: to measure people's relative capacity to finance their government. A person who consumes more typically has a greater ability to pay than a person who consumes less, and a person who earns higher wages usually has a greater ability to pay than a person who earns lower wages. But neither of these measures in isolation may provide an adequate index of overall economic well-being. Neither a wage tax nor a consumption tax will tax heavily a wealthy person who lives frugally from interest, dividends, rents, and royalties but earns no wages. An income tax base is a more comprehensive measure of a person's ability to pay than either wages or consumption.

There is little reason to eliminate entirely the income tax. Achieving low tax rates for everyone and a simple tax system for the vast majority of Americans can be accomplished by replacing part of the income tax with a consumption tax. In 1992, outgoing Treasury secretary Nicholas F. Brady offered one alternative: a revenue-neutral and distributionally neutral enactment of a 5 percent value-added tax to replace the income taxes of all taxpayers with incomes below $30,000 or so. In 1994 former senators Jack Danforth and David Boren also proposed combining a value-added tax with a more narrowly targeted income tax. Variations on this theme merit serious attention by Congress.

A few basic facts reveal the potential to eliminate the income tax for most people by enacting a federal retail sales or value-added tax. Putting aside any potential reductions in government spending or a burst of revenues from increased economic growth, it would take about a 20 percent value-added tax to replace completely the revenues from the individual income tax. An additional 4 percent VAT would replace corporate income tax revenues.[8] A 10 percent value-added or sales tax would raise about $360 billion of revenues in 1999, about one-half the total $730 billion expected to be raised that year by the individual income tax.[9] Thus, without any additional revenues from base broadening, spending cuts, or economic growth, such a tax would allow the income tax to be cut to half its current size. A 12 percent VAT would allow both the individual and corporate income taxes to be cut in half; a 15 percent VAT—the typical European rate—would allow an additional $100 billion of income tax relief.

Because, as we have seen, a flat-rate value-added or retail sales tax does not burden families similarly to the current income tax, simply halving income tax rates across the board would not be appropriate. But consider these additional facts. Based on IRS data for tax returns for 1993, tax returns with adjusted gross income (AGI) above $75,000 paid one-half of all the income taxes for that year although they accounted for only 7.5 million of the 107 million returns filed, or less than 7 percent of the total.[10] This means that, in principle, without any changes in the current income tax, a 10 percent value-added tax would allow eliminating from the income tax rolls 100 million tax returns with adjusted gross income of less than $75,000.

Moreover, the tax filers with incomes above $75,000 paid taxes at an average rate of just under 21 percent of AGI, so that a 10 percent value-added tax would allow exemption of all tax returns below $75,000 of adjusted gross income combined with a flat-rate 21 percent tax on the total adjusted gross income of returns above $75,000. By applying the current minimum-tax rules to these people or slightly increasing their tax rates, deductions for charitable contributions, medical expenses, and home mortgage interest could be allowed. Alternatively, broadening the tax base by eliminating other tax breaks might permit retention of these deductions without increasing the tax rate.

If the income tax threshold were lowered, say to $50,000, additional possibilities occur. Again based on 1993 data, a 10 percent tax on the adjusted gross income of tax filers between $50,000 and $100,000 coupled with a 20 percent tax on the adjusted gross income of filers with AGI above $100,000 would raise more than 110 percent of the revenues necessary to replace one-half the individual income tax. Thus, if a new 10 percent value-added tax were coupled with income tax base broadening, there would be greater flexibility.[11] An exemption for some level of Social Security payroll taxes could serve as a simple and effective replacement for the earned-income tax credit and prevent a tax increase for low-wage workers.

These simple illustrations demonstrate that introducing a 10–15 percent value-added tax into the federal tax system offers enormous potential to simplify the income tax, perhaps removing as many as 100 million families from the income tax rolls.[12] It would also make the federal tax system much more economically efficient and friendlier to savings and capital formation without introducing the inherent unfairness of completely substituting a consumption tax for income taxation.

The combination of a 10–15 percent VAT with a 20 percent flat-rate income tax on incomes above $75,000 to $100,000 would mean that high-income taxpayers would pay a 20 percent tax on their income and a 10–15 percent tax on their consumption. At lower levels of income people would pay only the VAT.

In addition to substantially reducing the current tax burden on savings for everyone, this regime would also remove many of the inefficiencies and inequalities of the current income tax. At a 20 percent rate, tax favors would be worth less, and their repeal might be easier politically. Capital gains could be taxed at the same rate as ordinary income. The marriage penalty would be eliminated. Distortions due to inflation would be eliminated for most people and substantially reduced for all others. If rules to prohibit employers from discriminating in their pension or health insurance plans in favor of highly compensated employees were retained, employer provision of both health coverage and retirement income might be saved.[13]

If an income tax charitable deduction were retained, charitable contributions would continue to be tax-preferred relative to either consumption or savings for those higher-income individuals whose charitable giving is now most influenced by the tax break. If some income tax deduction for home mortgage interest were retained for the acquisition of an owner-occupied home, homeowners should not experience a precipitous decline in the values of their homes.

If 2 percent of the VAT were dedicated to reducing corporate income tax rates, the corporate tax rate could also be cut to 20 percent. This would stimulate corporate investments and encourage capital to be invested in businesses located in the United States. Tax advantages for particular investments or kinds of businesses would become far less valuable and many might be repealed. This system would reduce substantially the shift in the tax burden to labor-intensive industries that would occur if the corporate income tax were completely replaced by a VAT.

Changes of the sort I am suggesting here would return the income tax to its pre–World War II status, when it supplied progressivity to the United States tax system by limited application only to people at the top of the income tax scale. This is the "Back to the Future" tax reform.

The Missing Fairness Link—a Tax
on Wealth?

Many of the proposals for replacing the income tax with a consumption tax would also eliminate the estate and gift taxes. These taxes are imposed on transfers of wealth to younger generations and are quite complex, although they produce relatively little revenue. The estate tax accounted for about 11 percent of federal revenues at its zenith in 1946, but it has never produced more than 2.5 percent of federal revenues since the end of the Second World War. Today it accounts for only about 1 percent of federal revenues.

The federal taxes on gifts and bequests are, however, the only federal taxes on wealth and have made a significant contribution to the progressivity of the nation's tax system. Despite their low revenue yield, estate and gift taxes have long contributed roughly one-third as much to the progressivity of the nation's tax structure as have progressive tax rates in excess of the average individual income tax rate.[14] Indeed, Steve Forbes's heirs' tax savings from repeal of the estate tax would easily have funded his presidential campaign to enact a flat tax.

This is not the occasion for an extended discussion of estate and gift taxes, which, to be sure, have significant structural problems of their own, and are also unpopular, particularly with small business owners and farmers. But I question whether repeal of such an important element of progressivity without any replacement is appropriate now, given the widespread evidence that the distribution of wealth in the United States has become more unequal in recent years. Protecting family farms and businesses from having to liquidate to pay estate taxes is no reason for exempting large liquid estates from tax. Wealth inequality has always been greater than income inequality, and several recent studies suggest that distributions of recent wealth increases have greatly favored the wealthy. For example, one study claims that the top 1 percent of wealth holders enjoyed two-thirds of the increases in financial wealth during the 1980s.[15]

A direct tax on wealth of 0.5 percent, as imposed by Germany, would provide about $75 billion annually, approximately 1.5 percent of total income tax revenues.[16] But an annual wealth tax would be difficult to administer and would raise constitutional questions.

Taxing gifts and inheritances to individuals as income under the income tax system I have proposed here would exempt transfers to people without substantial other income and would reduce the top rate on such transfers to 20 percent from its current high of 55 percent. Such a tax probably would raise as much revenue as the existing estate and gift taxes even if gifts of up to $10,000 a year continued to be exempt from the tax. Alternatively, a so-called accessions tax could be imposed, which would tax gifts and inheritances to the recipients at progressive rates that would depend on the total amount of gifts or bequests they receive during their lifetimes. Or the current estate and gift taxes should be retained and improved.

The major argument for eliminating the estate and gift taxes, of course, is to remove this tax on savings and, by so doing, stimulate economic growth. Unsurprisingly, the evidence about the effect of these taxes on the national savings level is uncertain and controversial. But, as usual, true believers abound. One law professor even argued for repeal of the estate and gift taxes on the ground that repealing this tax, which applies only to the wealthiest 1 percent of the population, would increase the wages of the least advantaged members of our society.[17] He failed, however, to offer one shred of evidence that this kind of wage increase would actually occur.

To Forgive Is Divine

Any major change in the nation's tax system should be coupled with a tax amnesty for people who owe taxes and penalties under prior law. Virtually all of the states have had at least one tax amnesty and some have had two. Some European countries have also had tax amnesties. These amnesties permit people who have failed to file tax returns or who have underpaid taxes to come forward during some specified period of time to clear up their delinquent tax status by paying the taxes they owe without fear of civil or criminal penalties. Despite their popularity in the states and calls for them from time to time by members of Congress and by Bob Dole in his presidential campaign, the IRS and the Treasury Department have always opposed a federal tax amnesty, and there never has been one.

State tax amnesties have generally been most successful when they have been coupled with either a substantial increase in state tax enforcement efforts or a major change in state tax structures. California's campaign slogan "Get to us before we get to you" is typical of the carrot and stick approach that has worked well in the states.

A major change in the federal tax structure would be the perfect occasion for a federal tax amnesty to clean up the existing enforcement backlog. An amnesty might also provide a burst of short-term revenues to aid the transition to a new tax structure. Although the states have generally exceeded their expectations about the revenues to be collected through an amnesty, federal tax authorities have always predicted that an amnesty would produce minimal net revenues. However, if substantial additional revenues were produced by an amnesty, greater transitional relief could be financed. Treasury's long-standing concern that a federal tax amnesty would actually harm tax enforcement in the long term because people would expect the amnesty to be repeated would be substantially reduced if Congress structured the amnesty as an integral part of a once-in-a-lifetime restructuring of the federal tax system.

People would be encouraged to clean up their outstanding tax problems and move forward together into the new tax world. As the old saying goes, "To err is human, to forgive divine."

Short-Term Politics
Trump Long-Term Goals

The prospects for enacting a major restructuring of the nation's tax system necessarily, but unfortunately, will turn on whether a majority in Congress and the president see short-term political advantages from taking a new direction. Short-term politics tend to trump long-term economic goals. The legislation passed by Congress in 1995 makes this point vivid. In 1995, as part of its budget proposals, Congress passed major tax-reduction legislation for the first time since 1981. Surprisingly, this major tax relief—$245 billion over a seven-year period—contained little that would further the long-term tax reform goals of its supporters. The 1995 legislation, which was vetoed by President Clinton, would have done virtually nothing to simplify the tax law and would have provided only a few small changes intended to encourage savings.

Three-fifths of the total tax cuts, nearly $150 billion, were to be spent on a new tax credit for families with children. This tax cut reflected a major political priority of important constituencies of the Republican Party, particularly the Christian Coalition and the Family Resources Council. It also fulfilled a politically popular promise of the House Republicans' 1994 "Contract with America." But this tax cut did nothing to simplify the tax law for the average American, nothing to encourage additional savings, and nothing to improve people's potential to earn income. Lest there be any doubt of its political origins and motivations, the Republicans who voted for it made the first installment of the tax cut payable in October 1996, a few weeks before the presidential election. The paperwork burden of people having to file separate returns to claim this credit was considered well worth the potential political payoff. As this chapter has shown, many more useful and important tax cut opportunities exist.

The key point is this: Congress's short-term policy priorities are often disconnected from its long-term policy goals. There seems little basis for optimism about the prospects for fundamental tax reform so long as Congress remains transfixed in an effort to secure short-term political advantages.

The International Wild Card

Making tax law at the end of the twentieth century is very different from at the century's beginning. Our nation's ability to

fashion a tax law that makes the necessary and appropriate compromises among the goals of equity, economic efficiency, and simplicity is now limited by the globalization of economic activity.
Because capital, in particular, is extremely mobile across international boundaries, every nation's sovereignty over its own tax policy is constrained. For example, any nation's ability to implement
high and steeply progressive rates on capital income—perhaps because its view of tax fairness demands such rates—can be thwarted
by citizens shifting wealth into foreign corporations and to other
entities that employ the capital abroad. The globalization of capital markets, with their ability to transfer capital rapidly across borders, coupled with the movement toward greater European
economic unification, has made it more difficult for any one country to impose disproportionate taxes on capital or on capital income. As nations compete for investments, they tend to reduce
their taxes on capital to make such investments more attractive.
This may stimulate an international "race to the bottom"—a
beggar-thy-neighbor policy—which will undermine each nation's
independent tax equity goals. Many people, including tax officials
of the OECD and the European Community, have expressed concerns that such a race to the bottom is already under way.

The flows of capital, from the United States to other countries
and from other countries, particularly Western Europe, Japan, and
Canada, into the United States, are enormous. Today, U.S. persons
own more than $2 trillion in foreign assets, and foreign persons,
including foreign governments, own more than $2 trillion of U.S.
assets. In 1994 alone U.S. assets abroad increased by more than
$125 billion and foreign-owned assets in the United States in-
creased by more than $290 billion. U.S. purchases and sales of se-
curities on foreign markets were $850 billion in 1995. In 1970,
most U.S. corporations that had operations abroad received a relatively small portion of their income from foreign sources, typically
10 to 20 percent. Today, most of these same companies receive
more than one-half of their income from abroad. As international
taxation has become more important to these companies, they
have become much more aggressive and worldly-wise in their tax-
planning techniques. There is a considerable risk, even if a change

in tax policy were to prove successful in increasing national savings, that rather than trickling down and throughout the American economy, the benefits from such increased savings could flow across the sea. Many of the tax reform proposals now being advanced are motivated at least in part by a desire to modernize America's tax system to enhance the competitiveness of American businesses in the world economy and to attract capital to the United States from abroad.

Not only capital moves across national borders. In January 1996 the University of Miami held a conference for tax planners that included a session called "Tax Advantaged Traveling for You and Your Money: Expatriation and Foreign Trusts."[18] In 1995, Congress became concerned with loopholes in the existing income and estate taxes that allow people to avoid paying large amounts of U.S. taxes by renouncing their citizenship and moving abroad. The president and the Congress proposed so-called Benedict Arnold amendments to eliminate the practice. The most notorious case involved the billionaire Kenneth Dart, president of Dart Container Corporation, a Styrofoam cup manufacturer. Mr. Dart in 1993 renounced his American citizenship and left his home in Sarasota, Florida, darting to the Central American nation of Belize (formerly British Honduras, south of Mexico on the Caribbean Sea), in the process saving millions of dollars in U.S. taxes. In 1995, the Belize government urged the U.S. State Department to allow it to open a consulate in Sarasota, Florida, where Mr. Dart's wife, children, and other relatives live. Kenneth Dart apparently was to be appointed counsel to the United States from Belize and thereby, as a diplomat, would become free to come and go as he pleases, freeing him from a restriction that limits him to 120 days a year in this country. Dan Miller, Sarasota's Republican congressman, said, "The Sarasota area is not known for its concentration of Belizean nationals," and speculated that the choice of a location for the consulate where Mr. Dart's family lives was no coincidence.[19] Florida's representative on the House Ways and Means Committee, Sam Gibbons of Tampa, a Democrat, was only a bit more forgiving: "I do believe that Dart ought to be allowed to live with his family. But I also think he should pay his taxes in order to do so."[20] In 1996

Congress passed legislation to restrict somewhat such tax avoidance opportunities.

The emergence and maturation of global financial markets increases the likelihood that the tax systems of the developed countries will tend to look more and more alike. In the late 1980s, many European and other nations rushed to imitate the income tax rate reductions of our 1986 Tax Reform Act. This presented striking evidence of the tendency of different countries' tax systems to converge. The internationalization of the world economy has made it far more difficult for the United States, or any other country for that matter, to enact a tax system radically different from those in place elsewhere in the world. In today's worldwide economy, we can no longer look solely to our own navels to answer questions of tax policy.

As Chapter 13 tells, the greatest disparity between this nation's tax system and those of our trading partners is their greater reliance on consumption taxes. The OECD countries, on average, collect nearly one-third of their tax revenues from consumption taxes, and over the past thirty years consumption taxes have more than doubled in these nations as a percentage of gross domestic product.[21] The convergence of nations' tax policies clearly points the United States toward increased taxation of consumption, perhaps as I suggest here, as a substitute for a large part of the income tax.

But the unique consumption tax proposals that seem to be the most viable politically in the United States raise new problems of their own. In today's world, capital moves much more rapidly than government policies can respond. The difficulties this causes, the inability to "go it alone" in tax policy, create serious problems for proponents of both the flat tax and the Nunn-Domenici "USA" tax, two novel, untried, and untested tax regimes. Both of these proposals, for example, would make the United States a tax haven for foreign capital, because we would no longer tax income earned by foreigners. It would be folly, however, to count on our trading partners to sit idly by watching their nation's capital move to the United States. At a minimum, we should expect them to revise their tax laws to make sure that their corporations and residents will not enjoy disproportionate tax advantages by investing in the United

States rather than at home. This can be done rather easily by adopting a foreign tax credit system such as we and a number of other countries now have. Other nations might also move aggressively to tax income in their countries owned by U.S. corporations and residents. On the other hand, they might join the tax haven game by attempting to make capital investments in their countries even more attractive than we do, but, given their levels of taxes and public spending and the makeup of their tax systems, this does not seem a very likely alternative.

Neither the flat tax nor the Nunn-Domenici USA consumption tax is easily conformed to the practice prevalent in the world of taxing only consumption within the nation's borders. There are currently more than 100 countries with value-added taxes in place and virtually all of them tax consumption within their nation's borders by taxing imports and exempting exports. The flat tax exempts imports and taxes exports, directly contrary to the prevalent world practice. As Chapter 14 tells, this also presents an enormous domestic political hurdle to enactment of the tax. The USA tax would tax consumption by U.S. citizens and residents anywhere in the world. It would be unthinkable under that tax to allow a deduction for consumption abroad similar to the deduction allowed for savings. Moreover, there is no practical way to collect the personal-level USA tax on consumption in the United States by foreign residents, something that a standard form of value-added or retail sales tax accomplishes routinely. Finally, the size and scope of international trade are important factors in making the subtraction-method value-added tax advanced for businesses under both the flat tax and the USA tax more difficult to collect than the credit-method VATs used in Europe and elsewhere.

For all of these reasons, I would urge that the consumption tax enacted by the United States be a credit-method value-added tax of the sort commonly in place elsewhere in the world. One great advantage of the proposal I have advanced here—a 10–15 percent value-added tax, a 20–25 percent individual income tax applicable only to people with incomes in excess of $75,000 to $100,000, and a 20–25 percent corporate income tax—is that this system conforms to our own ethical standards for fairness in taxation without varying drastically from tax systems in place elsewhere in the world.

Conclusion

The proposal for a major restructuring of the federal tax system that I have offered here responds to the problems of the existing income tax and puts in place a tax system that is both fair and conducive to economic growth. For the vast majority of Americans the 10–15 percent value-added tax would completely replace the income tax. They would not be required to file any tax returns and would never have to deal with the IRS. Their savings would be completely tax-free. Income tax penalties for marriage would disappear. Replacing the earned-income tax credit with a Social Security tax exemption would eliminate the need for the working poor to file tax returns simply to claim the credit. People engaged in illegal activities who now also evade income taxes would pay taxes on their purchases of goods and services.

Retaining an income tax with a 20–25 percent tax rate schedule for families with incomes above about $75,000 to $100,000 would ensure that tax reform not become an occasion for shifting the tax burden away from high-income families to the middle class. I have described in this chapter ways to make this low-rate income tax limited to upper-income families much simpler and more conducive to savings than current law. A greatly simplified income tax should apply to small businesses to ease their compliance burdens. The opportunity this tax restructuring presents to reduce the corporate tax rate to 20–25 percent would help American businesses to become more competitive in the world economy. This kind of tax system demonstrates that it is possible for U.S. tax policy to be simpler to comply with and to advance economic growth without abandoning this nation's long-standing commitment to tax fairness.

Whatever combination of taxes we choose, we cannot allow the restructuring of our tax system to become an occasion for exploding national deficits. To do so would undermine the opportunity of such a change to increase national savings and, in turn, to expand national output and wealth. In addition to savings by businesses and families, the government plays an important role in determining the aggregate level of savings. Total national savings generally consist of the portion of income that is not consumed by either households or the government. One of the key benefits of reducing or eliminating government deficits is to curb government dissaving. Much of the impetus for replacing the income tax with some form of consumption tax is the view that a consumption tax will be more friendly to savings. It is crucially important that such a shift not serve to reduce substantially total government revenues since increasing federal deficits would tend to offset any benefits of increased private savings.

16

Seeking Protection
from the Politicians

People who want a major restruc-
turing of the nation's tax law confront a serious dilemma. Assume
(heroically) success, a transformation of the current tax law into a
simple, fair, even pristine, revenue-raising mechanism. How will we
keep it that way?

Today, public polls serve as the guide to policymaking; special-
interest money is the 800-pound gorilla of the tax legislative
process; and politicians with political courage are an endangered
species. Every proponent of the flat tax, for example, insists that it
will cut everyone's taxes, yet lose no revenue or increase the deficit.
Promising a tax cut for all is the political currency of the tax reform
movement. In such circumstances we would indeed have to be
Pollyanna to expect our politicians to resist pressures either from
the public for broad incentives, such as for homeownership, or

from narrower interests for special tax breaks, such as for oil drilling or ethanol in automotive fuels. What will prevent a new assortment—or even the old assortment—of incentives, special privileges, and loopholes from reappearing?

Congressman Dick Armey and his allies claim that protection from future political tinkering lies in a flat tax rate. They insist that a flat tax with few or no deductions and exclusions would be a stable tax law. They claim that to raise or lower taxes for one person or company, Congress would have to raise or lower taxes for all. The *Wall Street Journal* agrees: "If all taxpayers pay a single rate, a higher rate is an increase for all. The decisive advantage of the flat tax is that politicians will no longer be able to divide and conquer."[1] Dick Armey claims that the flat tax would have a "chilling effect on the lobbying industry and transform the entire political culture in Washington."[2] Steve Forbes echoes this sentiment by claiming that moving to a flat tax would so fortify Congress that it would thereafter resist all pleas from special interests for narrowly targeted tax breaks.

This is palpable nonsense. There is nothing in a flat tax that would prevent a future Congress from adding a special tax break for drilling for oil, spending money on research, building low-income housing, rehabilitating historic structures, giving works of art to a museum, or even buying a house. What guarantees that once a flat rate always a flat rate? What is to prevent Congress, for example, from enacting a 10 percent surtax on people who earn more than $250,000? There is one of those in current law.

Bill Archer, the chairman of the House Ways and Means Committee, is far closer to truth when he insists that repeal of the Sixteenth Amendment of the Constitution—the amendment that authorizes an income tax—should be part of any move to replace the income tax with a consumption tax. And it is far from clear that even repeal of the Sixteenth Amendment would offer sufficient protection. The Constitution grants Congress broad taxing powers even without that clause. The corporate income tax, for example, was upheld as an excise tax on doing business in corporate form before the Sixteenth Amendment became law.

But Congressman Archer's suggestion to marry tax reform

and fundamental or even constitutional political change strikes an important chord. Bill Archer recognizes that the current tax reform movement has coalesced two political impulses, linking a desire to reform, or perhaps even remove, the federal income tax with an urge to reform our political process. As I have demonstrated in prior chapters, much of the public's anger with the current income tax is rooted in the tax law itself, but the anti-tax movement is also spurred by deep public disappointment, even antipathy, for the political process that produces this law. The public is searching, therefore, not only for new tax policies to replace those that they believe to have failed, but also for new mechanisms to limit congressional discretion. The American people no longer believe, if they ever did, that what a politician says today—or even the laws Congress makes today—will guide tomorrow's conduct. Today taxes are cut, tomorrow they will rise. Today we rip the income tax out by its roots, tomorrow it blossoms again.

The desire to limit political discretion lies at the heart of proposed new limits on the political process. This is what explains public acclaim for a balanced budget amendment, why people applaud term limits for senators and representatives, why Bill Archer wants to repeal the Sixteenth Amendment, why Bob Dole and Dick Armey want to require more than a 50 percent majority vote in the Congress to change the tax laws.

In our political system, there are four strategies for inhibiting congressional discretion. First, although the framers wisely made it difficult to do so, we can amend the Constitution either to declare certain substantive legislation out of bounds or to provide procedural safeguards. Indeed, our Constitution contains both kinds of provisions: the substantive limitations in Article 9, Section 4, on "capitation" or "other direct" taxes and the Sixteenth Amendment permitting the taxation of income; and the procedural limitation of Article 1, Section 7, that "[a]ll Bills for raising Revenue shall originate in the House of Representatives." Second, the judicial branch, in interpreting the Constitution, particularly the Supreme Court, can strike down legislation as unconstitutional, thereby limiting congressional discretion. Third, one Congress can pass legislation that is designed to constrain actions of future Congresses, such as the Gramm-Rudman Act and the Budget Acts of 1990 and 1993. Finally, Congress can revise its rules for considering or enacting legislation; examples include the Senate's 60-vote requirement to stop a filibuster or to add certain amendments to budget legislation.

However, none of these limitations on congressional action is problem free. The essential difficulty with such ideas is their tension with the nation's constitutional structure for governance. The Constitution provides that the legislative function must be performed by a Congress whose membership changes frequently. The entire House of Representatives and one-third of the Senate must stand for election every two years. The legislative function in our majoritarian system of government is designed to be responsive to changes in the tastes and composition of the voting public as well as to variations in the nation's economic or social circumstances. The typical public complaint is about the difficulty of change, about legislative inertia enshrining the status quo. If we really want to adopt procedures to make it more difficult to change the tax law, we should be sure we have the tax law we really want to keep. If we are going to empower a minority to block future changes, we'd better like what we've got. We should not fall into the trap of believing that restructuring the tax law or the procedures for changing the tax law will rid us of the pathologies of our political system.

The Constitution Stops Where the Internal Revenue Code Begins

In the states, the tax limitation movement frequently took the form of an amendment to the state constitution. Proposition 13, for example, changed the California constitution to limit the ability of local governments to raise property taxes and to require a two-thirds majority in the state legislature to raise certain others. Eight other states changed their constitutions in connection with tax limitation measures, with four requiring specific voter approval to override tax limitations, and the others requiring a two-thirds majority vote by the state legislature. On April 15, 1996, 243 members of the House of Representatives—not enough—voted for a constitutional amendment to require a two-thirds majority in both chambers of Congress on legislation to raise revenue. The process for constitutional change at the federal level is much more cumbersome than in the states. As the long but ineffective efforts to add a balanced budget amendment or a line item veto to the nation's constitution show, we should hesitate to rely on constitutional amendments to remedy defects in our lawmaking process.

Nor will the courts protect us from the whims of our elected politicians. Since the end of the nineteenth century, constitutional constraints on the legislative process for writing tax legislation first eroded, then disappeared. For all practical purposes, the Constitution now stops where the tax law begins.

Constitutional challenges to tax rules are common. For example, tax increases due to inflation and the income tax penalties on marital status have been challenged as unconstitutional. Before Congress acted to restrict income tax increases due to bracket creep, a number of taxpayers mounted constitutional challenges to the imposition of the inflation penalty. For example, Brad Warren claimed that the "inflation tax" was unconstitutional "taxation without representation" because its tax increase was never enacted by the Congress and signed into law by the president. Mr. Warren and others also contended that all paper money (Federal Reserve notes) should be valued relative to gold, rather than by their face value. Both arguments were rejected by all the courts that heard such contentions.[3]

A somewhat more creative claim was advanced by Arthur Causland, who deducted on his tax return an "inflation loss." The Tax Court, which heard his case, did not deny that inflation had reduced Arthur's purchasing power and, at the same time, had pushed him into a higher tax bracket. The court offered the following non sequitur as its basis for disallowing the deduction he claimed: "No deduction is available for a loss in the purchasing power of the United States dollar. The inflation loss claimed by petitioners is in the nature of a purely economic loss."[4]

Both the marriage penalty and the additional tax on being single also have been challenged as contrary to the Constitution. Vivien Kellems mounted a constitutional attack on the income tax

THE DECLINE (AND FALL?) OF THE INCOME TAX

rate schedules, challenging the validity of the additional taxes paid by single people because the income-splitting benefits of joint returns were permitted only to married couples. In her case, the Tax Court determined that the constitutional issue "hangs on . . . whether this court 'perceives' a rational basis for the distinction drawn between married and single persons for purposes of the applicable rates of taxation."[5] The Tax Court found such a rational basis "since it is conceivable Congress believed that married persons generally have greater financial burdens than single persons," although the court emphasized that the constitutionality of the statute did not require any finding that Congress actually had held such a belief.[6] This, of course, was lucky for the IRS lawyer, since she would have had difficulty demonstrating that Congress held this belief and also had enacted a tax penalty on certain married couples.

On the other side of this issue, a married couple, James and Joan Druker, challenged the constitutional validity of the marriage penalty. James, who was a federal prosecutor, went to great lengths to ensure that his constitutional attack on the marriage penalty would not threaten his law enforcement job or result in any serious civil or criminal penalties. He simply wanted the courts to take seriously the Supreme Court's characterization of the right to marry as a fundamental right protected by the U.S. Constitution.[7] James met with several IRS intelligence agents and, based on their advice, he attached to both his and his wife's tax returns a letter informing the IRS that he was married but nevertheless was calculating his tax under the single person's rate schedule in order to challenge the constitutional validity of the marriage penalty. In an effort to dot every *i* and cross every *t*, James, following a suggestion of the IRS intelligence officers, provided his wife's Social Security number for cross-reference with the letter attached to his return and included his Social Security number in a similar letter attached to Joan's return. As James summed up his behavior at their Tax Court trial: "In short, I have made every effort that I could to act in good faith at this time and to avoid any sort of concealment of our marital status from the Internal Revenue Service."[8]

James learned in the very opening moments of his Tax Court

trial that his constitutional challenge was an uphill struggle. Just minutes after he had taken his seat in the courtroom, the Tax Court judge, Theodore Tannenwald, Jr., admonished him: "You know perfectly well that the marriage penalty is constitutional." When Druker countered that neither the court of appeals nor the Supreme Court had "yet faced this question," the judge responded: "Be my guest."[9] Needless to add, the Tax Court used very few words in dismissing the Drukers' constitutional arguments.

On appeal, the United States Court of Appeals for the Second Circuit (which sits in New York City) took the Drukers' constitutional claims more seriously. Ultimately, however, that court, in an opinion by one of its most respected judges, Henry Friendly, also held that the United States Constitution accorded the Drukers no protection against the marriage penalty. Judge Friendly insisted that the marriage penalty did not "absolutely prevent" anyone from getting married, nor did it place any "direct legal obstacle in the path of persons desiring to get married." He added that it was "altogether absurd to suppose Congress had any invidious intent to discourage or penalize marriage—an estate enjoyed by the majority of its members."[10] Tax accidents happen, and that Congress does not fix them for decades apparently is of no constitutional moment.

The appellate court then added insult to injury. It prevented the Drukers from refiling a joint return as a married couple, thus imposing on them the even higher taxes that resulted from the rate schedule applicable to married couples filing separately. Then, as a bit of frosting, the court imposed an additional 5 percent penalty on both James's and Joan's returns for "intentional disregard of rules and regulations." The Tax Court had rejected the IRS's efforts to apply this penalty, believing that the Drukers should "not be penalized for seeking to litigate this issue." But although the court of appeals agreed with the Tax Court that there was nothing "furtive or fraudulent" in the Drukers' behavior, it concluded that the penalties nevertheless applied. Given the amount of money they had to pay, Judge Friendly's exegesis about the seriousness of the Drukers' constitutional claim offered them little comfort.

As my last piece of evidence to confirm the futility of constitutional challenges to the tax law, I offer the lawsuits complaining that the 1982 Tax Act violated mandatory constitutional procedures. The framers of the Constitution gave primacy in tax matters to the House of Representatives, the legislative body supposedly closest to the people. The Constitution contains an "origination clause" (Article I, Section 7, Clause 1), which states: "All Bills for raising Revenue shall originate in the House of Representatives; but the Senate may propose or concur with amendments as on other Bills."

The House of Representatives in 1982 had passed a very minor piece of tax legislation that, in less than twenty-five pages of statutory language, would have lowered revenues by about $1 billion over the subsequent five-year period. When this legislation got to the Senate, its entire substance was deleted, and it was replaced with more than 600 pages of statutory amendments to the Internal Revenue Code that were estimated to raise almost $100 billion during the next three years. The Senate amendment was accepted virtually intact by a House-Senate conference. The conference agreement was then passed by both chambers of Congress and signed into law by President Reagan.

Several disgruntled taxpayers challenged the constitutional validity of this legislation on the ground that, since the House bill would have reduced revenues, this measure to raise revenues originated in the Senate in violation of the Constitution's origination clause. Several courts of appeals heard these cases, and all easily found them without merit and upheld the legislation. Since these disputes had not even produced a difference of opinion in the lower courts, the Supreme Court refused to take a case, thereby ending the matter.

This episode, in effect, renders the origination clause a nullity, with no practical significance whatsoever. As law professor Boris Bittker put it:

> To be sure, the House can prevent the Senate from taking any action on taxation by refraining from originating *any* tax legislation; but even if the Senate were allowed to originate a tax bill, it could not become law

without House concurrence, so it hardly matters which chamber acts first. Since it takes two to tango, what difference does it make whose foot first touches the ballroom floor?[11]

The only difference is that the Constitution says that bills for raising revenue must originate in the House.

A variety of constitutional hurdles stymied tax legislation prior to the adoption of the Sixteenth Amendment in 1913, and resolution of constitutional issues remained critical in the very early days of the income tax. But, with the exception of one now archaic case dealing with the taxation of stock dividends, constitutional challenges to the income tax statute have all failed. After the constitutional validity of the income tax was settled by the ratification of the Sixteenth Amendment in 1913, the authority of the Congress in the field of taxation has not been seriously challenged.

But this is not the way it has to be. In Germany the constitutional court struck down an income tax penalty on marriage as an unconstitutional violation of the constitutional provision providing that marriage and the family must enjoy the "special protection" of the state. The German courts also held that a tax exemption for an amount that provides a minimal standard of living was constitutionally compelled. In contrast, by a vote of 7 men to 2 women the Canadian Supreme Court held that no allowance for child-care expenses was constitutionally required.[12]

The tax system of Germany has not collapsed because of judicial meddling. Here the United States Supreme Court routinely tells our state governments how the federal Constitution limits their taxing powers. But no constitutional revival is likely to restrict congressional power over the federal tax law. In principle, the Supreme Court could limit Congress's ability to ignore constitutionally mandated procedures for writing tax laws, prohibit it from departing from fundamental constitutional values, and stop it from preferring particular taxpayers when there is no rational basis for disfavoring others similarly situated. These are traditional judicial functions. Congress has no constitutional mandate other than to act in the public's interest. But, given our long history of judicial deference to congressional discretion even when serious constitutional challenges have been mustered, it would be myopic to look to the courts to protect the long-term integrity or stability of tax reform.

Can Congress
Limit Its Own Discretion?

Proposition 13 made sure that a vote of two-thirds of the California legislature was necessary to raise taxes, but Proposition 13 changed the California constitution, and constitutional change is not likely to happen at the federal level. Rather than requiring constitutional amendment, virtually every proposal for major restructuring of the federal tax code attempts to legislate greater stability into the tax law through some new requirement limiting the ability of Congress to change course by a simple majority vote.

In January 1995, on the first day of the new Congress, the new House Republican majority changed the rules of the House of Representatives to require a 60 percent majority to adopt any increase in income tax rates. Obviously this change was intended to make raising taxes more difficult, and in 1995 and 1996 the House voted several times to waive the requirement in order to pass legislation. Congressman Dick Armey's flat-tax proposal would require a similar 60 percent supermajority of both the House and Senate to raise tax rates, to create multiple tax rates, to lower family allowances, or to create a tax loophole (whatever that may mean). Bob Dole proposed a similar supermajority requirement to raise tax rates.

Congressman Richard Gephardt, the leader of House Democrats, has also gotten the message. His tax reform proposal would require a national referendum to increase tax rates, thus proposing for the nation the kind of public approval that his home state of Missouri requires for state tax rate increases. Gephardt said that requiring a national referendum would "end the temptation to start raising tax rates by doling out loopholes." However, a requirement for public approval of congressional tax legislation would be unprecedented at the federal level, and not something Congress seems likely to embrace.

The history of legislative limitations on the discretion of Congress is not especially promising if the goal is to restrict the flexibility of future legislators. The Gramm-Rudman budget limitations of the 1980s had only limited success in making Congress confront deficit spending and an expanding national debt. New budget limitations enacted in 1990 and 1993 have not fared much better. The congressional ceiling on the total amount of federal debt has become a bad joke, a blunt political weapon that now serves no useful purpose in limiting total federal borrowing.

The Senate's 60-vote requirement to shut off a filibuster, on the other hand, has often served to allow a Senate minority to block change, as has the Senate's so-called Byrd Rule, which requires 60 votes for certain amendments to budget legislation. A supermajority voting requirement, therefore, does have the potential to entrench the status quo and to make existing laws more stable, assuming that a simple majority of the House or Senate cannot get rid of the supermajority requirement.[13] A national referendum would raise even greater hurdles for change.

As I have indicated, an important question is whether such supermajority voting requirements are consistent with the fundamental majoritarian precepts of our political system. The very purpose of frequent elections for Congress is to permit new majorities to enact new laws. Supermajority requirements that can be eliminated by a majority vote of a subsequent Congress may turn out to be little more than window dressing. In 1996 Congress held hearings on adding such supermajority requirements to the U.S. Constitution. If the requirement of a supermajority vote is limited to tax rate increases, it may have a reasonable chance of enactment but it may also be of limited effect.

As Congressman Armey's proposal shows, determining just what laws should be subject to a supermajority restriction is a quite difficult matter. This is why, after considerable debate, House Republicans limited their 60-vote requirement in 1995 to increases in tax rates. A tax rate increase is pretty easy to spot. A supermajority voting requirement for *all* tax changes is unrealistic. Too many policy options are available, and there inevitably will be great flexibility for future Congresses to tinker with the tax law. A supermajority requirement limited to tax rate increases does not serve to inhibit much congressional mischief and may, in some circumstances, block the best course of action.

It is simply not practical in our system of government to remove congressional discretion over the tax law. Rather than looking to limit congressional action over the tax law, we should change our political culture to eliminate the tax law as a playground for special interests. A good place to begin is with our system of campaign finance. A political system is sick when changing the tax law, or threatening to change it, is the most effective way to fill the campaign coffers of members of Congress. But this is the way it is.

Diving for Dollars

If tax lawmaking is, as so many have claimed, a group contest, either for the privilege of paying the least or among conflicting ideologies, it becomes critical to know who has access to lawmakers, whose claims will be heard in the legislative process. Despite our enduring national commitment to equal power for all individuals behind the curtain of the voting booth, in the halls of Congress, money talks. And money gets listened to.

The costs of running for public office have multiplied and, as a result, fundraising has become every member of Congress's preoccupation. It now costs $5 million on average to run for the Senate in a competitive state, and the record-setting contest between Diane Feinstein and Michael Huffington in 1994 in California cost a total of $42 million, far outpacing the previous record of $24 million spent in the 1984 North Carolina Senate contest between Senator Jesse Helms and Governor James B. Hunt, Jr. A race for the House of Representatives can easily cost $1 million or more. In 1994 a total of $720 million was spent on House and Senate races, compared to less than $200 million in 1978. (It is not hard to think of better uses for that kind of money.) Adjusted for inflation, congressional campaign expenditures in 1992 were more than twice as great in real terms as twenty years earlier. As Jesse Unruh, one of California's premier politicians, was fond of saying, "Money is the mother's milk of politics." Each year, more and more political milk is consumed.

Under campaign finance laws, while maximum contributions of individuals and corporations are limited in amount, political action committees (PACs) may spend unlimited amounts on behalf of candidates they favor. In 1972 they contributed $8.5 million to House and Senate candidates; twenty years later in 1992 they contributed more than twenty times that much, more than one-third of all Senate campaign funds and more than one-fifth of all House campaign contributions. The number of PACs grew from 608 in 1974 to 4,600 in 1992; corporate PACs increased from 89 to 1,900 during that period.[14] A good committee assignment coupled with a "good voting record" is a magnet for donations. No committee assignment is better than the Ways and Means or Finance Committee.

In the decade from 1980 to 1990, Ways and Means Committee Chairman Dan Rostenkowski received $1.7 million in speaking fees or honoraria from businesses and organizations with an interest in tax legislation.[15] In 1991–1992 Bob Packwood received $3.3 million in contributions from PACs and individuals contributing the maximum allowable under the law; John Breaux, who received $2,225,000, finished second. Dan Rostenkowski received $1.3 million, only a few hundred thousand less than in the entire decade of the 1980s.[16] This is how fundraising has expanded.

The new breed of freshman House Republicans elected in 1994 did nothing to change fundraising business as usual. They raised a total of $5 million from special-interest PACs in the first six months after taking office. Representatives Jon Christensen of Nebraska and John Ensign of Nevada both found their positions on Ways and Means to be the path to gold. Congressman Ensign raised $600,000 in 1995, half from PACs, and Mr. Christensen raised $670,000 in 1995, $266,000 from PACs. House Republicans even maintain a "report card" of "friendly" or "unfriendly" corporate donors used to rate lobbyists who seek access to the House Republican leaders.[17]

PACs, which now have enormous influence over the direction of campaign funding, seem to have become similarly influential in guiding policy decisions.[18] Unsurprisingly, important contributors and fundraisers now have great influence in the legislative process. Their point of view is always heard by key members of Congress.

Perhaps it was coincidence that Seagrams Company, which received a $40 million tax break in 1986, had paid speaking fees to three Ways and Means and five Senate Finance committee members. Perhaps it was coincidence that eleven insurance companies, which had contributed more than $33,000 to Rostenkowski, shared, along with four other companies, in a $119 million "transition" rule in the 1986 legislation.[19] Perhaps it is coincidence that the Ways and Means Committee holds an annual "members day," where narrow tax legislation, usually targeted for certain contributors to and constituents of committee members, is taken up. Perhaps, but I don't think so.

This is not the place to describe or evaluate the various campaign finance reforms that have been floated in recent years. Personally, I am attracted to ideas like Bruce Ackerman's suggestion that campaigns should be financed only from credit cards or vouchers that are distributed in equal amounts to the voting public. He calls this "red-white-and-blue money" and would treat the use of "greenbacks" to contribute to political campaigns "as a form of corruption similar to the use of greenbacks to buy votes."[20] But there are serious questions about the constitutional validity of such an idea in light of previous Supreme Court campaign finance decisions. And given Congress's reluctance to root out the pathologies of current campaign finance laws, there is little reason to expect this sort of legislation anytime soon. Perhaps only when the momentum of the term limits movement seems unstoppable will Congress turn seriously to campaign finance reform as a less threatening alternative. Something must be done.

As a nice counterpoint to the vast sums of money contributed to members of the tax-writing committees of Congress, consider the following comments concerning the retirement of George Lefcoe from the Los Angeles County Regional Planning Commission:

> He did say that a mistake might have been that he re- tired before, and not after, Christmas. "I really missed the cards from engineers I never met, the wine and cheese from development companies I never heard of and, es- pecially, the Honey baked ham from, of all places, Forest Lawn [a well-known Los Angeles mortuary and ceme- tery], even though the company was never an applicant before the commission when I was there," Lefcoe said.
>
> "But because I miss them is why I think it was a good idea I resigned," he added. "I do not think it is wise to stay in public office for too long a time."
>
> Lefcoe used the ham from Forest Lawn as an illus- tration:
>
> "My first Christmas as a commissioner—when I re- ceived the ham—I tried to return it at once, though for the record, I did not because no one at Forest Lawn seemed authorized to accept hams, apparently not even for burial. My guess is that no one of the many public ser- vants who received the hams ever had tried to return it," said Lefcoe.
>
> "When I received another ham the next Christmas, I gave it to a worthy charity," Lefcoe recalled. "The next year, some worthy friends were having a party, so I gave it to them. The next year I had a party and we enjoyed the ham.
>
> "In the fifth year, about the 10th of December," said Lefcoe, "I began wondering, where is my ham? Why is it late?"
>
> Lefcoe sighed and laughed. "So much for the se- duction of public officials. It was then I thought it was time to retire though it took me two more hams and three years to finally do it."[21]

George Lefcoe's hams from Forest Lawn are nothing compared to the amount of pork members of Congress routinely receive and dispense, but Lefcoe understood even the hams to be corrupting. If they can't reform the process, more members of Congress should follow George Lefcoe's example.

Notes

1: Introduction

1. Richard Goode. "Overview of the U.S. Tax System," in *The Promise of Tax Reform,* ed. Joseph Pechman (Englewood Cliffs, N.J.: Prentice-Hall, 1985).
2. "Bob Dole's Speech in Chicago Outlining His Economic and Tax Plans," *New York Times,* August 6, 1996, p. A14.
3. Dirk Johnson, "Voices from the Grass Roots: Anger Over Partisan Politics," *New York Times,* August 27, 1994, p. A1.
4. Quoted in Bruce Wgr, "A New Tune: Freedom Not to Pay Taxes," *New York Times,* July 5, 1995, p. D8.
5. Quoted in Jeffrey L. Yablon, "As Certain as Death—Quotations about Taxes," *Tax Notes,* 69 (December 25, 1995): 1665.
6. Quoted in Phil Kuntz, "A Day in Washington Is Just Another Day to Raise Moe Dollars," *Wall Street Journal,* October 23, 1995, p. A1.
7. Quoted in Myra Navarro, "Lawmakers Face Elderly on Medicare," *New York Times,* October 23, 1995, p. B8.
8. See Michael J. Graetz, "Paint-By-Numbers Tax Lawmaking," *Columbia Law Review,* 95 (1995): 609.
9. William Safire, "The 25% Solution," *New York Times,* April 20, 1995, p. A23.

10. Editorial, "Reform for the Millennium," *Wall Street Journal,* January 4, 1996, p. A10.
11. Sidney Ratner, *Taxation and Democracy in America* (New York: Octagon Books, 1980), p. 18.
12. Samuel Eliot Morrison, *Oxford History of the United States* (New York: Oxford University Press, 1927), p. 182. The history in this section is taken from Michael J. Graetz and Deborah H. Schenk, *Federal Income Taxation: Principles and Policies,* 3d ed. (New York: Foundation Press, 1995), pp. 4–14.
13. *Springer v. United States,* 102 U.S. 586 (1880).
14. *Pollack v. Farmers' Loan & Trust Co.,* 158 U.S. 601 (1895).
15. *Brushaber v. Union Pacific Railroad,* 240 U.S. 1 (1916).
16. The figures in the text describe only debt owed to the public and not debt owed within the government, such as to the Social Security Trust Fund.
17. Alan J. Auerbach, *The U.S. Fiscal Problem: Where We Are, How We Got There, and Where We're Going* (Cambridge, Mass.: The National Bureau of Economic Research, 1994).
18. Congressional Budget Office, *Reducing the Deficit: Spending and Revenue Options* (Washington, D.C.: Government Printing Office, August 1996); see also Perry D. Quick and Thomas Neubig, "Tax Burden Comparison: U.S. v. the Rest of the G7," *Tax Notes,* 65 (December 14, 1994): 1409.
19. T.S. Adams, quoted in Ratner, *Taxation and Democracy,* p. 14.
20. Charles Kingson, "The Coherence of International Taxation," *Columbia Law Review,* 81 (1981): 1151.

2: It's a Sin to Get a Mexican Divorce

1. Daniel R. Feenberg and Harvey Rosen, "Recent Developments in the Marriage Tax," *National Tax Journal,* 48 (1995): 91.
2. Ibid.
3. *Congressional Record,* 80th Cong., 1st Sess., Vol. 93, pp. 5837–5840 (May 27, 1947).
4. Randolph E. Paul, *Taxation in the United States* (Boston: Little, Brown & Co., 1954), p. 275.
5. House Committee on Ways and Means, *Tax Treatment of Single Persons and Married Persons Where Both Spouses Are Working,* 92nd Cong., 2nd Sess., April 10, 1972.
6. This was demonstrated mathematically by Edwin S. Cohen, assistant secretary of the Treasury for tax policy, in 1972 testimony before the House Ways and Means Committee:

    Case 1 is a single person who earns $20,000.
    Case 2, two single persons each earn $10,000.
    Case 3, a husband earns $20,000 and a wife earns zero.
    Case 4, a husband and wife each earn $10,000.

    If we want no penalty on remaining single—and a large group insists upon this—Case 1 must pay the same tax as Case 3. A single person earning $20,000 pays the same tax as a married couple earning $20,000.

If we want no penalty on marrying, Case 2 must pay the same tax as Case 4. Two single persons earning $10,000 each pay the same tax as a married couple each earning $10,000.

If we want husband and wife to pay the same tax however they contribute to the family earnings, Case 3 pays the same tax as Case 4.

To summarize the tax results:

Case 1 equals Case 3.

Case 2 equals Case 4.

Case 3 equals Case 4.

Based on the fundamental mathematical principle that things equal to the same thing must be equal to each other, the result should then be that Case 1 equals Case 2, or, in other words, that the tax on a single person earning $20,000 equals the tax on two single persons each earning $10,000.

But that cannot be so if we are going to have a progressive income tax structure, and progressive taxation is a basic tenet of our income tax system. The tax on a single person earning $20,000—Case 1—must be greater than the total tax on two single persons each earning $10,000 if we are to have a progressive rate structure. . . .

It becomes apparent from this analysis that you cannot have each of these principles operating simultaneously, and that there is no one principle of equity that covers all of these cases. No algebraic equation, no matter how sophisticated, can solve this dilemma. . . . All that we can hope for is a reasonable compromise.

Hearings on Tax Treatment of Single Persons and Married Persons where Both Spouses are Working, before the House Ways and Means Committee, 92nd Cong., 2nd Sess. (1972).

7. Ibid.

8. Boris Bittker, "Federal Income Taxation and the Family," in *Collected Legal Essays*, ed. Boris Bittker (Littleton, Colorado: Fred B. Rothman & Co., 1989), p. 397.

9. Lawrence Malong, "America's Middle Class," *U.S. News & World Report*, March 30, 1981, p. 39.

10. These examples are from the testimony of Anne L. Alstott during the House Ways and Means Committee Hearings, Tax Provisions in the Contract with America Designed to Strengthen the American Family, January 17, 1995. The EITC in some cases creates an incentive for marrying, but at this end of the income scale a childless low-income worker generally has to marry a low-income nonworker with children for the marriage incentive to be significant. For example, if two workers each earning $5,000 and having one child marry, their combined EITC increases from $3,400 to $3,650, but if a childless worker earning $10,000 a year marries a nonworker with two children, the couple's EITC rises from zero to $3,650.

11. The precise amount of wealth necessary to produce $15,000 of after-tax income each year depends generally on prevailing rates of interest.

12. A few single people probably even took the advice offered to them by the usually dull publication *Tax Advisor,* and adopted their adult friend. As the *Tax*

Advisor put it: "In this case, head of household filing status could be selected with one adult taxpayer serving as the 'parent.' " *Tax Advisor,* April 19, 1995.

13. Transcript of *Boyter v. I.R.S.,* Tax Court case, p. 16.
14. Ibid., p. 18.
15. Ibid., attachment.
16. Internal Revenue Code, §143(a).
17. Bruce Olson, "Protesters Say Tax Reform Is Still Unfair to Married Workers," United Press International, October 8, 1981, B.C. Cycle.
18. *Boyter v. Commissioner,* 668 F.2d 1382 (1981), and lower court opinion in 74 T.C. 989 (1980).
19. "Divorced, and $18,000 Richer," *Washington Post,* February 3, 1981, p. B5.
20. Richard Haitch, "Tax Split," *New York Times,* February 15, 1981, Part 2, p. 49, col. 5.
21. Private Letter Ruling 78-35-076, 6/1/78.
22. Senate Finance Committee, Subcommittee on Taxation and Debt Management Generally, *Hearing on §.336, §.1247 and §.1877,* August 5, 1980, p. 187.
23. House Committee on Ways and Means, *Tax Treatment of Married, Head of Household, and Single Taxpayers,* 96th Cong., 2nd Sess., April 2, 1980, p. 164.
24. Richard Cohen, "There's No Justice in a Marriage Tax," *Washington Post,* November 11, 1979, p. D1.
25. House Committee, *Tax Treatment of Married, Head of Household, and Single Taxpayers,* p. 164.
26. Ibid.
27. In 1981 Congress reduced the marriage penalty somewhat for two-earner couples by allowing a special deduction of 15 percent of the earnings of the lesser-earning spouse. This provision was repealed in 1986.
28. Senate Finance Committee, Subcommittee on Taxation and Debt Management Generally, *Hearing on §.336, §.1247 and §.1877,* August 5, 1980, p. 186.

3: Chasing Chinchilla Coats
and Other Tax Shelter Aerobics

1. Address by Commissioner Egger, "New Directions in Tax Shelters," *Daily Tax Report,* Bureau of National Affairs, #210, p. J4; October 30, 1981.
2. Roscoe L. Egger, "The I.R.S. versus the Tax Shelter," *Best Review,* October 1985, p. 78.
3. Egger, "The I.R.S. versus the Tax Shelter"; Roscoe L. Egger, Address to a Meeting of the American Institute of Certified Public Accountants, October 4, 1983.
4. Senate Committee on Finance, *The Flat Rate Tax,* 96th Cong., 2nd Sess., September 12, 1982, p. 245 (testimony of Louis Harris, chairman and chief executive officer, Louis Harris and Associates).
5. Joint Committee on Taxation, *Pamphlet on Tax Shelters and Other Tax-Motivated Transactions,* February 17, 1983.
6. "CIA Director Testifies in Tax Court about Challenged Deductions," *Tax Notes Today,* July 9, 1984.
7. See Tom Furlong, "Grand Design of Wheeler-Dealer: John Galanis Thought Big—Now He's Accused of a Mammoth Scam," *Los Angeles Times,* July 12,

1987, Part 4, p. 1; James Bates, "Nearly 400 Claim Fraud in Tax Shelter Plan," *Los Angeles Times,* November 4, 1987, Part 4, p. 16. See also Frederick Unge-heuer, "Pied Piper to the Truly Rich: The U.S. Cracks Down on a Tax-Shelter Scheme," *Time,* April 6, 1987, p. 52.

8. *Mager v. Commissioner,* 47 T.C.M. (CCH) 1651 (1984); T.C. Memo 1984-211 (1984).

9. Frank Goss is quoted in Susan Dentzer, "How Americans Beat the Tax Man," *Newsweek,* April 16, 1984, p. 56.

10. *Congressional Record,* 98th Cong., 2nd Sess., 1984, 4:5599.

11. House Ways and Means Committee, *General Tax Reform,* 93rd Cong., 1st Sess., 1973, 886–887 (testimony of Martin Ginsburg).

12. *West v. Commissioner,* 88 T.C. 152 (1987).

13. Revenue Ruling 80-69, 1980–1 C.B. 55; *Chui v. Commissioner,* 84 T.C. 722 (1985).

14. See the complaint of the U.S. Justice Department in the District Court for the Western District of Pennsylvania against Australia Mining, reprinted in *Tax Notes Today,* December 31, 1984 (Doc. 84-8417).

15. The phrase is from GAO Deputy Director Werner Grosshans in February 28, 1983, testimony to the House Ways and Means Subcommittee on Oversight reported in Jonathan Berry Foreman, "Tax Consideration in Renting a Navy," *Tax Notes,* March 25, 1985.

16. Letter Ruling 8510032, reported in *Tax Notes,* March 18, 1985, pp. 1102–1103.

17. Quote by an unidentified aide in Thomas Edsall, "Efforts Fail to Control Tax Shelters," *Washington Post,* November 6, 1983.

18. Steve Kindel and Mark Gilbert, "The Beast that Ate Hollywood," *Financial World,* April 7, 1987, p. 26.

19. Susan Dentzer, "How Americans Beat the Tax Man," *Newsweek,* April 16, 1984, p. 56.

4: Disappearing Dollars

1. Robert D. Hershey, Jr., "Indexing Personal Income Tax," *New York Times,* January 11, 1983, p. D1.

2. "Economy Cuts Dollar's Purchasing Power in Half over 12 Years, Board Reports," *Bureau of National Affairs Daily Report,* May 24, 1982, p. A5.

3. C. W. Bastable and Steven L. Fogg, "Indexation: Will Taxpayers Get Its Benefits?" *Journal of Accounting,* 153 (January 1982): 56.

4. Bradly Graham, "Dole Pushes Legislation for Indexing Tax Rates," *Washington Post,* August 21, 1979, p. D6.

5. Thomas Humbert, "Tax Indexing: At Last, a Break for the Little Guy," The Heritage Foundation, March 22, 1983. Indeed, by 1980, the average marginal tax rate was 30 percent, compared to 25 percent during the Korean War and 21 percent in 1965, after President Kennedy's tax cut. Robert Barro and Chaiput Sahasakul, quoted in David Frances, "Reagan's Supply Side Experiment May Have Just Begun," *Christian Science Monitor,* July 25, 1983, p. 11.

6. The income referred to in the text is "adjusted gross income," which is taxable income plus personal exemptions and other itemized deductions or the standard deduction.

7. The 1983 Joint Economic Report on the February 1983 Economic Report of the President, Joint Economic Committee, March 3, 1983, describing estimates of the Joint Committee on Taxation.
8. Quoted in Floyd K. Haskell, "Retain Tax Indexing," *New York Times*, March 4, 1984, p. 21.
9. David A. Stockman, *The Triumph of Politics: The Inside Story of the Reagan Revolution* (New York: Harper & Row, 1986), p. 275.
10. Ibid. See also Richard Goode, "Lessons from Seven Decades of Income Taxation," in *Options for Tax Reform*, ed. Joseph A. Pechman (Washington, D.C.: Brookings Institution, 1984), pp. 13, 18–19.
11. The Congressional Budget Office, in February 1995, estimated that repeal of indexing would produce more than $150 billion over the next five-year period, and a similar estimate for the five-year period 1991–1995 was used by the Congress during consideration of the 1990 Budget Act. Such estimates, of course, are highly dependent on the rate of inflation assumed, but the 1995 Congressional Budget Office estimate assumes only an average annual rate of inflation of 3.3 percent. Timothy B. Clark, "Campaign Debate Over Tax Indexing Could Spill Over to 1985 Congress," *National Journal*, October 6, 1984, p. 1865. The Congressional Budget Office estimated in 1984 that if tax indexing were repealed, total tax revenues would have been $160 billion greater in total by 1989.
12. Reed Shuldiner, "Indexing the Tax Code," *Tax Law Review*, 48 (1993): 537, 544.
13. Likewise, capital losses are allowed to be used against only $3,000 of ordinary income, a dollar amount legislated in 1969. Inflation that has occurred since the provision first became effective in 1970 would have raised that amount to more than $12,000 had the $3,000 limitation been indexed. Ibid. Despite Congress's concerns with liberalizing the treatment of capital gains to stimulate investments, proposals to index this amount have been unsuccessful.
14. A more comprehensive list can be found in Shuldiner, "Indexing the Tax Code," p. 545, Notes 24, 26, 27.
15. Alan J. Auerbach, "The Corporation Income Tax," in *The Promise of Tax Reform*, ed. Joseph A. Pechman (Washington, D.C.: Brookings Institution, 1985), p. 69.
16. Ibid.
17. See C. Eugene Steuerle, "Tax Arbitrage, Inflation and the Taxation of Interest Payments and Receipts," *Wayne Law Review*, 30 (1984): 991.
18. C. Eugene Steuerle, *Taxes, Loans and Inflation: How the Nation's Wealth Becomes Misallocated* (Washington, D.C.: Brookings Institution, 1985), p. 56.
19. This example comes from C. Eugene Steuerle, *The Tax Decade: How Taxes Came to Dominate the Public Agenda* (Washington, D.C.: Urban Institute, 1992), p. 33.
20. Emil M. Sunley and Randall D. Weiss, "The Revenue Estimating Process," *American Journal of Tax Policy*, 11, (1992): 261, 283–284.
21. Department of the Treasury, *Integration of Individual and Corporate Tax Systems* (January 1992), p. 10. The data in the text are for nonfinancial business corporations.
22. For examples of common transactions, see Peter C. Canellos, "The Over-Leveraged Acquisition," *Tax Lawyer*, 39 (1985): 91.
23. Department of the Treasury, *Integration of Individual and Corporate Tax Systems*

(January 1992), p. 10. The data in the text are for nonfinancial business corporations.

24. The only comprehensive non-academic proposal for structural indexing of the tax law was advanced in a set of tax reform proposals released by the Treasury Department in 1984. Although other of Treasury's proposals formed the basis of President Reagan's March 1985 tax reform proposals that ultimately led to the 1986 Tax Reform Act, the indexing proposals were dropped from President Reagan's final suggestions.

25. For a criticism of the use of five-year revenue numbers in the legislative process, see Michael J. Graetz, "Paint-by-Numbers Tax Lawmaking," *Columbia Law Review,* 95 (1995): 609.

5: Dad Is Not at
the Dining Room Table Anymore

1. Internal Revenue Code, §179.
2. Boris I. Bittker and Lawrence Lokken, *Federal Taxation of Income, Estates and Gifts,* 2nd ed. (Boston, Mass.: Warren, Gorham & Lamont, 1990), p. 35–37.
3. *Harsaghy v. Commissioner,* 2 T.C. 484 (1943).
4. *Nelson v. Commissioner,* 25 T.C.M. (CCH) 1142 (1966).
5. *Pevsner v. Commissioner,* 628 F.2d 467 (5th Cir. 1980).
6. *Steiner v. Commissioner,* 524 F.2d 640 (10th Cir. 1975).
7. *International Artists, Ltd., v. Commissioner,* 55 T.C. 94 (1970). Both the Liberace story and the Nelsons' story are told in Cathy M. Kristof, "Truth or Dare? It's a Fine Line between Legal Tax Avoidance and Larceny," *Los Angeles Times,* February 26, 1995, p. D1.
8. *Bodzin v. Commissioner,* 60 T.C. 820 (1973); *rev'd* 509 F.2d 679 (4th Cir., 1975), *cert. denied* 423 U.S. 825 (1975).
9. *Commissioner v. Soliman,* 113 S.Ct. 701 (1992).
10. Internal Revenue Code, §280A.
11. Dean M. Maki, "Household Debt and the Tax Reform Act of 1986," C.E.P.R. Policy Paper No. 436 (Stanford University, November 1995).
12. Detailed discussions of interest deductibility can be found in Cheryl D. Block, "Trouble with Interest: Reflections on Interest Deductions after the Tax Reform Act of 1986," *University of Florida Law Review,* 40 (1988): 631, 689–754, and Curtis Jay Berger, "Simple Interest and Complex Taxes," *Columbia Law Review,* 81 (1981): 217.
13. Internal Revenue Code §3121(b)(7) and (x).
14. David Cay Johnston, "IRS Inquiry: Is Worker at I.B.M. Really a Contractor?" *New York Times,* July 6, 1995, p. D3.
15. A detailed history of H & R Block can be found in Brian Settle, "Behind the 17 Reasons: Bloch's Road to Success," *Business First—Buffalo,* January 20, 1986, p. 26.
16. David Hallerman, "Sitting Down with a Tax Expert: Your Computer," *New York Times,* March 2, 1995, p. C6.
17. See Greg Anrig, Jr., "The Pros Flunk Our New Tax Test," *Money,* March 1989, p. 110.

18. Edwin S. Cohen, *A Lawyer's Life: Deep in the Heart of Taxes* (Arlington, Va.: Tax Analysts, 1994).
19. G. E. Holmes, "Is It Not Time to Simplify the Income Tax," *Bulletin of the National Tax Association,* 11 (1926): 195, quoted in Boris I. Bittker, "James S. Eustice," *Tax Law Review,* 45 (1990): 1, 3.

6: Have We Become
a Nation of Tax Cheaters?

1. Bill Clinton's assistant secretary for tax policy, Leslie Samuels, in May 1995 told the American Bar Association that the U.S. "voluntary tax system" is the envy of the world, reprinted in *Tax Notes,* May 29, 1995, p. 1137.
2. Quoted in Michael J. Graetz, "Can the Income Tax Continue to Be the Major Revenue Source?," in *Options for Tax Reform,* ed. A. Pechman (Washington, D.C.: Brookings Institution, 1984), pp. 59–60.
3. Tom Herman, "Tax Report," *Wall Street Journal,* June 14, 1995, p. 1.
4. The Egger quotations are from "The Tax System How Fair? The Payers How Honest?" *New York Times,* March 4, 1984, p. 38.
5. IRS commissioner Egger said that 75,000 additional revenue agents could be added to the IRS before their additional costs equaled the additional revenue they would produce (*Tax Notes,* September 2, 1985, p. 1048). April 29, 1985, marked something of a low point, when the General Accounting Office (GAO) told Congress that the IRS needed a larger budget than it was willing to ask for. GAO emphasized that IRS personnel had increased less than 3 percent in the decade 1976–1986, while tax-return filings had increased 46 percent, a 25 percent increase for individuals alone (*Tax Notes,* May 6, 1985, p. 570).
6. See House Committee on Ways and Means, *Hearing to Consider Tax Compliance Act of 1982 and Related Legislation,* 97th Cong., 2d Sess., p. 14. (Capital gains is second largest category of unreported income.)
7. James S. Henry, "Noncompliance with U.S. Tax Law: Evidence in Size, Growth, and Composition," in *Income Tax Compliance,* ed. P. Savitchi (Chicago: American Bar Association, 1983), p. 17.
8. Internal Revenue Service, *Individual Tax Gap Estimates for 1985, 1988, and 1992* (Pub. No. 1415, April 1, 1996).
9. Ibid.
10. Janet Novak, "You Know Who You Are, and So Do We," *Forbes,* April 11, 1984, p. 88.
11. Jeffrey A. Dubin, Michael J. Graetz, and Louis L. Wilde, "The Changing Face of Tax Enforcement, 1978–1988," *Tax Lawyer,* 43 (1990): 893.
12. Internal Revenue Code, §§6111, 6112, 6707, 6708, and 7408.
13. Internal Revenue Code, §§6651, 6652, 6676, 6678, 6686, and 6701.
14. Internal Revenue Code, §§6041A, 6050E, 6053(c), 6059, 6678, 6706, 6708, 7201, 7203, 7305, 7206, and 7207.
15. Internal Revenue Code, §6622. See also §§6601, 6660, and 7205; §§6111, 6112, 6621(d), 6700, 6707, 6708, and 7408; §§3406, 6045, 6050E, 6050H, 6050I, 6050J, 6050K, and 6693.

Notes

16. Jeffrey A. Dubin, Michael J. Graetz, and Louis L. Wilde, "The Changing Face of Tax Enforcement, 1978–1988," *Tax Lawyer,* 43 (1990): 893.
17. For 1992, the IRS estimated it collected $3.1 billion from document matching and $5.2 billion from audits of individual tax returns. IRS Pub. No. 1415, April 1, 1996.
18. Jim Newton, "Electronic Filing Scams Are Taxing Resources of the IRS," *Los Angeles Times,* April 12, 1994.
19. David Cay Johnston, "IRS Scrutiny Forces Delays in Some Refunds," *New York Times,* May 30, 1995, p. D1.
20. Lee A. Shepard, "The IRS and Civil Disobedience," *Tax Notes,* March 4, 1985.
21. United States Justice Department, *Manual on Tax Protesters,* July 1994, §40.14.
22. Paul W. Valentine, "Police Sergeant Guilty in Scheme to Reduce Taxes," *Washington Post,* September 12, 1984, p. C1.
23. Ellen Cates, "U.S. Attorney: Church was a Tax Dodge for 700 Cops," United Press International, June 25, 1994.
24. Don Van Natta, Jr., "11 Officers are Accused of Failure to Pay Taxes," *New York Times,* July 17, 1996, p. B3.
25. Don Van Natta, Jr., "600 Are Suspected in Plot to Evade Taxes on Income," *New York Times,* July 18, 1996, p. A1.
26. Warren Richey, "Man Charged with Using IRS to Discredit Enemies," *Fort Lauderdale Sun Sentinel,* December 29, 1994, p. 4B.
27. United States Justice Department, *Manual on Tax Protesters,* July 1994, §40.14.
28. David Cay Johnston, "The Anti-Tax Man Cometh," *New York Times,* July 5, 1995, p. D1.
29. Theresa Tritch and Mary L. Sprouse, "*Money* Audits the Clintons," *Money,* April 1994, p. 84.
30. Staff of U.S. Joint Committee of Internal Revenue Taxation, *Examination of President Nixon's Tax Returns for 1969 through 1972* (Washington, D.C.: Government Printing Office, 1974).
31. Internal Revenue Service, *Individual Tax Gap for 1985, 1988, and 1992* (Pub. No. 1415, April 1, 1996).
32. This notion stems, at least in part, from the basic cost-benefit calculation that underreporting produces lesser benefits at lower rates of tax. Where criminal fraud penalties are not applicable, however, lower tax rates will also reduce the costs of underreporting, since these are always a percentage of the tax due and the cost-benefit calculation will remain unchanged. When government auditing and collections are included as a factor in the tax compliance calculus, lowering rates might even suggest greater, rather than lesser, noncompliance. Michael J. Graetz and Louis L. Wilde, "The Decision by Strategic Nonfilers to Participate in Income Tax Amnesties," *International Review of Law and Economics,* 13 (1993): 271.

7: A Visit to the Sausage Factory

1. See John F. Witte, *The Politics and Development of the Federal Income Tax* (Madison: University of Wisconsin Press, 1985), p. 166.
2. Much of the description of the tax legislative process during this period is

taken from Michael J. Graetz, "Reflections on the Tax Legislative Process: Prelude to Reform," *Virginia Law Review,* 58 (1972): 1389.

3. Joseph Kraft, "Power to Destroy," *Washington Post,* December 7, 1969.

4. Elizabeth Drew, *Politics and Money: The New Road to Corruption* (New York: Macmillan, 1983), p. 66.

5. Rosina B. Barker and Jasper L. Cummings, Jr., "Interview with the Honorable Dan Rostenkowski," *ABA Section of Taxation Newsletter,* Winter 1996, p. 12.

8: Rosie Scenario
Becomes the Belle of the Ball

1. C. Eugene Steurle, *The Tax Decade* (Washington, D.C.: Urban Institute, 1991).

2. Phil Gramm, *This Week with David Brinkley,* September 16, 1990.

3. Elizabeth Drew, *Politics and Money: The New Road to Corruption* (New York: Macmillan, 1983), p. 92.

4. Ibid., p. 92.

5. Ibid., pp. 40–46.

6. Timothy B. Clark, "Selling Tax Breaks—If Both Parties Benefit, Then Why Is Congress Unhappy?" *National Journal,* 13 (December 19, 1981): 2238.

7. William Safire, *Safire's New Political Dictionary* (New York: Random House, 1993), p. 672.

8. For an excellent description of how the 1986 Tax Reform Act made it through Congress, see Jeffrey H. Birnbaum and Alan S. Murray, *Showdown at Gucci Gulch: Lawmakers, Lobbyists, and the Unlikely Triumph of Tax Reform* (New York: Random House, 1987). See also Joseph Minarik, "How Tax Reform Came About," *Tax Notes,* 37 (December 12, 1987): 1359.

9. Ronald Reagan, "Encroaching Control: Keep Government Poor and Remain Free," *Vital Speeches of the Day,* 27 (1961): 677, quoted in Marvin A. Chirelstein, "Back from the Dead: How President Reagan Saved the Income Tax," *Florida State University Law Review,* 14 (1986): 207.

10. Rosina B. Barker and Jasper L. Cummings, Jr., "Interview with the Honorable Dan Rostenkowski," *ABA Section of Taxation Newsletter,* Winter 1996, p. 12.

11. Birnbaum and Murray, *Showdown at Gucci Gulch,* p. 161.

12. Ibid., pp. 204–233.

13. Minarik, "How Tax Reform Came About," p. 1359.

14. Joel Slemrod, "The Economic Impact of the Tax Reform Act of 1986," in *Do Taxes Matter?,* ed. Joel Slemrod, (Cambridge, Mass.: MIT Press, 1990).

15. *Tax Reform Act of 1986,* §1608.

16. Internal Revenue Code, §170(m).

17. Ibid., §512 (b)(15).

18. Birnbaum and Murray, *Showdown at Gucci Gulch,* pp. 146–147.

19. Ibid., pp. 240–243.

9: The Madness of Two Georges

1. "Bush, Republicans Agree to Postpone Capital Gains Plan to Get Clean Budget Bill," Bureau of National Affairs, *Daily Tax Report,* November 3, 1989, p. G3.

Notes

2. Gerald E. Auten and Joseph J. Cordes, "Policy Watch: Cutting Capital Gains Taxes," *Journal of Economic Perspectives,* 5 (1991): 181, 187.

3. Lee A. Sheppard, "Equity Swaps: The Other Shoe Drops," *Tax Notes,* 67 (May 8, 1995): 721.

4. Floyd Norris, "For Wall Street, A New Tax Break," *New York Times,* March 29, 1994, p. D1.

5. Michael Kinsley, "The GOP's Tax Scam," *New Republic,* December 12, 1994, p. 16.

6. George R. Zodrow, "Economic Analysis of Capital Gains Taxation: Realizations, Revenues, Efficiency and Equity," *Tax Law Review,* 48 (1993): 419, 476–477.

7. James M. Poterba, "Capital Gains Tax Policy Toward Entrepreneurship," *National Tax Journal,* 42 (1989): 375.

8. Zodrow, "Economic Analysis of Capital Gains Taxation: Realizations, Revenues, Efficiency and Equity," pp. 419, 469.

9. Charles A. Cooper, Michael A. Carvin, and Vincent J. Colatriano, "The Legal Authority of the Department of the Treasury to Promulgate a Regulation for Indexation of Capital Gains," Memorandum for Dr. Lawrence A. Hunter, National Chamber Foundation, Washington, D.C., August 17, 1992.

10: Sin Looks Pretty Good
When the Alternative Is Taxes

1. Cedric T. Sandford, *Successful Tax Reform: Lessons from Analysis of Tax Reform* (Bath, U.K.: Bath Fiscal Institute, 1993); Ken Messere, "Taxation in Ten Industrialized Countries Over the Last Decade: An Overview," *Tax Notes International,* 11 (August 21, 1995): 512.

2. Christopher Ruhm, "Alcohol Policies and Highway Vehicle Fatalities," *NBER Working Paper,* January 1996, p. 5195.

3. These data come from Congressional Budget Office, *Federal Taxation of Tobacco, Alcohol Beverages, and Motor Fuels,* August 1990.

4. Ibid. See also Congressional Budget Office, *Reducing the Deficit: Spending and Revenue Options* (Washington, D.C.: Government Printing Office, August 1996).

5. Michael Wines, "Republicans Push for Repeal of Gas Tax," *New York Times,* May 1, 1996, p. A16.

6. *Imus in the Morning,* May 7, 1996.

7. Messere, "Taxation in Ten Industrialized Countries," p. 532, *n.* 16.

8. Congressional Budget Office, *Reducing the Deficit: Spending and Revenue Options,* February 1995, pp. 401–402.

11: Read My Hips

1. These events were recounted in numerous newspaper accounts, the best of which is William Rectenwald, "Insurance Forum Turns Catastrophic for Rostenkowski," *Chicago Tribune,* August 18, 1989, p. 1.

2. Reischauer testimony to the Joint Economic Committee, July 11, 1990, based on Congressional Budget Office's *Economic and Budget Outlook: An Update* (1990).

3. "Putting the T Back in the Budget," *Economist,* June 30, 1990, p. 27.

4. Tom Kenworthy, "Rep. Gingrich Steps Back onto Political Highwire," *Washington Post,* October 3, 1990, p. A8.

5. Dan Goodgame, "Read My Hips," *Time,* October 22, 1990, p. 26; Richard Morin and Paul Taylor, "Polls Show Plunge in Public Confidence," *Washington Post,* October 16, 1990, p. A1.

6. John Yang, "How Budget Cutters Worked Up a $60,000 Appetite," *Washington Post,* January 23, 1991, p. A15.

7. Ann Devroy, "Breaking Tax Pledge a Mistake Bush Says," *Washington Post,* March 4, 1992, p. A1; Andrew Rosenthal, "Bush Says Raising Taxes Was His Biggest Mistake," *New York Times,* March 4, 1992, p. A1.

8. "President Needle," *New York Times,* March 5, 1992, p. A26; "Flip, Flop, . . . Flip?" *Washington Post,* March 5, 1992, p. A20.

9. I am dealing here only with debt owed to the public and not debt owed within the government, such as the Social Security Trust Fund.

10. See, e.g., J. Bradford DeLong and Lawrence Summers, "Equipment Investment and Economic Growth: How Strong Is the Nexus?," *Brookings Papers on Economic Activity,* 2 (1992): 157; cf. Jane G. Gravelle, *Tax Subsidies for Investment: Issues and Proposals,* Congressional Research Service, No. 92-2055, February 21, 1992.

12. Just the Facts, Ma'am

1. Michael J. Graetz, "Paint-by-Numbers Tax Lawmaking," *Columbia Law Review,* 95 (1993): 609, 642. See also Congressional Budget Office, *The Incidence of the Corporate Income Tax* (Washington, D.C.: Government Printing Office, March 1996).

2. This story is told in Charles E. McLure, Jr., and George R. Zodrow, "The Study and Practice of Income Tax Policy," in *Modern Public Finance,* ed. John M. Quigley and Eugene Smolensky (Cambridge, Mass.: Harvard University Press 1994), pp. 173–176. The Hausman study is Jerry A. Hausman, "Labor Supply," in *How Taxes Affect Economic Behavior,* ed. Henry J. Aaron and Joseph A. Pechman (Washington, D.C.: Brookings Institution, 1981).

3. McLure and Zodrow, "The Study and Practice of Income Tax Policy," p. 177.

4. Don Fullerton, "Comments," in *Modern Public Finance,* p. 87.

5. In 1983, for example, Robert A. Stranger, who published the *Stranger Review* (which previously had been called the *Tax Shelter Review*), estimated that public offerings of tax shelters in such things as real estate, cattle, and the movies would total more than $8 billion in 1983, compared to $4.2 billion in 1982. Mr. Stranger estimated that probably another $6 billion would be raised privately for tax shelter deals, but other experts put this number as high as $25 billion.

6. Herbert Stein, "Will a Tax Cut Help Dole?" *New York Times,* July 31, 1996, p. A15.

7. A. B. Atkinson, *Public Economics in Action: The Basic Income/Flat Tax Proposal* (Oxford: Oxford University Press, 1995), p. 155.

8. Wassily Leontief, Presidential Address to the American Economics Association,

December 29, 1970, in *Essays in Economics* (1985), reprinted as "Theoretical Assumptions and Non-Observable Facts." See also his "Academic Economics," *Science,* July 9, 1982, p. xii, where he stated: "Year after year economic theorists continue to produce scores of mathematical models and to explore in great detail their formal properties; and the econometricians fit algebraic functions of all possible shapes to essentially the same sets of data without being able to advance, in any perceptible way, a systematic understanding of the structure and operation of a real economy."

9. McLure and Zodrow, "The Study and Practice of Income Tax Policy," p. 203.
10. Letter to Laura Tyson, chair of the Counsel of Economic Advisors, from Senator Daniel Patrick Moynihan, July 28, 1993, reprinted in Daniel Patrick Moynihan, "Congress Builds Its Coffin," *New York Review of Books,* January 11, 1996, p. 34.
11. T. S. Adams, "Ideals and Idealism in Taxation," *American Economic Review,* 18 (1928): 12.
12. Louis Eisenstein, *The Ideologies of Taxation* (New York: Ronald Press, 1961), p. iii.
13. Ibid., p. iii.
14. Ibid., pp. 12–13.
15. Ibid., pp. 13–14.
16. Douglas Adams, *The Hitchhiker's Guide to the Galaxy* (New York: Harmony Books, 1979), pp. 179–180.
17. See *Omnibus Budget Reconciliation Act 1993,* §13201 (making provisions retroactive) and §13201(d) (allowing payment in installments).
18. See Michael J. Graetz, "Tax Policy at the Beginning of the Clinton Administration," *Yale Journal of Regulation,* 10 (1993): 561, 569 (illustrating the tax penalty on marriage for high-income taxpayers); see also Anne L. Alstott, "The Earned Income Tax Credit and the Limitations on Tax-Based Welfare Reform," *Harvard Law Review,* 108 (1995): 533, 559–564 (demonstrating the tax penalty inherent in the earned-income tax credit).
19. See *Federal Register,* 35 (1970): 19114–19115.
20. *Uruguay Round Agreements Act,* Public Law 465, 103rd Cong., 2nd Sess. (1994) §712.

13: Taxing What You Spend
Instead of What You Make

1. Bernard D. Reams, Jr. (ed.), *United States Revenue Acts, 1909–1950: The Laws, Legislative Histories and Administrative Documents,* Vol. 1 (Buffalo, N.Y.: William S. Hain & Co., 1979). *Internal Revenue Hearings Before the Committee on Finance of the U.S. Senate—The Proposed Revenue Act of 1921,* 67th Cong., 1st Sess., May 9–27, 1921, testimony of Chester A. Jordan, public accountant of Portland, Maine, p. 487:

Before the law came into effect I had three or four men in my employ. Since being obliged to undertake all of these problems for my clients I am obliged to employ seven or eight men and two or three women. Those men are college graduates and they are employed about six

months of the year on tax work. I believe that if the tax law were simplified as it should be I might not be obliged to employ more than half
that number.

2. Reams, *United States Revenue Acts, 1909–1950,* Vol. 1, "Internal Revenue Hearings Before the Committee on Ways and Means of the U.S. House of Representatives," July 26–29, 1921, pp. 144, 153.

3. *Report of the Secretary of the Treasury,* 1942, p. 92–95, 408–421.

4. Frank V. Fowles, "Administration Leans to Value-Added Tax to Help Solve National Fiscal Crisis," *National Journal,* 6 (1972): 210.

5. Congressional Budget Office, *Reducing the Deficit: Spending and Revenue Options*
(Washington, D.C.: Government Printing Office, August 1966), p. 16. See also
Committee on Fiscal Affairs, Directorate for Financial, Fiscal and Enterprise
Affairs, Organization for Economic Co-operation and Development, "The
Taxation of Profits in a Global Economy: An Overview of the Main Issues"
(1992), p. 34; Joint Committee on Taxation, Committee on Ways and Means,
U.S. House of Representatives, "Factors Affecting the International Compet-
itiveness of the United States," 102nd Cong., 2nd Sess., May 30, 1992, p. 321.

6. Ibid., and Joint Committee on Taxation, House Committee on Ways and
Means, "Factors Affecting the International Competitiveness of the United
States," 102nd Cong., 2nd Sess., May 30, 1992, p. 321.

7. There is considerable dispute in the literature as to how much of the disparity of wealth holdings is explained by life-cycle savings. See, e.g., A. B. Atkinson, *The Economics of Inequality,* (2nd ed. Oxford; Clarendon Press, 1983), pp.
76–77.

8. Norman Daniels, *Am I My Parents' Keeper?: An Essay on Justice between the Young
and Old* (New York: Oxford University Press, 1988), p. 41.

9. See Thomas A. Barthold, "How Should We Measure Distribution," *National Tax
Journal,* 46 (1993): 29, 192.

10. Herbert Stein, "Regarding Henry. . . ," *Wall Street Journal,* January 30, 1996, p.
A18.

11. Joel Slemrod, "What Makes Some Consumption Taxes So Simple and Others
So Complicated?" (presented at the Conference on Fundamental Tax Reform, Stanford University, California, December 1995), p. 3.

12. Vito Tanzi, *Taxation in an Integrating World* (Washington, D.C.: Brookings Institution, 1992).

13. Congressional Budget Office, *Effects of Adopting a Value-Added Tax* (1992);
Slemrod, "What Makes Some Consumption Taxes So Simple," p. 7.

14. Joint Committee on Taxation, House Committee on Ways and Means, "Factors Affecting the International Competitiveness of the United States," 102nd
Cong., 2nd Sess., May 30, 1992, p. 50.

15. Ibid., p. 32.

16. U.S. Treasury Department, *Report on Integration of the Individual and Corporate
Tax Systems: Taxing Business Income Once* (1992), p. 5.

17. See, for example, Alan J. Auerbach and Laurence J. Kotlikoff, "Demogra-
phies, Fiscal Policy and U.S. Savings," in *Tax Policy and the Economy,* ed. L. Summers (1990).

18. Alan Auerbach, "Tax Reform Capital Allocation, Efficiency and Growth"

(1995); Ronald A. Pearlman, *Transition Issues in Moving to a Consumption Tax: A Tax Lawyer's Perspective*" (Washington, D.C.: Brookings Institution, 1996).

19. Michael J. Boskin, "A Framework for the Tax Reform Debate," in *Frontiers of Tax Reform* (Stanford, Calif.: Hoover Institution Press, 1996), p. 24; William Gale, Speech to the National Commission on Economic Growth and Tax Reform, July 26, 1995, Washington, D.C.
20. "Information Technology Industry Could Be Hurt by Flat Tax, USA Tax, Survey Shows," *BNA Daily Tax Report,* February 15, 1996, p. G5.
21. Edwin S. Cohen, *A Lawyer's Life: Deep in the Heart of Taxes* (Arlington, Va.: Tax Analysts), pp. 438–439.
22. W. C. Hazlitt, *English Proverbs and Proverbial Phrases* (London: J. R. Smith, 1869), p. 366.

14: The Flat Tax, the "USA" Tax, and Other Uncommon Consumption Taxes

1. Alvin C. Warren, Jr., "The Proposal for an 'Unlimited Savings Allowance'," Tax Notes, 28 August 1995.
2. Algebraically, $t(s-p)=ts-tp$.
3. Recent international studies demonstrate sizable costs to businesses of complying with any credit-method value-added tax, particularly for small businesses. See, e.g., Cedric Sandford and John Hasseldine, *The Compliance Costs of Business Taxes in New Zealand* (1992).
4. David Bradford, "What Are Consumption Taxes and Who Pays Them?," *Tax Notes,* April 18, 1988, p. 383; Charles E. McLure and George Zodrow, "A Hybrid Approach to Direct Taxation of Consumption," *Tax Notes,* December 5, 1995.
5. Robert Hall and Alvin Robushka, *The Flat Tax,* 2nd ed. (Stanford, Calif: Hoover Institution Press, 1995), p. 55.
6. Ibid.
7. Moreover, once a married couple's exemption level is exceeded, a flat rate of tax ensures that a married woman's tax rate will not vary with the level of her husband's income. Finally, it accomplishes these goals without reintroducing into the tax law any disparity based on where people live; the tax would be the same whether the state has a community-property law or not.
8. A Brookings Institution study found that the distribution of income among U.S. families remained virtually unchanged between 1950 and 1970 despite the progressive income tax. See Joseph A. Pechman and Benjamin A. Okner, *Who Bears the Tax Burden?* (Washington, D.C.: Brookings Institution, 1974).
9. The material that follows is adapted from Michael J. Graetz, "To Praise the Estate Tax, Not to Bury It," *Yale Law Journal,* 93 (1983): 259.
10. Charles O. Galvin and Boris I. Bittker, *The Income Tax: How Progressive Should It Be?,* (Washington, D.C.: American Enterprise Institute, 1969), pp. 56–58, 31.
11. I have never been able to locate the source of this quote, despite having offered a prize for anyone who could. See "To Praise the Estate Tax, Not to Bury It," p. 278, Note 115.
12. William Safire, "The 25% Solution," *New York Times,* April 20, 1995, p. A23.

13. Martin Ginsburg, "Life Under a Personal Consumption Tax: Some Thoughts on Working, Saving and Consuming in Nunn-Domenici's Tax World," *National Tax Journal,* 48 (December 1995): 585.
14. See, e.g., U.S. Congress, Joint Committee on Taxation, *Estimate of Federal Tax Expenditures for Fiscal Years 1988–1997* (Washington, D.C.: Government Printing Office, April 24, 1992).
15. Ibid.
16. See Richard K. Green, Patrick H. Hendershott, and Dennis R. Capozza, "Taxes, Mortgage Borrowing and House Prices," paper prepared for Brookings Conference on the Economic Effects of Fundamental Tax Reform, Washington, D.C., February 15–16, 1996.
17. "A Flat Tax: Is It a Threat to Retirees' Security?", *New York Times,* July 9, 1995, p. F5.
18. Robert E. Heitzman and the American Academy of Actuaries, Report on Consumption Taxes and Pensions, quoted in *BNA Pension and Benefits Reporter,* January 22, 1996, p. 278.
19. Transcript of Senate Finance Committee Hearings on Flat Tax Proposals, May 18, 1995, p. 29.

15: Back to the Future

1. See Congressional Budget Office, *Baby Boomers in Retirement: An Early Perspective,* Ch. 2 (1996), and Edward I. Wolff, *Top Heavy: A Study of Increasing Inequality of Wealth in America* (New York: Twentieth Century Fund, 1995).
2. Roberta Kirwan, "Why Seniors Don't Marry," *Money,* July 1995.
3. See, for example, Lawrence Summers and Christopher Carroll, "Why Is U.S. National Saving So Low?", *Brookings Papers on Economic Activity,* 18 (1987): 2, and Alan J. Auerbach and Laurence J. Kotlikoff, "Demographics, Fiscal Policy and U.S. Savings," in *Tax Policy and the Economy,* ed. L. Summers (Cambridge, Mass.: MIT Press, 1990), pp. 73–101.
4. J. Gokhale and J. Sabelhaus, "Understanding Postwar Decline," in *U.S. Saving: A Cohort Analysis,* Brookings Paper in Economic Activities, 1996; Laurence J. Kotlikoff, *Generational Accounting* (New York: Free Press, 1992).
5. See, e.g., Martin Feldstein, "Would Privatizing Social Security Raise Economic Welfare?," NBER Working Paper No. 5281 (1995).
6. See, e.g., The World Bank, *Averting the Old Age Crisis* (Washington, D.C.: The World Bank, 1995).
7. "Would Privatizing Social Security Raise Economic Welfare," pp. 22–23. (The present value of the actuarially estimated liabilities due current workers and retirees minus the present value of Social Security taxes they would pay.)
8. American Institute of Certified Public Accountants Tax Division, *Flat Taxes and Consumption Taxes: A Guide to the Debate* (New York: AICPA, 1995).
9. Congressional Budget Office, *Effects of Adopting a Value-Added Tax* (1992).
10. These returns accounted for 31 percent of total adjusted gross income.
11. In practice, of course, things are not so simple. For example, an exemption of returns at $75,000 and below, with either the current regular tax, a 21 percent flat-tax rate, or the current alternative minimum tax applicable to peo-

ple above that level, would produce unacceptably high marginal rate cliffs that would need to be ameliorated through phaseouts, and some mechanisms would be necessary to provide equivalent relief to the nearly 6 million people who claimed earned-income tax credits in 1993. An exemption from some level of Social Security taxes could serve this purpose well.

12. The number of people is greater than the number of tax returns because of the many returns, particularly joint returns of married people, that include more than one person's income.

13. If the tax inducement at the 20 percent rate proved too low, mandatory pensions or additional government subsidies might be needed.

14. The estate tax applies only to the wealthiest 1 percent of people who die in any year. Michael Graetz, "To Praise the Estate Tax, Not to Bury It," *Yale Law Journal*, 93 (1983): 259.

15. Edward N. Wolff, *Top Heavy: A Study of the Increasing Inequality of Wealth in America* (New York: Twentieth Century Fund, 1995).

16. Ibid., p. 43.

17. Edward J. McCaffery, "The Uneasy Case for Wealth Transfer Taxation," *Yale Law Journal*, 104 (1994): 283.

18. The session was led by Caroline S. McCaffery, of a large New York law firm; Program for the Thirtieth Annual Phillip E. Heckerling Institute on Estate Planning, University of Miami School of Law.

19. Karen DeWitt, "Exile's Effort to Return Puts Focus on Tax Loophole," *New York Times*, October 1, 1995, p. 14.

20. Karen DeWitt, "Expatriate Avoiding Huge Tax Bill Tries Loophole For Return," *New York Times*, October 3, 1995, p. 5A.

21. Ken Messere, "Taxation in Ten Industrialized Countries in the Last Decade: An Overview," *Tax Notes International*, 11 (August 21, 1995): 512.

16: Seeking Protection from the Politicians

1. "The Flat Tax: Why Not?" *Wall Street Journal*, January 3, 1996, p. A18.

2. Dick Armey, "How Taxes Corrupt," *Wall Street Journal*, June 19, 1996, p. A20.

3. See, for example, *Warren v. Commissioner*, 45 T.C.M. 240 (1982); *Birkenstock v. Commissioner*, 646 F.2d 1185 (7th Cir. 1981); *Hellerman v. Commissioner*, 77 T.C. 1361 (1981).

4. *Causland v. Commissioner*, 35 T.C.M. 262 (1976).

5. *Kellems v. Commissioner*, 56 T.C. 556, 558 (1972).

6. Ibid., p. 559.

7. See, e.g., *Zablocki v. Redhail*, 434 U.S. 374 (1978).

8. *Druker v. Commissioner*, 77 T.C. 869, Transcript of proceedings, p. 7.

9. Ibid., p. 5.

10. *Druker v. Commissioner*, 697 F.2d 46. (2nd Cir. 1982), *cert.* denied 461 U.S. 957 (1983).

11. Boris I. Bittker, "Constitutional Limits on the Taxing Power of the Federal Government," *Tax Lawyer*, 41 (1987): 3, 5.

12. These examples are from Hugh Ault, "Comparative Income Taxation," forthcoming, presented at Harvard Law School, May 13 and 14, 1996.

13. This is more likely if the supermajority requirement is in the form of an amendment to the rules of the House and Senate than if contained in tax legislation itself. See Neera Tanden, "The Future Is Not Ours to Know: Supermajority Voting Requirements and Political Stability," unpublished manuscript, Yale Law School, 1996.

14. Roger H. Davidson and Walter J. Olesak, *Congress and Its Members* (Washington, D.C.: Congressional Quarterly Press, 1985), pp. 78–79.

15. David L. Bartlett and James B. Steele, *America: What Went Wrong* (Kansas City: Andrews & McMeel, 1992), pp. 193–194.

16. Larry Makinson and Joshua Goldstein, *Open Secrets: The Encyclopedia of Congressional Politics* (Washington, D.C.: Congressional Quarterly Press, 1994), pp. 112, 168.

17. Scott Shepard, "Focus on Money and Politics," *Atlanta Journal and Constitution,* December 20, 1995, p. 16A.

18. Susan B. Glasser, "Rostenkowski Locked in Critical 'Symbolic' Primary Race," *Roll Call,* February 24, 1992.

19. Ibid.

20. Bruce Ackerman, "Crediting the Voters: A New Beginning for Campaign Finance," in *The American Prospect Reader in American Politics,* ed. Walter Dean Burnham (Chatham, N.J.: Chatham House Publishing, 1995), pp. 218–231.

21. Sam Hall Kaplan, "When He Missed the Ham, He Quit," *Los Angeles Times,* January 25, 1987, Part VIII, p. 2.

Index

ability, ideology of, 183–84
accessions tax, 268
accounting, 50, 51, 195, 240, 253, 256–57
Ackerman, Bruce, 290
Adams, John, 14
Adams, T. S., 182–83
ad valorem energy tax, 156
alcohol tax, 13–14, 22–23, 150–54, 158, 159, 167, 222
Alexander, Lamar, 226, 259
Alien and Sedition Acts (1798), 14
alimony, 239
All-Savers Certificate, 125
American Academy of Actuaries, 238
American Association of Retired Persons (AARP), 115, 216

American Bar Association, 50, 51
American Petroleum Institute, 157
amnesties, 268–69
"angel of death" loophole, 144
annuities, tax-deferred, 134
Anthony, Berle, 6
anti-abuse rules, 64, 230
Archer, Bill, 4, 168, 191, 197, 201–2, 278–79
Armey, Dick, 4, 164, 191, 197, 215, 216, 217, 218, 219, 222, 226, 232–33, 234, 238, 240, 278, 279, 286, 287
Armstrong, Bill, 56–57, 65
art works, 94
assets:
    exchanges of, 94, 143–44
    government-owned, 187, 188

assets (*continued*)
  price of, 147, 199, 208, 231
  sale of, 59, 64, 143, 147, 187, 188,
    208, 214, 231, 246
  seizure of, 91–92
  transfer of, 189
Atkinson, A. B., 180
audits, tax, 5, 51, 80, 90, 92–94, 95,
    97–100, 106, 184
Auerbach, Alan, 208
Australia, 73, 201, 207
automobile industry, 76–77, 241, 247
Autotote Company, 144

Babbitt, Bruce, 136
Baird, Zoë, 78
Baker, Jim, 56–57
balanced budget amendment, 8, 18,
    188, 279
Bankers Trust Company, 143–44
banking, 62–63, 143–44, 200
bankruptcies, 63
Bank Secrecy Act (1970), 98
Barr, Joseph, 113, 262
barriers and deterrents, ideology of,
    183–84
beer, 153–54
Belize, 272
Bennett, Diane, 127
Bennington College, 46
Bentsen, Lloyd, 86, 139, 170
Bermuda, 202
Bismarck, Otto von, 115
Bittker, Boris, 284–85
Bloch, Henry, 81–82, 260
Bloch, Richard, 81–82
H & R Block, 81–82
Bodzin, Steve, 73
bonds:
  government, 235, 237–38, 254
  interest on, 134, 190, 262
  junk, 63
  municipal, 259
Boren, David, 157, 264
Boskin, Michael, 208–9
Boyter, David and Angela, 35–40, 221
bracket creep, 53–58, 61, 65–67, 91,

126, 134, 135–36, 151, 250, 266,
    281
Brady, Nicholas F., 166, 264
Breaux, John, 157, 289
BTU content, 155, 156
Buchanan, Pat, 169, 197, 226
Budget Act (1990), 136, 145, 147–48,
    151–52, 162–70, 188, 280
Budget Act (1993), 121, 145, 170–74,
    186, 188, 280
Budget Act (1995), 246, 257
Budget Enforcement Acts (1990), 117
budget summit (1990), 163–68
Budweiser, 153–54
buffalo ranches, 45
Bush, George, 18, 86, 121, 130,
    140–42, 146–48, 160, 162–70,
    171, 174, 183
business accrual accounting
    procedures, 253, 256–57
Business Council, 174
business transfer tax, 217
BusinessWeek, 4
"buy-a-tax-break" deals, 126–28
Byrd, Robert, 166
Byrd Rule, 287

California, 5, 23, 52–53, 111, 121, 122,
    280, 286
Calio, Nick, 168
campaign financing, 7, 119, 125,
    288–92
capital:
  income from, 58, 59–60, 64, 66,
    146–47, 209
  labor vs., 178, 210, 223, 224
  losses of, 58
  markets for, 203, 209, 255, 265, 271,
    272, 273–74
  venture, 142–43, 145–46
capital gains tax, 56, 59, 64, 66, 94,
    120, 140–48, 150, 165, 167,
    170, 172, 183, 189, 218, 240,
    266
Carter, Jimmy, 4, 120, 133, 141, 173
Casey, John, 2
Casey, William, 43

cash flows, 253, 256, 257
Causland, Arthur, 281
charities, 12, 46, 102, 145, 231–32, 234, 235, 238, 259, 265, 266
Charles I, King of England, 22
Cheslow, Joe, 104
child-care expenses, 58, 69, 70–71, 192, 219, 228, 259, 260, 270, 285
child support, 98, 239
chinchilla breeding, 43–45, 91
Christensen, Jon, 289
Christian Coalition, 270
cigarette tax, 150, 151–53, 158, 159, 167
Civil War, 15
Clinton, Bill, 18, 35, 104, 121, 130, 136, 144, 148, 152, 156, 157, 160, 170–74, 175, 183, 186, 242, 246, 270
clothing, work, 71–73, 228, 229
coal, 24, 155
Cohen, Edwin, 87
Cohen, Richard, 38
collectibles, 94
Common Cause, 119
common law, 30–31
Commonwealth Edison, 138
"community charge," 263
community property scheme, 30–31
commuting, 69, 74, 228, 229, 230
competition, foreign, 14, 49, 241–42, 272
computers, 8, 83, 106
Conable, Barber, 39
Conference Committee, 175
Congress, U.S.:
  legislation drafted by, 6–7, 30–34, 111–92, 203–4, 243, 279–81, 284–92
  public opinion on, 51, 67
  Republican control of, 173, 191–92, 196–97, 286
  special interests and, 7–8, 51, 115–16, 119–20, 125, 204, 277, 278, 288–92
  staff of, 117–18
  televised coverage of, 115, 175–76

Congressional Budget Office (CBO), 19, 117, 158, 178, 185, 206
Connally, John, 210
Connally, Tom, 31
Constitution, U.S., 3, 15–16, 101, 103, 146–47, 188, 210, 233–34, 262, 268, 278, 279, 280–86, 287, 290
consumer price index, 55, 251
consumers, 199–200, 202, 220
consumption tax, 195–243
  fairness of, 220–26
  implementation of, 234–43
  income tax vs., 4–5, 10, 12, 14, 112, 131, 149–59, 166–67, 169, 179, 195–243, 245, 263, 264–66, 273, 275
  products targeted by, 13–14, 22–23, 24, 41, 42, 150–59, 167, 172, 222
  on sales, 4, 14, 22, 66, 105, 155, 159, 191, 199, 200, 205–6, 210, 212, 216, 217, 218–19, 220, 221, 222, 223, 240, 258, 261–62, 264, 274
  simplification of, 205–6, 213, 226–32
  types of, 212–43
Contract with America, 148, 170, 173, 270
Coolidge, Calvin, 133, 182
Cooper, Charles, 147
corporate welfare, 126, 127
corporations:
  audits of, 95
  borrowing by, 63
  credits for, 126–28, 138–39, 171–72, 190, 235–36
  investment in, 207, 248–49
  multinational, 209, 230, 240, 261, 271
  multi-state, 199
  taxation of, 8, 10, 21, 56, 63–64, 84–85, 95, 105, 125, 133, 135, 166, 171–72, 178, 181, 182, 196, 197, 201, 208, 210, 217, 219, 221, 230, 248, 262, 264, 274, 275, 278
credit cards, 76, 247

criminal tax enforcement, 98–100
C-SPAN, 115, 175–76
currency exchange rates, 241

D'Amato, Alphonse, 238
Danforth, Jack, 264
Daniels, Norman, 203
Darman, Richard, 165–66
Dart, Kenneth, 272
debt:
  financing by, 64, 145–46
  national, 20, 49, 57–58, 124, 142,
    171, 287
  personal, 61–64, 74–77, 91–92
deductions:
  child-care, 70–71
  elimination of, 5, 131, 242
  interest, 62–63, 64, 75–77, 134
  itemized, 58, 134, 228–30
  meals and entertainment, 87, 135,
    230
  medical, 92–93
  standard, 29, 42, 56, 66, 93, 126,
    134, 213, 218, 219, 258–59, 260
  for tax shelters, 42, 44, 45, 48
  timing of, 65
  see also exemptions
defense spending, 162
Deficit Reduction Act (1990), 121
Del Monaco, Rocco, Sr., 103
DeMille, Cecil B., 33
Democratic Party, 124, 125, 130–31,
    136, 140, 141, 142, 148, 150, 151,
    165, 166, 167, 173, 174, 196, 233,
    263
dependents, 69, 77–78, 96, 103, 228
depreciation allowance, 47, 56, 60, 66,
    70, 77, 125, 230
Depression, 16
Diefenderfer, Bill, 133
diesel fuel tax, 157, 159
disabilities, 115
dividends, 126, 181, 218, 219, 240,
    248, 285
divorce, 29, 31, 35–40, 239
"Divorce for Fun and Profit" (Boyter
    and Boyter), 36

Dodge, Mrs., 190, 262
Dole, Robert, 4, 5, 20, 37, 122, 124,
    157, 166, 174, 175, 179, 191,
    197, 226, 228, 259, 269, 279,
    286
Domenici, Pete, 191, 197, 214, 215,
    217, 220, 231, 239, 252, 273
Douglas, Paul, 180
Drew, Elizabeth, 119
Drexel, Katherine, 138
Druker, James and Joan, 282–83

earned-income tax credit (EITC), 34,
    57, 66, 85–86, 118, 141, 169,
    218–19, 249, 259, 260, 265, 275
Economist, 163
economists, 180, 208, 241, 247
economy, U.S.:
  efficiency of, 11, 187, 192, 242
  foreign competition and, 14, 49,
    241–42, 272
  as market economy, 11, 223–24
  taxation and, 10, 11–12, 17, 18, 23,
    25, 134–37, 145, 167, 170,
    177–82, 187, 200, 209, 225, 234,
    236–39, 244–45, 248, 258, 259,
    268, 275
education, 198, 208, 224, 246, 247
Egger, Roscoe, 42, 90–91
Eisenstein, Louis, 183–84
elderly, 130, 160–62, 216, 250–53
Emerson, Ralph Waldo, 88
employees, domestic, 69, 78–80,
    228–29, 237
energy taxes, 24, 41, 42, 121, 150,
    154–59, 167, 172, 222, 242
Ensign, John, 289
entrepreneurs, 41
equipment, business, 41, 60, 70, 172,
    187
equity:
  home, 76, 247–48, 260
  horizontal, 185
  ideology of, 183–84
  swaps of, 143–44
estate taxes, 10, 15, 21, 96, 127–28,
    201, 267–68, 272

executives, corporate, 126, 143–44
exemptions:
dependency, 69, 77–78, 96, 103, 228
for disabilities, 115
elimination of, 228–32, 234, 235–36
personal, 5, 55–56, 58, 66, 101, 126, 204, 213, 221, 265
see also deductions
exports, 158, 200, 241, 274

false church schemes, 101–2
Family Resources Council, 270
farming, 41, 42, 95
Federal Reserve, 101, 129, 179, 180
Feinstein, Diane, 288
Feldstein, Martin, 179
Ferguson, Carr, 51
Fifth Amendment, 101
Filene, Edward A., 6
filibusters, 280
Florio, Jim, 122
Foley, Mark, 7
Foley, Tom, 168
Forbes, Steve, 4, 5, 197, 212, 215, 216, 217, 218, 219, 222, 226, 232–33, 251, 267, 278
foreign exchange rate, 182
forms, tax:
business, 206
false information on, 98–100, 102, 103
filing of, 18, 23, 96, 103, 106–7, 275
joint-return, 30, 31, 35, 282–83
preparation of, 8, 81–84, 101, 114, 260
simplification of, 213, 226, 227, 228, 229, 259–60
1040A, 259
1040EZ, 259
1098, 260
1099, 93, 100, 103, 260
understatement on, 96–97, 100, 104, 105
W-2, 74, 93, 100, 260
W-4, 103
Fortune, 4
401(k) plans, 63

Fourth Amendment, 101
Fowler, Robert F., 102
Foxe, Fanne, 112
Franklin, Benjamin, 14
Friendly, Henry, 283
fringe benefits, 229, 235, 259
Fullerton, Don, 179

Gale, William, 209
Garfield, James A., 15
gas tax, 24, 41, 42, 155, 156, 157, 158, 159, 172, 222
Gates, Bill, 143
General Agreement on Tariffs and Trade (GATT), 158, 187
General Electric, 127, 190, 262
General Motors, 138–39
Gephardt, Richard, 5, 153–54, 226, 286
Germany, 207, 241, 285
Gibbons, Sam, 114, 272
gift taxes, 10, 12, 15, 21, 104, 203, 267–68
Gingrich, Newt, 4, 124, 142, 164, 168, 169, 170, 187, 197, 259
Ginsburg, Martin, 45, 227
Giuliani, Rudolph, 102, 103
Goldman, Marvin, 250
Goldwater, Barry, 43
Goodman, Richard, 38
goods and services, 199, 216–17, 219, 221
Goss, Frank, 45
government, federal:
assets owned by, 187, 188
budget of, 8–9, 18, 116–18, 142, 185–87, 234–35, 253, 256–57
deficits of, 18–20, 22, 49, 57, 86, 116–17, 124, 129, 132, 135, 136, 146, 149, 152, 157, 158, 162–63, 167–74, 180, 181, 184–88, 208, 218, 226, 256–57, 275–76
public opinion on, 6, 7–8, 51, 67
reduction of, 93, 131, 232–36
services provided by, 25
shutdowns of, 168–69

government, federal (*continued*)
  spending by, 7, 18–19, 20, 55, 57,
    65, 106, 116–17, 124, 128–29,
    162–63, 180, 186, 191–92,
    234–35, 245, 255
  tax shelters used by, 46–48
  see also Congress, U.S.
Gramm, Phil, 124, 187, 226, 233
Gramm-Rudman Act (1985), 117,
    162–63, 167, 186, 188, 280,
    287
Grant, Ulysses S., 15
Great Britain, 173–74
Greenspan, Alan, 129
Greenspan Commission, 129
Griswold, Erwin N., 189
gross domestic product (GDP),
    18–19, 20, 171, 177, 201
Gulf War, 156, 163

Hall, Robert, 213, 216, 219
Hamilton, Alexander, 13, 22, 23, 111,
    196
Hampden, John, 22
Harris, Fred, 115
Harsaghy, Helen Krusko, 71–72, 73
Hausman, Jerry, 178–79
Havens, Richie, 6
health insurance, 86, 152, 160–62, 173,
    200, 214, 219, 230, 235, 236–37,
    250, 252, 256, 257, 259, 266
heating oil, 155, 156, 159
Heitzman, Robert E., Jr., 238–39
Helms, Jesse, 288
Hicks, Dean Harvey, 102
highway construction, 156
Hill, John, 7
Hitchhiker's Guide to the Galaxy, The
    (Adams), 185
Hobbes, Thomas, 202
Holmes, Oliver Wendell, 6
horses, Arabian, 45
House Budget Committee, 117, 118
House Government Operations
    Committee, 79
housekeeping, 69, 78–80, 228–29, 237

House Select Revenue Subcommittee,
    119
House Ways and Means Committee, 4,
    31, 32, 33, 38, 45, 111–20, 174,
    189, 289, 290
housing, 53, 207, 209, 236, 237, 246,
    247–48, 277, 278
Huffington, Michael, 288
Hunt, James B., Jr., 288

imports, 158, 200, 241, 274
Imus, Don, 157
income:
  adjusted gross (AGI), 113, 264–65
  business, 94, 95
  capital, 58, 59–60, 64, 66, 146–47,
    209
  disposable, 8
  equality of, 203, 204–5, 267
  fixed, 53
  illegal sources of, 201, 275
  interest, 61–64, 126, 134
  investment, 18, 30, 31, 41, 42–43,
    49, 76, 125, 231
  lifetime, 204
  net, 59
  unearned, 141
  unreported, 94
  withheld, 187
income tax:
  avoidance of, 41, 42, 50–51, 89–107,
    113, 206, 213, 272–73
  brackets for, 8, 53–58, 61, 65–67,
    91, 126, 134, 135–36, 151, 250,
    266, 281
  constitutionality of, 15–16, 101,
    210, 280–86
  consumption tax vs., 4–5, 10, 12, 14,
    112, 131, 149–59, 166–67, 169,
    179, 195–243, 245, 263, 264–66,
    273, 275
  credits for, 60, 125, 126–28, 137–39
  distribution of, 23–24, 63, 64,
    135–36, 167, 182, 185, 196, 220,
    222–26, 240, 242, 245, 254, 258,
    266

elimination of, 131, 196, 197,
     209–10, 222–23, 263, 264, 278
establishment of, 15–16, 196, 222,
     235, 262
fairness of, 3–4, 30–32, 48, 200, 203,
     204
forms for, *see* forms, tax
"gap" in, 105
increases in, 8, 17, 53, 55, 56, 57,
     121, 124, 132, 133, 136,
     163–70, 172–73, 174, 189, 233,
     287–88
minimum level of, 113–14, 134,
     190–91, 262–63, 265
penalties for, 46, 50, 95, 96–97, 100,
     105, 186, 268–69, 283
progressive, 12, 16, 21, 33, 132, 161,
     183, 196, 197, 201, 204, 214, 219,
     220, 221, 222–26, 234, 240, 266,
     267, 271
protests against, 8, 22–23, 32–33,
     52, 101–4
public opinion on, 3–8, 31, 48, 84,
     106, 113, 132–33, 139, 160,
     197, 212–14, 216, 242, 245, 249,
     279
reductions in, 4, 5, 16, 17, 55, 56,
     57, 65, 66, 94, 105, 121–22,
     124–26, 131, 141, 142, 158, 160,
     170, 173, 181, 191–92, 270, 277,
     279
reform of, 3–9, 118–20, 123–24,
     130–39, 141, 176, 177–80, 185,
     192, 212–14, 225–26, 232,
     234–45, 252, 269–70, 272,
     275–76, 277
refunds on, 93, 100
reporting procedures for, 93, 95,
     97, 98, 100, 106
see also taxation
independent contractors, 79
indexing, tax, 56–58, 59, 64, 65–67,
     147, 152, 154
Individual Retirement Account (IRA),
     62–63, 125, 181, 187, 198,
     246–47

inflation, 52–67
bracket creep and, 53–58, 61,
     65–67, 91, 126, 134, 135–36, 151,
     250, 266, 281
capital income and, 58, 59–60, 64,
     66, 146–47
consumption taxes and, 151–53
depreciation for, 59–60
federal deficit and, 163
interest income and, 61–64
penalties and, 97
premium for, 61
property taxes and, 52–53
rate of, 128, 135
revenues and, 53, 151
tax timing and, 65
Information Technology Association
     of America, 210
inheritance taxes, 10, 15, 21, 96,
     127–28, 201, 267–68, 272
Inman, Bobby Ray, 78
interest:
on bonds, 134, 190, 262
deductions for, 62–63, 64, 75–77,
     134
income from, 61–64, 126, 134
on investments, 47
mortgage, 58, 63, 64, 69, 75, 76, 77,
     93, 229, 234, 237, 248, 259, 260,
     265, 266
on national debt, 171
rate of, 163, 179, 237
taxation of, 218, 229, 240, 247–48,
     260
Internal Revenue Code:
amendments to, 87, 123, 284
arbitrary nature of, 87
complexity of, 8, 18, 64, 65, 68–88,
     116, 134, 143, 215, 227, 228–30,
     240, 242, 243
constitutional challenges to, 280–86
definitions in, 103
enforcement of, 91–100
legislation on, 6–7, 30–34, 111–92,
     203–4, 243, 279–81, 284–92
loopholes in, 42, 144, 190, 272, 286

Internal Revenue Code (*continued*)
reform of, 24–25, 105, 243
repeal of, 5
simplification of, 70, 86, 87–88,
106–7, 131, 132, 134, 187, 200,
205–6, 213, 226–32, 242–43, 244,
245, 258–62, 265, 270
text of, 92–93
Internal Revenue Service (IRS):
administration of, 86–87, 93, 98,
228
budget of, 99
elimination of, 4, 5, 213, 240
rulings by, 43, 45, 47, 71–72, 282–83
Intuit, 83
inventories, 59–60
investments:
capital for, 142–43, 145–46
in corporations, 207, 248–49
credits for, 47, 66, 134, 146–47, 150,
190, 221, 227, 231
foreign, 181, 272, 273–74
income from, 18, 30, 31, 41, 42–43,
49, 76, 125, 231
interest on, 47
quality of, 44, 190, 248–49
rate of, 45, 50, 198, 207–8, 244
taxation of, 179, 181, 183, 262
transactions for, 93
"Is It Not Time to Simplify the
Income Tax?," 87–88

Jackson-Hewitt Tax Service, 82
Japan, 20, 22, 153, 201, 207, 241, 247,
271
Jefferson, Thomas, 14, 111
job-related expenses, 69, 70, 247
John Paul II, Pope, 138
Joint Budget Resolutions, 117, 186
Joint Committee on Taxation, 114,
117–18
Jones, Jim, 120
Jordan, Chester, 195

Kaptur, Marcy, 45
Keefer, Gary D., 91–92

Kellems, Vivien, 32–33, 38, 40, 221,
281–82
Kemp, Jack, 4, 145, 177, 191, 197, 250,
259
Kemp Commission, 4–5, 252
Kemp-Roth bill, 66
Kennedy, Edward M., 257
Kennedy, John F., 16, 17
Kerrey, Bob, 254, 255, 257
Kinsley, Michael, 144
Knowland, William, 30–31
Koch, Ed, 33
Korean War, 17
Kozien, Leona, 161–62
Kraft, Joseph, 116
Kuttner, Robert, 5

Lasser, J. K., 83
lawyers, tax, 44, 50–51, 80, 240
Lear, Norman, 43
leasing, auto, 76–77
Lefcoe, George, 291–92
Leno, Jay, 168–69
Leontief, Wassily, 180
leveraged buyouts, 63, 248
Liberace, 73
life insurance, 219, 235, 246,
259
Life Science Church, 102
Lincoln, Abraham, 15, 164
line item veto, 8
living standards, 12, 54, 285
loans, 61–64, 74–77, 98, 215, 219, 247,
260
Long, Russell, 6, 56, 115, 137–38
Louisiana State University, 137–38
Lugar, Richard, 4, 191, 197

McClellan, John, 30–31
McClure, Charles, 181
McGovern, George, 43
Mack, Connie, 216
McKinley Tariff Act (1890), 15
McLaughlin Group, 4
Mager, Howard, 44–45
market economy, 11, 223–24

marriage penalty, 7, 29–40, 91, 186, 215, 221, 234, 250, 266, 275, 281, 282–83, 285
Marsh and McClennan, 127
Marx, Karl, 132
Massachusetts, 121
Maxwell, Nancy, 7
Medicaid, 55, 261
Medicare, 17, 21, 55, 78, 129, 160–62, 167, 169, 208, 221, 222, 249–58
Medicare Catastrophic Coverage Act (1988), 160–62
Mellon, Andrew, 16, 133, 225
Merrill, Steve, 226
Mexican-American War, 101
Michel, Robert, 168
middle class, 21, 43, 54, 70, 121, 126, 130, 167, 170, 172, 230, 246, 275
mileage allowance, 74
Mill, John Stuart, 195–96, 202
Miller, Dan, 272
Mills, Ogden, 195
Mills, Wilbur, 8–9, 32, 111–16, 175
Mitchell, George, 12, 141, 142, 146, 147, 148, 164, 183
Mobil Corporation, 85
Mondale, Walter, 121, 132, 136
Money, 83–84, 104
money supply, 129, 281
Morgenthau, Henry, 196
mortgages, 58, 63, 64, 69, 75, 76, 77, 93, 229, 234, 237, 248, 259, 260, 265, 266
Motion Picture Association, 48–49
movies, 41, 42, 45–46, 48–49
Moynihan, Daniel Patrick, 182
mutual funds, 59, 68, 209

Nader, Ralph, 119
National Association of Realtors, 125
National Chamber Foundation, 146–47
National Federation of Independent Businesses, 115–16
National Taxpayer's Union Foundation, 146–47

National Women's Party, 32
Navy, U.S., 46–48
Nelson, Ozzie and Harriet, 72
New Republic, 132
New York Times, 36, 103–4, 133, 170, 216
Nixon, Richard M., 103, 104, 114, 116–17, 172, 196, 210
"no change" letter, 92
nonprofit organizations, 231–32
North American Free Trade Agreement (NAFTA), 158
Norton, Eleanor Holmes, 259
Nunn, Sam, 197, 214, 215, 217, 220, 239, 252, 273

Occidental Petroleum, 127
offices, home, 69, 73–74, 228, 229
oil, 24, 41, 42, 125, 154–59, 235, 236, 238, 278
Omnibus Budget Reconciliation Acts, 117, 184–85
Organization for Economic Cooperation and Development (OECD), 20, 22, 199, 201, 207, 271, 273

Packwood, Robert, 132, 133, 138, 175, 289
Panetta, Leon, 170
partnerships, 41, 219
"passive losses," 48
Pataki, George, 121
Paul, Randolph, 31
payroll tax, 10, 12, 16, 17, 21, 129–30, 169, 187, 196, 197, 209–10, 215, 221, 222, 223, 233, 249, 250, 252, 254, 255, 265
Penn, William, 101
pension funds, 61–62, 63, 145, 209, 238–39, 245, 246, 253, 256, 259, 261, 266
Pevsner, Sandra, 72
"Philadelphia Nun" provision, 138
political action committees (PACs), 115, 125, 289–90

pollution, 154, 155, 158
Pond, Phyllis, 38
precautionary savings, 203
preparers, tax, 8, 81–84, 101, 260
presidential campaigns:
    of 1976, 4
    of 1984, 132
    of 1992, 121, 169, 183, 214, 263
    of 1996, 4, 160, 197, 226
prices:
    alcohol, 151–53
    of assets, 147, 199, 208, 231
    housing, 53, 237
    increases in, 178
Price Waterhouse, 49
productivity, 49
property taxes, 5, 13–14, 23, 52–53,
    54, 75, 111, 121, 122, 223, 234,
    237, 258, 263, 280, 286
Proposition 13, 5, 23, 52–53, 111, 121,
    122, 280, 286

Quicken, 83

Randolph, William, 209
rates, tax:
    brackets for, 53–58, 61, 65–67, 91,
        126, 134, 135–36, 151, 250, 266,
        281
    flat, 4–5, 8, 16, 40, 66, 123, 131,
        179, 180, 183, 191, 197, 204, 208,
        212–43, 258, 262, 265–66, 273,
        277–78
    fluctuations in, 11, 20, 53, 62–63, 65,
        94, 147, 149, 166, 181, 198, 265
    foreign, 232
    multiple, 205, 221–22, 231, 232, 286
    single, 5, 131, 183, 213, 215, 219,
        221, 226, 231, 258
    top, 126, 127–28, 136, 141–42, 145,
        186
    zero, 231–32
"read my lips" pledge, 163–65
Reagan, Ronald, 16, 56, 65, 66, 91–92,
    93, 120, 121, 124, 128–32, 135,
    140–41, 160, 164, 167, 171, 175,
    179, 196, 284

real estate, 41, 42, 49, 60, 62, 94, 125,
    237
reasonable basis standard, 50–51
recessions, 163
referendums, 286–87
Reich, Robert, 259
Reischauer, Robert, 162
religious organizations, 101–2, 138
rents, 69, 75, 218, 228, 229
Republican Party, 125, 132, 136, 140,
    141, 147–48, 150, 151, 162, 164,
    166–67, 169, 173, 191–92,
    196–97, 240, 270, 286
restaurants, 96
retailers, 60, 198, 199, 205, 206, 217
retirement, 62–63, 125, 181, 187, 198,
    201, 209, 219, 230, 235, 238,
    245–47, 250–53, 255, 256
returns, tax, see forms, tax
Revenue Act (1926), 87–88
Revenue Act (1932), 16
Revenue Act (1936), 87
Revenue Act (1942), 196
Revenue Act (1978), 141
Revolutionary War, 22, 111
Ribicoff, Abe, 115
"rifle-shot transition rules," 137
Robushka, Alvin, 213, 216, 219, 238
Rogers, Diane Lim, 209
Roosevelt, Franklin D., 16, 171, 204
Rostenkowski, Dan, 6, 12, 112–13,
    114, 119–20, 132, 138, 161–62,
    168, 175, 289, 290
Rowland, John, 122

safe-harbor leasing, 126–28
Safire, William, 5, 11, 225–26
savings and loan industry, 49, 125, 237
savings rate, 21, 50, 68, 155, 179, 181,
    183, 198, 200, 202, 203, 207–9,
    215, 239, 244–53, 256, 257, 266,
    268, 270–76
Schiff, Irwin A., 103–4
Seagrams Company, 290
self-employment, 69, 70, 93, 95, 206,
    219, 229
Senate Budget Committee, 117, 118

Senate Finance Committee, 42,
    114–20, 135, 138–39, 157, 168,
    174–75, 195, 289, 290
sequestration, 162–63, 167
shelters, tax, 41–51
    deductions for, 42, 44, 45, 48
    elimination of, 179
    government, 46–48
    for health insurance, 236–37
    interest income and, 62
    for personal consumption, 230
    schemes for, 41–51, 62, 66, 67, 68,
        91, 114, 134, 274
"ship money," 22
ship rentals, 46–48
Simon, William, 224–25
Simpson, Alan, 254, 255, 257
single status, 31–33, 38, 40, 221, 260,
    281–82
Sixteenth Amendment, 3, 15–16,
    101, 210, 222, 262, 278, 279,
    285
slavery, 13–14
Smith, Adam, 12, 263
Smith, Dan T., 225
Smith, William French, 43
Smithsonian Institution, 46
Social Security, 249–58
    finances of, 34, 54, 55, 57, 58, 69,
        78, 79, 80, 126, 128, 167, 172,
        181, 208, 227, 230, 236, 246,
        249–58, 260, 275
    legislation on, 16, 129–30
    number assigned for, 91, 96, 100,
        282
    payroll tax for, 10, 12, 16, 17, 21,
        129–30, 169, 187, 196, 197,
        209–10, 215, 221, 222, 223,
        233, 249, 250, 252, 254, 255,
        265
    privatization of, 253–56
    trust funds for, 251, 253
Social Security Act (1935), 16
Soliman, Nader E., 73–74
South Carolina, 205
Specter, Arlen, 4
"speedup," 187–88

spending caps, 162–63, 167
Standard and Poor, 254
Stark, Fortney "Pete," 45, 119
stated dollar thresholds, 58
Stathis, Jennie, 100
Stein, Herbert, 179–80, 205
Steiner, Carol, 72–73
Stockman, David, 128–29
stocks, 59, 76, 94, 143–44, 254, 255–56
    dividends from, 126, 181, 218, 219,
        240, 248, 285
summits, budget, 163–68, 175
Sununu, John H., 147, 165, 166
supermajority requirements, 287–88
supply-side economics, 16, 137
Supreme Court, U.S., 15, 16, 30,
    73–74, 279, 282, 284, 285, 290
surtaxes, 233, 278
Swanson, Gloria, 33
syndication, 49

Tannenwald, Theodore, Jr., 283
"target savers," 208
Tariff Act (1816), 14
Tariff Act (1894), 15
tariffs, 14–15, 24, 158, 187, 198
Tax Act (1981), 124–28
Tax Act (1982), 284
"Tax Advantaged Traveling for You
    and Your Money," 272
taxation:
    anecdotes about, 189–91, 262–63
    budget process and, 116–18,
        185–87, 234–35, 256–57
    compliance with, 8, 10, 25, 32–33,
        38–39, 86–87, 89–107, 192,
        205, 206, 242, 249, 260, 261,
        275
    consumption, *see* consumption tax
    death and, 14
    economic impact of, 10, 11–12, 17,
        18, 23, 25, 134–37, 145, 167, 170,
        177–82, 187, 200, 209, 225, 234,
        236–39, 244–45, 248, 258, 259,
        268, 275
    excise, 14, 21–22, 150, 151, 153,
        159, 169, 187, 198, 223, 278

taxation (*continued*)
  fairness of, 3–4, 10, 11, 12, 13, 24, 40, 133, 137, 153, 185, 187, 201–5, 220–26, 240, 244, 258, 262, 263
  flat, 4–5, 8, 16, 40, 66, 123, 131, 179, 180, 183, 191, 197, 204, 208, 212–43, 258, 262, 265–66, 273, 277–78
  history of, 13–24
  ideology of, 182–84
  international, 20, 22, 199, 201, 207, 270–75
  laws for, *see* Internal Revenue Code
  minimalization of, 35, 39, 184
  mix of, 11, 21–22, 24
  over-, 21, 60
  policy on, 177–92
  political impact of, 7, 8, 22–24, 80–81, 103, 106, 121–22, 151, 152–59, 203–4, 216, 269–70, 277–92
  power of, 22–23, 146–47, 284–86
  predictions for, 119, 125, 127, 128–29, 177–80
  principles of, 10–13
  questions on, 10–11, 181–82
  rates of, *see* rates, tax
  regressive, 222, 223
  representation and, 111, 281
  revenue from, 3, 9–10, 13, 20–22, 24, 53, 56, 57–58, 86, 105, 124, 125, 130, 131, 135, 144–45, 149–50, 151, 185, 186–88, 200, 235, 244, 246, 276, 277, 281
  sales, 4, 14, 22, 66, 105, 155, 159, 191, 199, 200, 205–6, 210, 212, 216, 217, 218–19, 220, 221, 222, 223, 240, 258, 261–62, 264, 274
  social impact of, 6–7, 13, 35–40, 152–59, 222, 236–39, 244–45, 259
  state and local, 10, 20, 23, 52–53, 75, 85, 93, 201, 210–11, 213, 221, 234, 237–38, 260, 261–62, 269, 285, 286
  timing of, 65, 143, 144, 231, 232

  types of, 9–10
  uncommon, 212–43
  value-added (VAT), *see* value-added tax (VAT)
  wars and, 14, 15, 17, 101
  see also income tax
Tax Court, U.S., 36–37, 43, 45, 71–72, 282–83
Tax Reform Act (1969), 113–16
Tax Reform Act (1986), 17, 48, 51, 66, 119–20, 123–24, 130–39, 145, 149, 179, 185, 190, 226, 227–28, 242, 247, 259, 273
Tax Reform Commission, 177
Taylor, Humphrey, 91
Thatcher, Margaret, 263
Thoreau, Henry David, 23, 101
Thrasher, Paul, 6
tickets, sports, 137–38
tips, 90, 96
Tisch, Preston, 43
tobacco tax, 150, 151–53, 158, 159, 167
transportation, 69, 74, 228, 229, 230
Treasury bonds, 254
Treasury Department, U.S., 47, 63, 120, 131, 141, 147, 181, 227–28, 269
"trickle down" economics, 202
Triumph of Politics, The (Stockman), 128–29
TurboTax, 83
two-tier tax enforcement, 93–98

Ulman, Al, 112, 120, 196
unemployment compensation, 187
uniforms, 71–72, 73
Uniform Savings Allowance (USA) tax, 214–15, 216, 219, 220, 226, 227, 231, 237, 239, 240, 252, 273, 274
United States-Canada Free Trade Agreement, 158
United States Strategic Petroleum Reserve, 157
Universal Life Church, 102

university endowment funds, 61–62
Unruh, Jesse, 289

vacation-divorces, 35–40
value-added tax (VAT), 264–66
    as consumption tax, 22, 66, 112,
        150, 155, 196, 197, 205, 208, 210,
        212, 214, 216, 220, 221, 222, 226,
        240, 258, 264–66, 275
    credit-method, 199–200, 206, 217,
        274
    subtraction-method, 217–18
Veblen, Thorstein, 202
Vietnam War, 23, 113
Volker, Paul, 129

waitresses, 89–90, 96
Wall Street Journal, 12, 36, 199, 233, 278
Ward, Benjamin, 102
Waring, Hilde, 250
War of 1812, 14
Warren, Brad, 281
War Widows of America, 32
Washington, George, 23
Washington Post, 37, 129, 164, 170
wealth:
    "common pool" of, 202
    paper, 53

redistribution of, 11–13, 132, 171,
    204–5, 222–26, 267
taxation of, 10, 20, 21, 143–44, 148,
    165, 183, 190–91, 196, 198, 202,
    223, 245, 267–68
Weil, A. Lorne, 144
West, Joe, 45–46
Whiskey Rebellion (1794), 22–23
Whitewater affair, 104
Whitman, Christine, 122
wholesalers, 60, 201
Wilshire 6000 index fund, 255
Wilson, Woodrow, 171, 182
window, budget, 185, 187
wine, 154
women:
    single, 32–33
    in workforce, 34, 38, 40
World War I, 17
World War II, 17, 32, 196, 204
Wright, Jim, 136
WWL, 138

Yale Health Plan, 150
Your Income Tax (Lasser), 83
Yves St. Laurent clothes, 72

zero bracket, 231–32